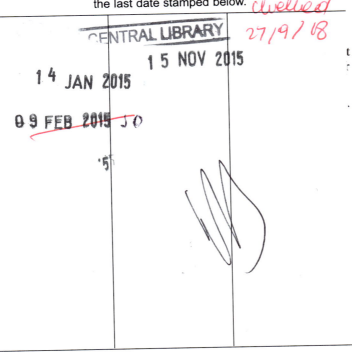

I, Durga Khote

An Autobiography

Translated from Marathi by Shanta Gokhale

With an Introduction by Gayatri Chatterjee

OXFORD
UNIVERSITY PRESS

791.430924

OXFORD
UNIVERSITY PRESS

YMCA Library Building, Jai Singh Road, New Delhi 110 001

Oxford University Press is a department of the University of Oxford. It furthers the
University's objective of excellence in research, scholarship, and education
by publishing worldwide in

Oxford New York

Auckland Cape Town Dar es Salaam Hong Kong Karachi Kuala Lumpur
Madrid Melbourne Mexico City Nairobi New Delhi Shanghai Taipei Toronto

With offices in

Argentina Austria Brazil Chile Czech Republic France Greece Guatemala
Hungary Italy Japan Poland Portugal Singapore South Korea Switzerland
Thailand Turkey Ukraine Vietnam

Oxford is a registered trademark of Oxford University Press
in the UK and in certain other countries

Published in India by Oxford University Press, New Delhi

© Oxford University Press 2006

The moral rights of the author have been asserted
Database right Oxford University Press (maker)

First published 1976
Second Impression 2006
Oxford India Paperbacks 2007

ISBN-13: 978-0-19-569243-3
ISBN-10: 0-19-569243-8

MR. Omayal Achi MR. Arunachalam Trust was set up in 1976 to further education and
health care particularly in rural areas. The MR. AR. Educational Society was later
established by the Trust. One of the Society's activities is to sponsor Indian literature. This
translation is entirely funded by the MR. AR. Educational Society as part of its aims.

Typeset in Goudy 10.5/12.5
by Sai Graphic Design, New Delhi 110 055
Printed in India by De-Unique, New Delhi 110 018
Published by Oxford University Press
YMCA Library Building, Jai Singh Road, New Delhi 110 001

Contents

List of Illustrations — vi
Remembering My Mother • Bakul Khote — vii
Translator's Note • Shanta Gokhale — xiv
Durga Khote: The Contour of a Life and Work — xvii
  • Gayatri Chatterjee

1. The Laud Family Home — 1
2. My Marriage — 16
3. My Mother's Home — 36
4. Memories of the Marathi Stage: 1910–26 — 42
5. The Dawn of Prabhat — 55
6. Departure for Kolhapur — 58
7. After the Dawn — 62
8. Maya Machhindra and After — 66
9. Dongersey Road: A New Life — 78
10. Kolhapur: Shalini Studio — 83
11. Fate Strikes Again — 86
12. The Boys' Future — 92
13. From the Frying Pan into the Fire — 95
14. Europe: The First Encounter — 104
15. Bakul and Harin — 112
16. The Theatre Again — 116
17. The Boys Marry — 124
18. Fact Films — 132
19. Durga Khote Productions — 135
20. 1964 — 138
21. Tours Abroad — 143
22. The UNESCO's World Women's Conference — 153

23. The Body's Debt   157
24. Life: A Void   161
25. A Different View   167
26. Some Moments of Joy   170
27. A Film on Fifty Years of Filming   173
28. My Friends in the Film World   179
29. Looking Back Now   183

Glossary   189
Appendix   193

Illustrations (between pp. 80–1)

1. Durga Khote as Jijabai in *Sambhaji*
2. As Rani Taramati in *Ayodhyecha Raja*
3. Mubarak and Durga Khote in *Saugadi* (Marathi) produced by the actress
4. As Rani Kilotala in *Maya Macchindra* (Marathi)
5. As Rani Taramati in *Ayodhyecha Raja* (Marathi)
6. Durga Khote in *Pratibha* (Marathi)
7. As Rani Kilotala, with a cheetah at her feet, in *Maya Macchindra*
8. Durga Khote in the palace with attendants—as Jodhabai in *Mughal-e-Azam*
9. A studio shot
10. Durga Khote and her family
11. With Yeshwantrao Chavan and Indira Gandhi
12. Durga Khote with Nargis, Jawahar Lal Nehru, and Raj Kapoor
13. At the Peking Language School, as member of the Indian delegation which visited China in 1954

(Photographs: Courtesy Bakul Khote)

Remembering My Mother

M other did not discuss the writing of her autobiography with anyone in the family. It was written three years into her farm 'Retreat' at Jhirad, her own space, totally, for the first time in her life. Although we never talked about it, I believe she chose the medium of the autobiography to come to terms, for herself, with the swings of fate, the initial joys, the enormous tragedies, and the overreaching successes in rising above them, and the inevitable turmoil and disappointments of her life. In the process, I believe, she ultimately found her peace.

In writing this note, one wonders at the capacity of the human mind to draw on memories and even mental images from seventy-five years ago, starting at the age of six years on the sets of *Ayodhyecha Raja* at Prabhat Films, Kolhapur. I have no memories of my parents prior to 1930; no awareness of the traumas of the first six years of her married life in the Khote family.

The only real parenting came from my mother, despite her frequent and protracted absences between 1930 and 1938 when she worked in Kolhapur, Calcutta, Pune, and Madras, trying to put in place a dependable financial life in an unstable and problematic profession of a film actor. She was certain she would not want her sons to be exposed to the personal hazards of the film industry, and made sure we never got involved in it. There was no parenting from my tragically inadequate and lost father. The intermittent 'parenting' by my maternal grandmother was essentially in a physical supervisory and disciplinary role.

There are few memories of life with my mother in those early years up to 1937. The earliest were those of the sets and shooting of

Ayodhyecha Raja where I wept copiously seeing her 'suffering' in the role of Taramati. The next abiding memories are those of being with her as the honoured guest at the Kolhapur Palace (*Wada*), and participating with her in the extraordinary hunting experiences with the Kolhapur ruling family—pig-sticking on horseback; following in cars with greyhounds chasing hares; and the most amazing of all, sitting on horse-drawn coaches with trained cheetahs which would be released to chase black buck across open country. It was an incredible and indelible experience she brought into the life of a young boy. Harin, my younger brother, was too young and so stayed behind at the Wada. I don't remember my father being with us on these occasions. Then there were memories of the marvellous sets and exciting shooting of *Maya Macchindra*, and of Sundari, the trained cheetah at Mother's feet.

There are no memories of Calcutta (New Theatres), other than her account of the luxury of travelling in the railway saloon of a Parsee friend who was a senior Railway official. Nor memories of her at Prabhat, Pune, for *Amarjyoti*, other than the immense campus across vast acres of open rolling land of the studios, ancillary buildings, and housing colony for the owners. However, over this period and between the ages of eleven and thirteen years, I remember the sad experiences of seeing my father again and again under two distressing circumstances—his gasping for breath in severe asthmatic attacks and bouts of deep dejection, and depression in the face of a wasted and lonely life, about which my mother could do nothing but grieve from afar.

1937 was a watershed and determining year in our relationship. That August we experienced the immense trauma of my father's death—of a heart attack while sitting in a parked car on a Bombay street. My mother and I were in Pune; she was in the middle of the only, and sadly, disastrous attempt at producing a feature film, *Soungadi* (Nataraj Films). I have no recollection now of the funeral or the mourning following it. But sitting beside my father's body in the drawing room of our Doongersey Road house I felt a sense of change within me. What seems like two or three days after all the funeral and condolence ceremonies were over, Mother was sitting in an armchair in the alcove to the right of the entrance in front of her bedroom. She made me sit on a stool by her side, put her arm around my shoulders, and looking straight into my eyes, said, 'Bakya (the Marathi diminutive for Bakul), you are now the man of the house!' I can still see the scene in my mind's eye. And from then on, our relationship was more of trusted friends than mother and son. That incident was to mark and shape my development into adulthood and my future working life to a mature professional career through the 1940s.

Despite her strong sense of being an independent, liberated, almost rebellious woman, Mother was deeply rooted in the Laud and Khote families' traditions regarding rituals and religious ritual and spiritual issues, and she stood by that tradition as strongly as her social independence in her secular life. She was now a Hindu widow, with only one path ahead—withdraw from public life and confine oneself to the family in a widow's white weeds. This is exactly what she did, forsaking extraordinary achievements in her career and her public acclaim. Her view of widowhood was further compounded by the distress of the collapse of her venture into feature film production, Nataraj Films.

Into 1939, the family coffers, which she and her father had filled only in the previous decade, were running dry. In 1930, her profoundly wise, practical, and supportive father had launched her on the mission of providing a sound financial future for her family. And once again he came to her rescue. He told her she had done her duty according to tradition, she had to now get back to her career to provide for her children. We were then living with my maternal grandparents. Practical and strong-minded, she took his advice and went back to her film career. Just as well, as soon thereafter her father, the only other earning member and provider in the Laud-Khote families, died unexpectedly. She now remained the sole provider and financial pillar.

This was also a defining point and an example of her unusual parenting role in my life. I finished my schooling from Cathedral School in December 1939 with excellent results in the Senior Cambridge school-leaving examination. I was 15 years old. But what now? She decided she could not organize the financial resources needed for higher education and qualifications for the usual high-income careers—law, medicine, engineering. She sought advice from friends and enrolled me in a short diploma course in commerce at

Davar's College of Commerce, while she networked to find for me an early training opportunity that would also give me an income. This materialized in late 1940 through the husband of one of her college friends—an apprenticeship with the American oil company Caltex, which I started from January 1941 at the age of sixteen, at their Delhi district office on a stipend of Rs 75 per month. She sent me Rs 100 every month for my board and lodge expenses and I even managed to save Rs 20 in a bank account. She signed a certificate of consent for Caltex to employ her minor son. This act of faith and fortitude symbolizes her parenting, guidance, and support from afar which has enabled me to achieve, with God's grace, a fulfilling and successful life of a wide range of social, cultural, and professional experiences.

Over those ten critical formative years in the life of a young man from 1941 to 1950, between the ages of seventeen and twenty-seven, I was largely living away from Bombay, coming home for short spells between job changes. She was also on the move and away from home for long stretches because of her professional life. Looking back, I see three ways in which her parenting *ashirwads* (blessings) that could work from afar. First, the relationship of 'trusted friends', established that sad August of 1937 when sending me off to Delhi to embark upon being 'the man of the house' at the age of sixteen. She never, ever communicated the slightest chink in that 'armour of trust', by thinking or worrying that I may fail or do something foolish or unacceptable. Respecting this trust and living up to it became part of my being.

The second powerful instrument of distance parenting was mother's nationwide public stature and heroic image, admiration, and affection she enjoyed as a result of her successful career in films. She had admirers everywhere. For me this meant that initially at Delhi (1941–3) and later at Karachi (1943–9), a number of eminent and wonderfully warmhearted admirers became close family friends and took over her parenting role, with tremendous development and cultural benefits for her beloved son. She achieved similar parenting benefits for my brother Harin through my step-father Mohammad Rashid.

I believe the third ashirwad was her sense of spiritual faith in divine benediction and in prayers to attain a link with the Divine.

As mentioned earlier, she believed in traditional religious rituals as an expression of faith. This was totally devoid of any doctrinaire attitudes or sectarianism in religious belief. This faith in the Divine brought into her life two extraordinary gurus in Bombay—Kamalbaba of Jogweshari, a devotee and disciple of Sri Saibaba of Shirdi, and through him into becoming a devotee of Sri Saibaba and visiting Shirdi on a number of occasions; and Bandalshahbaba, a judge of the Madras High Court who was crippled by a stroke and had then strangely acquired, like one possessed, widely venerated spiritual powers and a large following.

Mother had unusual experiences with these two gurus, which illustrate what I mean by this third aspect of her distance parenting. As her life and career were never without some turmoil and concern, she visited these two gurus fairly regularly for the comfort of their presence and blessings. On one such occasion, I think it was a Sunday afternoon in 1946, she was sitting with Kamalbaba and he suddenly turned to her and said: '*arre, arre, woh gadha kya kar raha hai?*' She did not understand him at that time, but in retrospect it was the moment I had met with an accident in Karachi while driving to work at the airport. I had fallen asleep at the wheel on that warm afternoon and rammed into a bullock cart. Fortunately I woke up just in time to apply the brakes before the full impact of the crash could be felt. The cart was smashed, the radiator of my car bashed in, but there was no other damage. Her other extrasensory experiences that I know of were with Bandalshahbaba. During that period—I don't remember the chronology and it does not matter—she was going through a difficult income tax case. One day there was a ring at the door of her apartment and someone from Bandalshahbaba's entourage was at the door to tell her Baba had asked them to drive him to her house because as a cripple he was not mobile. That was all. The income tax case was settled favourably soon after the incident. Some time later, Bandalshahbaba died unexpectedly. The night before his death, Mother had a strange dream in which she saw herself standing beside the gravestone of someone clearly important as it was decorated. Later, when she visited Bandalshahbaba's *mazaar* in the Grant Road area, it looked exactly like the one she had dreamt of before he died.

I have no doubt in my mind that her prayers for her sons, and later her grandchildren, fortified by her faith in divine benedictions to which I had been witness, were the shield of protection and guidance for her family. This included my stay in Karachi for almost three years, and through the Partition, in the home and under the guardianship of Maryam and Hatim Tyabji, the Chief Justice of the Sind High Court. They chose to become my foster parents, so to speak. I came back to Bombay in 1949.

My mother's resilience in dealing with the unusual and unexpected in her life never failed. It was always a challenge to manage the somewhat unsteady waters of life with Rashid. Then, in 1953, I dropped the bombshell about my interest in marrying a European girl. Concerned as she must have been at this development and with my proposal that the young lady come to Bombay for three months to see whether it would 'work out', she, with her sense of trust in me and innate openness and generosity of heart, accepted it with enthusiasm. She even bravely chaperoned us during the high-profile trial, including three weeks of travelling by car to south India through the heart of Maharashtra (Pune and Kolhapur) to the British- dominated planters' fest at Coonoor and Ootacamund where I was to arrange and manage a week's PR programme for Air India. With genuine affection, grace, and happy participation she went on to host my wife's family from Montreal, the Catholic church wedding, and even a live-in daughter-in-law!

A joint family with an independent, though traditional, Indian mother-in-law and an equally independent-minded western daughter-in-law, particularly as they went on also to become business partners, was never going to be easy. My admiration and deep gratitude to the two most important women in my life for their innate wisdom and forbearance to make it work to the end. While Rashid's paddling in unsteady waters was another difficult dimension, divine benediction prevailed by bringing in three glorious Lakshmis—our daughters, Anjali, Rekha, and Priya—who became a significant element in cementing the family.

The tragic loss of Harin at the age of thirty-six was the gravest blow my dear mother had to face in life. She could never fully reconcile herself to the sense of guilt in leaving him to battle alone the travails of adolescence in the inhospitable Laud household. She perhaps felt that that experience led to his stressful inner personality which took its toll through his heart attack at that early age. I would like to believe that the tragic void of Harin's loss was filled in some measure by her splendid co-parenting of our three daughters to their great benefit in personal development, as in their Indian roots and family bonding.

The three girls and their grandmother had very strong bonds of affection and joy. The memories of these bonds continue for them through their inheritance of a part of her 'retreat' of 'peace and resolution', in the Jhirad farm.

Thank you, Mother—Bandu, as you liked me to call you—for your ashirwads. We are so proud of and grateful for your life which has brought such joy and richness to the collective lives of your family.

The Khote family also wishes to convey—on its behalf and also on behalf of the many admirers of my mother—deep gratitude to Mini Krishnan and Oxford University Press for making the story of her extraordinary and inspiring life available through this translation of her autobiography (originally written and published in Marathi).

I am particularly grateful to Mini for her suggestion that I write this piece, 'Remembering my Mother', instead of the usual 'Author's Note'. Not being sufficiently versed in Marathi to read the original, the English translation gave me greater insight into many important aspects of my mother's life, and in writing this piece I have the wonderful opportunity to offer this personal tribute to her.

BAKUL KHOTE

Translator's Note

It was almost fifteen years ago that I first came across *Mee, Durga Khote*, a spirited account by the actress of her life and work in the Indian film industry. She had made a serendipitous (and initially disastrous) entry into the world of films at a time when women from 'respectable' families were forbidden from stage and screen. Films were just learning to talk then, in the early 1930s, and she learned to talk, walk, and sing with them. She finally carved for herself an impressive career spanning half a century. We had grown up in times when films were frowned upon. Young children from educated homes were given books to read, not taken to see films. But Prabhat Films were an exception. They were not 'mere entertainment'. They told edifying stories and explored the cinematic medium and art of acting in new ways. That is how we got to see Prabhat Films to which Durga Khote had contributed so much of her beauty and talent.

What impressed me about *Mee, Durga Khote* was the multi-faceted personality of the writer as it came through. One had read other autobiographies by her contemporaries. There was much personal agony there but not too much insight into the profession and certainly no experience of the outside world. Durga Khote, on the other hand, was not a just a suffering woman exploited by the world of men—as Leela Chitnis or Hansa Wadkar projected themselves to be in their autobiographies. Though her life was marked by tragedy and she knew what pain was, she also had a lively mind and an adventurous spirit, to both of which she gave full play wherever she went, whatever she did. She had gone out into the world, explored it with zest, and made her own assessments about what she had seen. All these experiences are recorded in her narrative, in a style that is both trenchant and lively.

When I was the Arts Editor of the Bombay edition of the *Times of India*, I would occasionally publish translated excerpts from the works of artists on the Arts page. I forget now what the commemorative occasion was that gave me the right newspeg to translate and publish a short excerpt from the first chapter of *Mee, Durga Khote*. I remember how much I enjoyed doing it. I also remember thinking that one day I might want to translate the book in full. The idea lingered for many years, regularly revived by Durga Khote's son Bakul, who was very keen to see his mother's story published in English. When Mini Krishnan joined Oxford University Press I knew she was the person to whom I could send a few sample excerpts of translation for an opinion. Mini Krishnan is an editor for whom publishing translations of Indian language texts has become something of a mission. I have known her for years, met and heard her at seminars on translation, have worked with her on a translation project, and have come to trust her judgement implicitly. She gave my proposal and the translated excerpts a careful reading and got back to me with an affirmative response.

When I began translating from Marathi into English almost forty years ago, translation theory and studies were unheard of. I translated for a very simple reason. I know two languages and have a certain way with words. It seemed right that I use these skills to give Marathi drama, fiction, and autobiographies a larger readership. Though I did not work to a theory, one principle had always governed my efforts—fidelity to the original. I had never allowed myself to feel tempted to 'improve' on the author's work, even when I was translating my own novel or play where I might have been conceded the right to recreate rather than translate.

Yet, it was precisely this principle of fidelity that I appear to have forgotten in my first draft translation of *Mee, Durga Khote*. How did this happen? My hunch is that I got too comfortable with the story. The milieu was familiar. Durga Khote wrote in an urban idiom about an urban life. The distinction between author and translator got blurred. Unconsciously, I became a co-author! Fortunately, Oxford University Press sends translation drafts to reviewers. Mini Krishnan sent my first draft to two of the most distinguished names in Marathi-English translation for review. Their comments and suggestions brought me down to earth. I was not the co-author but the translator. So I got down to amending, rewriting, and refining, with many valuable inputs from Mini Krishnan, arriving in the end at a more satisfactory translation.

Durga Khote is a good storyteller with a distinct sense of style. Though occasionally derived from romantic literature, as when she describes the beauties of Nature, it is otherwise crisp and direct and often touched with humour. The text presented me with none of the more severe problems that bedevil the translator. Yet, the main problem remained—that of cultural transposition. Suddenly a word or phrase could spring up on the page that was so deeply rooted in some aspect of Marathi culture that English stood defeated before it.

Familial relationships were one such stumbling block. Raised in a large joint household, Durga Khote (née Laud) spent her early life in the midst of hordes of cousins, aunts and uncles, each with his or her designated place in the family's hierarchy. The term *leki-suna* appears often in this part of Khote's account. Rendered literally, it would have to be daughters and daughters-in-law of the house. Rather an unwieldy rendering, and bald to boot, without the embedded indication of the status in the family of leki or suna that is automatically suggested in the Marathi term. Marathi makes a further distinction between daughters who are still not married—and therefore living in the parental home—and those whose 'real' home is with their in-laws but who have come to their parental home for a brief stay. The former are plain 'leki' while the latter are *mahervashini*, maher being mother's home. The word carries a huge emotional charge. Mahervashini are to be pampered and spoilt because, for all you know, their real lives are full of pain, humiliation, and repression. What do you do with such a word in English?

And what do we do with *ghar-jawai*, literally 'home son-in-law', the man who, instead of taking his bride away to his father's home, moves into her father's home instead. The term causes eyebrows to be raised and mouths to turn down in contempt. Can a ghar-jawai be a self-respecting man? Having allowed his father-in-law to 'buy' him, he cannot command the respect that a man who is master of his own house, does. No English term can occupy the entire social space covered by ghar-jawai.

Yet, with all that, I would say *I, Durga Khote* comes close enough to *Mee, Durga Khote* for this translator not to feel like running away from the whole thing, an urge that she has grown familiar with over the last four decades.

SHANTA GOKHALE

Durga Khote: The Contour of a Life and Work

Learning about Shanta Gokhale's translation of Durga Khote's autobiography, friends and scholars were pleased. But they also raised many questions. For example, P. K. Nair immediately asked, 'Is there anything in her book to explain the tremendous dignity and strength exuded by the characters she plays? She is so regal and *manly*!' Whenever Durga Khote is mentioned, an image of the actress comes to mind—particularly to those who have seen her early films like *Amarjyoti*—proud and erect, wielding a sword, wearing the *nauvari*.[1] She is truly formidable; even Sohrab Modi, for example, seems dwarfed as she confronts him (to fall in love with him later) in *Prithi Vallabh*.

Her screen image was strengthened by the fact that Durga Khote came from an elite family of Maharashtra—and was also married into one. Every biographical account of hers informs the reader that she was the 'first actress from a respectable family to act in films'. Advertisements for her debut film had announced, 'Introducing the daughter of the famous solicitor Mr Laud'. Durga Khote knew how well her background was synonymous with family heritage, money, and all that comes with money, old and new. She begins her autobiography with an account of her childhood in their Kandewadi family home and provides details of traditions of the house that are dotted with accounts of the various experiences a girl child raised in such a joint family goes through. So, it is only well into the book before we realize how very gently she destroys what was earlier presented. Durga Khote's narrative is remarkable in how she also

---

[1] The Maharashtrian way of tying the sari, resembling men's way of wearing the *dhoti*, that enables a woman to sit astride a horse or 'fight like a man'.

records, alongside nostalgic details of a traditional past, the gradual impoverishment and decadence of both her families—natal and marital.

In addition to acting, Durga Khote also made documentary films and ran a production company. She attended seminars and film festivals (chairing the thirtieth National Film Festival of India) and headed several committees. There are easy successes, difficult obstacles, as also pathetic defeats—she writes about each of them in a deceptively calm manner. Whatever she did, Khote was mostly unaccompanied. Wherever she went, she travelled alone—something rare then and not too common even today. While reading pages carrying such details, I recalled *Aaram*, where she plays a rich widow. The first time we see Durga Khote in this film, she is in a private club sitting alone (head covered by her sari), sipping a cup of tea. The hero and the heroine (Dev Anand and Madhubala) and a friend too are at the table. She gets up, takes out a visiting card from her purse and offering it to the heroine, says: 'It seems, you all are pretending to be what you are not; perhaps you are in trouble. Why don't you come and see me in my house—I might be of help?'[2] Perhaps seeing her, filmmakers and scriptwriters were able to break out of the cliche that 'a woman seen alone in public is a "bad woman"'. Perhaps she inspired filmmakers to create new women characters—free-willed, intelligent, and dignified; like Saudamini in *Amarjyoti*, a rebel against patriarchy, a protector of other women, a pirate engaging in swordplay with her male adversary, played by none other than Chandramohan.

We tend to forget that Durga Khote acted in other roles, too. In her second film, *Ayodhyecha Raja*, the first to bring her acclaim, she portrays the tragic life of Rani Taramati, who is separated from her husband, the great Raja Harishchandra of Varanasi, is sold to a man who takes advantage of the situation, and whose son is killed. However, the same year she also played a queen with a cheetah at her feet in *Maya Machhindra*. Khote writes that her father and her children liked her to play only bold and strong characters, not ones where she suffered and cried. Perhaps we too prefer to remember her playing a strong individual. At times Khote chose her role carefully, rejecting offers; at times she accepted work because she needed the

---

[2] I am quoting from memory and this might not be the exact dialogue.

money—and all this she chronicles without lingering too much on any aspect, pleasant or unpleasant, glorious or ignominious. There is seldom a one-to-one correspondence between the roles an actor plays and the real self; but it could be argued that there *will* be readers who will expect such equations. They can then take the cue from Khote herself through her autobiography.

Durga Khote gained in stature as she groomed herself to be a true professional—treating acting as one of the ways women could earn a living. She reports her father telling her, after the failure of her first film[3]: 'I don't care what the rest of the film is like. But you have shown a way for women to earn a living.' She had joined films when she needed to provide for her family—her two sons—as her husband was reluctant or unable to do so. It is important to note that Durga Khote's autobiography shows that there can never be such simple co-relationships; she weaves her narrative between her personal life and her profession, giving almost equal importance to both.

THE IDEA OF AN AUTOBIOGRAPHY

Durga Khote's background and strong character notwithstanding, working in the film industry then could not have been easy; she could not have escaped what other actresses faced. But she provides few accounts of unpleasant experiences. Aware of the conditions women professionals faced in the film industry during that period, some readers have wondered whether Khote has adequately depicted the problems encountered by women actors in those days. As I read her accounts and went through the rigours of preparation for this piece, I pondered upon this literary genre—the autobiography. I wondered what and how much writers allow others to know—or inadvertently reveal; about writers' deliberations behind decisions to hide certain details and highlight others; about what one remembers and what one forgets or chooses to forget. On the other hand, there is the reader's expectations. A reader approaches an autobiography with some *a priori* expectations and curiosity. When the autobiography is by an actor, several factors come into play.

---

[3] A banal film called *Farebi Jaal* (Mohan Bhavnani, 1931). This silent film had ten minutes of sound, in which Khote sang a song.

There is the persona the actor created for herself or was created for her. In the case of the successful star, there is the aura. For an actor working within the studio system, known for typecasting actors (making an actor play the same role over and over again), there is a fixed image. In such cases, there is an already-established relationship with the readers, the same people who have been the audience, who have known that persona, been bedazzled by the aura or been familiar with that particular image. But, the question is how much the actor— in this case, the author—might herself complicate matters. Does she preserve her persona or try and create yet another, does she present herself as more splendid or fantastic, or does she dispel all mysteries, coming out as the ordinary person that she was? Does she provide explanations of her life as were made known to her readers through print and rumour?

Autobiographies are about how one ultimately perceives oneself. But at times, it is also about explaining how one was perceived by one's contemporaries. Also, in an autobiography, a performer makes clear her position in the tradition she had found herself, or had chosen for herself. Durga Khote is constructing for us a self and a narrative after her work is over—she made her last film in 1981 and the book was published in 1982. Her book title in Marathi is *Mee, Durga Khote*. This use of *mee* or 'I' in conjunction with the name, that is, the pronoun with the proper noun makes for a statement. Perhaps she is fully aware of the purpose the text is to serve? She knows what she wants to write; she also knows what is expected of her.

To think about such matters is to think of the very interesting phenomenon of the *atmacaritra* (autobiography, as it has come to be called in Marathi) in general, and the phenomenon of the prolific output of autobiographies by women in Maharashtra in particular.[4] In a way, while writing her autobiography Durga Khote is following both a contemporary trend and also an old tradition. So many individuals at so many points in the history of this land have thus constructed their 'I'. Let me briefly invoke this history.

---

[4] It will be prudent, even while asking such questions, to remain within this one location. This one story itself is the territory complicated and, little charted; it will be impossible to generalize about all regions, each of which has a vast repertoire of varied stories, circumstances, and histories.

Chakradhar, a prominent follower of the Mahanubhava sect, is generally acknowledged as the first to write an autobiography in Marathi. This work in prose was destroyed in a fire and a disciple re-composed it later (around 1276) by collating material from other people's writings and their collective memory of the earlier work. After him, several followers of this sect wrote autobiographical pieces. But this habit, perhaps, was particularly strong amongs members of the other important religious sect of Maharashtra, the Varkaris. Almost every *sant-kavi* or saint-poet's work contains autobiographical elements, especially those by Namdev, Tukaram, Janabai, and Bahina-bai. The latter is unfailingly mentioned as the first woman autobiography-writer in Maharashtra. 'Autobiographical writings are rarely found outside the tradition of individualism and the sense of the personal worth it inculcates. Yet, of the 473 *abhangs* of this seventeenth-century poet and philosopher that are available today, the first seventy-eight are an *atmanivedan*, an autobiographical account of her soul's journey through seven previous lives as well as through her present one.' (Tharu and Lalita 1991)

Bahina-bai had chosen Tukaram of Dehu as her guru, the most popular and revered saint-poet of Maharasthra, whose fame had spread rapidly in his lifetime. In a particular verse, he tells his God, 'It is good that you have made my songs travel far and wide.' Bahina clearly knew this would never be so in her case; and she provides the world with bonafides, as it were, through accounts of her *past and present* lives. She first draws up a spiritual lineage for Tukaram and the other important saints before him, and then places herself within that lineage. What she lacks in terms of a large following she tries to fill up by dotting her life's account with the representation of scores of miracles (there is hardly any in Tukaram's writing—he did not need them). As a Brahman's wife desiring to become a disciple of a lower-caste person, the obstacles before her were monumental: her husband beat her till she was *kukurkundali*, curled up on the ground 'like a dog'. She did not leave her husband as ascetic religious women usually do, but remained a *pativrata* serving him when he was ill. We can almost hear her chuckle when she writes how, convinced then of her dedication and faith, Bahina's husband had accompanied her to Dehu for a *darshan* of the guru.

There are several reasons why a look at this history is necessary to appreciate this work of Durga Khote. We must do this if we are to examine our attitudes as readers reading autobiographical works. Writing on the autobiography by Rashsundari Devi in Bangla, Tanika Sarkar comments: 'In its textuality and conditions of being, *Amaar Jeebon* was a nineteenth-century production, although Rashsundari seldom reflected upon her times. They gave her a publisher, a printer, a market for her writing. They created a modern readership that would want to read about an ordinary woman. They also gave her a language that she could write in—a vernacular prose, which was accessible to a neo-literate person with no training in the classical languages or in English.' (Sarkar 2000) Literary genres like the autobiography or the biography have strong links with colonialism, nationalism, and modernity. Autobiographies, in fact, are easier to understand when seen in this light, as something coming from the West and people taking to or imitating all that is new. It is the pre-colonial practices that are more difficult to understand and in need of better theorization. Discontinuities of cultural practices are clearly perceived, but the continuities remain hard to trace. Someone suggested the difference perhaps lies in the fact that the modern is secular and pre-modern is religious or sectarian. But we have counter-examples. For example, Muddupalani, a polyglot courtesan in the Thanjavur court in the eighteenth century, writes how beautiful and accomplished she was and so men, contrary to tradition, would dedicate their literary creations to her. But later, in the nineteenth century, Rashsundari writes about her love for Krishna. The more we research into history the curiouser it gets and we are then required to make changes in how we look at things.

Then there is the example of Nana Phadnavis, the great political figure in the Sepoy uprising of 1857, writing most boldly and unusually in 1761, details of what he saw to be sexual obsessions or aberrations in his own character. This 'confessional' mode is totally outside anything coming out of Indian tradition, and Nana's text might be taken as the first 'modern' piece of autobiographical writing. This perhaps is also when the term *atmacaritra* came to be established in the Marathi language.[5] In 1828, Colonel Briggs had translated Nana's manuscript and read it out before the members of the Royal

---

[5] The word *atmacaritra* does not feature in Molesworth, the Marathi-English dictionary first published in 1831, though there are several words compounded with *atma*.

Asiatic Society, London. When the Marathi manuscript was finally ready for printing in 1889, the publishers needed to come up with a specific word in Marathi for 'autobiography'.[6]

It is truly surprising how literary works travelled to distant places. Perhaps they were only a few got to read them; a few more heard them cited by others or as songs if they were in verse form. We are not discussing the strength of readership, but the act of someone writing the story of one's life for a desired or supposed readership. It is true of the nineteenth century that technologies like the print medium brought many changes in the lives of people and a greater number took to writing. At the same time, we cannot say that the beginning of the construction of the self was congruent only with the advent of technology. What emerges is the need to archive autobiographical writings, particularly when they are by artisans, women or common people not attached to a court.[7] We need to ask what *we* make of Bahina-bai's re-presentation of her highly-developed sense of selfhood. She too was ordinary—unknown and unsung— when she wrote; but there was a desire for self-construction. She did this from within a tradition of Bhakti that, among other things, *is* all about self-articulation. Rashsundari Devi, in writing about her spiritual self, was also partaking of the Bhakti tradition. So, religion did provide these two writers opportunities that otherwise would not be theirs. But then surely, a comparative study would reveal differences in each personality and the two respective texts. Issues like individualism, its construction, and subjective writing are seen as belonging only to the modern period—the nineteenth century, the colonial period, and thereafter. In fact, several moments in history act as catalysts, bringing about major changes for many individuals,

---

[6] The manuscript cover has inscribed on it '*punyashlokaache svataacha anubhavaacha svahasta likhita prakaran*'. Ram Bapat thinks this must be the title given by the person who made the fair copy from the writer's handwritten manuscript; so the man had written: 'A personal narrative of the honourable person's own experiences written by his own hands.'

[7] Proper studies of the many different modes of the autobiography are crucially needed; for example, the traditional custom of opening literary works with a self-introduction. There is a long discussion on Muddupalani (ca. 1730– 90), a poet, polyglot, and courtesan of Thanjavur, in Tharu and Lalita, cited above. What were such pieces called—surely there was a term—how else would audiences and critics allude to and discuss them?

and the literature of the period gets accordingly marked. So it is not so much looking at the past versus the present, but trying to see things in a historical perspective.

But do women's conditions change accordingly and as much? A woman and a man are situated together at any time in contemporary history, but she does not share in that equally with a man—their histories are always different. Not many women in the modern period could reap the benefits of modernity as men did; for those women who did, modernity did not come to them in equal terms. In fact, what we see is how women often write *in spite* of all odds and obstacles. And even they themselves construct their selves differently; and all this makes our task of reading autobiographies so much more challenging and interesting.

DURGA KHOTE: PERSONALITY AND PERSONAL ACCOUNT

Durga Khote's account is deceptively simple to read; but it raises all the issues that are involved when we are looking at a person's account of herself in the context of the larger history in which the writer, the piece of writing, and the act of writing are situated. For example, we might share with Pushpa Bhave her disappointment, for she had expected 'Durga-bai would talk more about her contemporaries, throw light on the hectic activity and excitement of the nationalist movement that was going on around her'. Khote's narrative actually contains some explanations, and shows that not all partake equally in contemporary history. When a very young Khote had come in contact with women involved in the national movement, she was consumed by a nationalistic fervour, wanting to leave school and serve the nation. But she did not ultimately join the movement. Khote explains how disappointed she was to observe indiscipline and a self-serving attitude even among those who were meant to lead. But her association with women like Avantikabai Gokhale rubbed off on her in other ways: in the way Khote went about her profession alone, in the way she valued hard work, training, and discipline. In fact, just three years into her career, she went to Calcutta to act in many important films of New Theatres (and formed many friendships there), but was not at all pleased to find the Calcutta studio less organized than Prabhat Films in Pune.

Through all her accounts of professional life there is a constant cry: she could not spend as much time with her sons as she would have liked to and they—one son in particular—suffered since the mother went to work and the father remained largely absent. As the book progresses, one realizes how much Khote valued her relationship with her sons. Many women in the late nineteenth and early twentieth centuries wrote about their fathers and husbands, people important in shaping the course of their lives (Bhagawat 2004). Pandita Ramabai, who wrote essays on different topics, explained, in an autobiographical piece, how her father's tremendous drive for women's education had directed her life's path, had made her into the person she was. Lakshmibai Tilak wrote about her life with her husband, a man who had defied society by embracing Christianity. Clearly these women knew who and what had shaped them and their lives. 'It would be simple-minded to posit a straight connection between female subjectivity and female writing to assume that the latter reflects the former in a direct, unmediated way.' (Tharu and Lalita 1991)

Prabhat's music director Keshavrao Bhole's book *Majhe Sangeet* is exhilarating to read, so rich is it in details and analyses of music, cinema, and the people who inhabited those worlds (Bhole 1934). A book like this also illustrates how men *can* totally disregard family or home life, make their profession their life, and write only about their work. But we could also wonder a bit about a subjectivity that discards life's major components—family members, other lives they have shared, close intimacies—as we find in many men's writings. Of course, that way of writing ensures that the text is all about the writer's sense of purpose and his confidence in his professional and other capabilities; and no doubt as readers we enormously enjoy that as well. It could be said that in the case of women's autobiographies, we see how closely family is linked with work or other aspects of life.

What makes *Mee, Durga Khote* such compelling reading is precisely because the 'I' or 'Mee' here is so multifaceted. It is marked by all the contradictions and paradoxes contained in Khote's rich and elite background; it chronicles the many pleasures and pains she went through as a woman going out to earn a living for herself and her family. And she writes about everything with almost the same degree of passionate attachment or dispassionate distance. We enjoy her writing as a testament of the multiplicity and ambivalence, the determination and confusion of the period she belongs to. We appreciate Khote's portrayal of herself as free-willed as well as chained by the opinions of others, capable of acting independently, and yet unable at times to take harsh decisions, putting an end to things that only brought her pain. 'In fact, for the writing woman, the act of writing itself reconstitutes her subjectivity in radically new ways. Yet, a woman's writing is far too easily related to the cultural world it came out of.' (Tharu and Lalita 1991)

Another popular actress of the same era and cultural world, Hansa Wadkar, follows a very different path in her autobiography, *Sangte Aika* (1970). The book's title, borrowed from her very successful film, makes a direct appeal to the readers: '(I am) telling (you); (you) listen!' At the age of seven Wadkar was sent to work in films and earn for the family and later her husband exploited and harassed her for her earnings. She is quite brutally graphic about the privation and abuse (even physical) she was subjected to. Wadkar's book is similar to Mee, *Durga Khote* in that it is as much about her personal life as about her profession; it is different in that it includes accounts of her amorous relationships and also of abuses (including sexual) by men who supported her in her work but took advantage of her.[8] It is easy to understand why, at the end of it all, Wadkar did not feel any hesitation in writing about *that* part of her life and profession. It is equally easy to understand why Khote would want to be silent about her personal life.

It is interesting how concerns about 'realism' and moralist stances become two sides of the same coin. People uncomfortable with Wadkar's autobiography would like to think such things could not be real. 'How do we know all that she has said actually did happen?' They would like to know what the men she wrote about thought: 'Such books are one-sided narratives and we do not know the "other side".' Some others appreciate Wadkar's book *because* it is bold; they would like to believe all she has said is true. Some applaud what

---

[8] At the time of the publication of Wadkar's book, the publisher had suppressed many names, for the men she discussed in the book were well known, and some still living.

they like and applaud it for being 'true'; for some, if an autobiography is filled with pleasant reminiscences it must be 'untrue', mere nostalgia; such readers would run down a work if it were lacking in morally or politically controversial material.[9]

Very different from any of the above-mentioned two works is the autobiography of Leela Chitnis, an educated actress who came from a middle-class family. Her autobiography, *Chanderi Duniyet*, is remarkable in that the actress shows tremendous awareness of her environment; she has allotted one chapter to making her point on how actresses in the film industry were treated shabbily by their male colleagues. Chitnis was married to a doctor who was a member of several reformist movements, including the Prarthana Samaj. She devotes much space in her book to another of her husband's friends— M. N. Roy and his Radical Humanist Movement. While she is quite matter-of-fact when she writes of her marriage slowly dissolving, she fondly remembers her initial involvement with the progressive plays she acted in and occasionally directed. Her roles in films could be seen as extensions of the naturalist plays staged by the political-social groups to which she and her husband belonged. This could be the reason her persona has been associated with that of an ordinary, often poor woman, type-cast as a doting mother. Interestingly, Chitnis was never cast in the *veerashree* or heroic-woman roles that came to Khote.

How does Durga Khote fare as a woman in the patriarchal world of cinema? There is very little of that in her autobiography. There is one moment in Khote's life that we know must have been particularly hard for her, but she has chosen to remain silent on that too. Her father and family regularly saw Marathi plays and attended every performance of the eminent theatre personality and female impersonator Bal Gandharva. In fact, the Gandharva Theatre Company regularly gathered at Mr Laud's house for play-readings of new projects, with other family members also attending. Contemporary journals and newspapers, such as the *Dnyanprakash*, report Bal Gandharva saying in a public meeting, 'When women from respectable families enter professional theatre, they are likely

---

[9] The other autobiographies are by the Marathi actresses Shanta Apte (who worked with Khote in some films), Snehalata Pradhan, and others.

to go astray. Durgabai Khote says she would work only with Govindrao Tembe.[10] Well, Tembe might be your guru but why insist on this?' Film-musician Vasant Desai writes in his reminiscence, 'Laudsahab sent a legal notice to Bal Gandharva asking him to give a clarification of the defamatory news report and warning criminal proceedings in its failure.' (Desai 1962: 127–200)[11] Khote saw Bal Gandharva's position as important to Maharashtrian cultural history; she saw Marathi theatre as important to the trajectory of her journey towards cinema. And so, she is silent about those very sad moments of her life. On the other hand, most touchingly, she recalls with tremendous pelasure her days of documentary film-making in the interiors of Orissa and other places, and her travels in Europe.

PERSONAL WRITING AND THE ARCHIVE OF THE SELF

The act of writing the atmacaritra is vastly complicated, carrying within it complex purposes and drives. An autobiography contains the thoughts and beliefs of the writer, things the writer lived and battled for, people who influenced her. An autobiography chronicles a writer's desires—fulfilled or not—and her achievements and failures. It is a cathartic act. For some, the act of writing makes it easier to live; it is also an act where a rebellious self emerges and stands out for all to see. We might not find signs of courage and rebellion within the life's account, but the act of writing itself is that. For some women, the act of writing an autobiography is a way of getting the attention that was otherwise denied to them.

What is important to notice is how many different kinds of autobiographies have originated from this one linguistic region and how many different terms are used to define them: *atmanirikshan* (self observation/examination) or *atmajigyasa* (self questioning) are modern terms. In the past, there have been *atmanivedan* (a surrender or humble presentation of one's self) and *atmavritta* (the trajectory of one's life). Recently, there have been more coinages like *atmasamarthan* or justification of one's *modus vivendi*. After the

---

[10] Durga Khote acted with Tembe as the male lead from *Maya Macchindra* onwards.

[11] I thank Urmila Bhirdikar for bringing this to my notice and translating this piece from Desai's book.

excitement of linguistic discovery, we realize all these words convey tendencies towards analysis, value judgment or, more importantly, the need to label something as identified.

If we want to be rid of *a priori* opinions and bias, we might also see the autobiography as something else—an archive of the self. This archive is a personal collection of 'things' or 'items' important and unimportant, information and events, desires and hopes, ideas and thoughts. The importance of personal history has grown in stature with the writings of Michael Foucault, who called the collection of autobiographical writing, whatever the form and stature, 'the murmuring of the world'. Or, following him, we can also use the term 'archaeology' and find traces of a larger history in such writings.

Daniel Favre points out to the number of anonymous and ordinary people, who would not be seen as playing any important role in History spelt with a capital 'H', who have written their memoirs, autobiographies, and confessionals. He calls his article *Vivre, Écrire, Archiver*—'To Live, Write, Archive'. He says the impulses behind the writing of all autobiographies are as strong as living and of storing objects and things, for one's self and for others. And when such a personal archive comes into our hands we take each and everything in it as part and indicative of a larger collective history. We do not start by sorting out the items according to their value; like good archaeologists, we know that everything here is valuable for our knowledge and understanding of that individual, of that time in particular, and of a larger history in general. Favre cites the French woman writer George Sand on this. Individuality for her was not merely one's 'drawing room of experience', and the expression within an autobiography 'makes sense only when merged with that of all others'—that is the way '*life* becomes *history*'. There is an acute need to better archive these archives of the self. Fortunately, there are several efforts in that direction and this series, starting out with the translation of *Mee, Durga Khote*, is an apt choice for a beginning.

GAYATRI CHATTERJEE

Films cited

Aaram, D. D. Kashyap, Hindi, 1951.
Amar Jyoti, V. Shantaram, Marathi, 1936.
Ayodhyecha Raja, V. Shantaram, Marathi/Hindi, 1932.
Maya Machhindra, V. Shantaram, Marathi, 1932.
Prithvi Vallabh, Sohrab Modi, Hindi, 1943.

Bibliography

Bhagawat, Vidyut (2004). *Stree-prashnachi Vatchal*, Pune: Pratima Prakashan.
Bhole Keshavrao (1934). *Maajhe Sangeet: Racana ani Digdarshan*, Mumbai: Popular Prakashan.
Bourdieu, Pierre (ed.) (2002). *Histoire et Archive de Soi*, in the series *Sociéte & Représentations*, Paris: Credhess.
Chitnis, Leela (1981). *Chanderi Duniyet*, Pune: Sri Vidya Prakashan.
Desai, Vasant Shantaram (1962). *Makhmalicha Padada*, Pune: Venus Prakashan.
Heilbrun, Carolyn G. (1988). *Writing a Woman's Life*, New York: Ballantine Books.
Sarkar, Tanika (2000). *Hindu Wife, Hindu Nation: Community, Religion and Cultural Nationalism*, New Delhi: Permanent Black.
Tharu, Susie and K. Lalita (1991). *Women Writing in India: 600 BC to the Early Twentieth Century*, New Delhi: Oxford University Press.
Wadkar, Hansa (1970). *Sangte Aika*, Pune: Rajhansa Prakashan.

I, Durga Khote

1

The Laud Family Home

The Laud family home in Kandewadi was as large as it was chaotic. It was neither *wada* nor manor, apartment block nor bungalow. It was like a beehive that grows bit by bit and keeps spreading. Yet there was a lot of vitality in that house. And a decided charm.

The house literally spilled over with joy and laughter all the way from the massive columns of the front porch to the family deity Manginbaay's shrine at the back. The columns were topped by carved horseheads. They were like the guardians of the house. As you stepped past them on to the verandah, you saw a staircase on the left. It led to the first floor. The door to the staircase was a small replica of the main door. Both were heavy and carved with images.

Four enormous chests stood on the verandah. They wore huge locks on their mouths that kept the secrets in their bellies safe. The chests contained not one or two but innumerable things for wedding celebrations—gigantic pots, pans, basins, and vats, expensive cotton mats and carpets. Behind the verandah was the *kood*. It was constantly buzzing with all kinds of activity. 'Kood' is a Goan Konkani word for what one might call a family room. We belong originally to Goa and the elders in the family speak Konkani at home. Our kood was ruled by the women of the house. The room was so large that it could easily accommodate sixty guests or more at a time for a sit-down meal. It had windows on all sides through which a gentle breeze blew day and night.

The windows had broad sills. One or other of the women was always to be found sitting there, one leg drawn up and tucked under. Thus seated, her hands would be busy stringing flowers or destalking tulsi leaves. The floor of the kood was made of sand and cement, red and satin-smooth. With the reflection of the gaslight on it, you might think somebody had drawn a *rangoli* on it. The red of the floor looked even more striking against the brilliant green of banana leaves laid out for a feast. It was an altogether alluring sight.

In front of the prayer room beyond the kood hung an ancient swing. It had been creaking away for years. Its finely-moulded chains were made of brass. On the top were carved parrots and peacocks. The chains were extremely beautiful. If you sat on the swing you could see the gods. They appeared to advance as you swung forward. Then they receded. It was a game for us.

Lord Mangesh of Mangeshi in Goa is our family deity. There was a lovely blackwood shrine in the middle of the *puja* room. In it was the mask of Lord Mangesh. The shrine was literally surrounded by all thirty-three crore gods. They made a dense crowd. Some had come from the women's maternal homes as their patron deities; some had granted boons to family members; some were images of heavenly stars governing family horoscopes; and the rest, countless in number, were photographs of any and every other god. This sacred congregation had co-existed peacefully in the puja room, under the gentle, steady flames of four tall oil lamps, showering their grace upon the Laud home.

The married women of the Laud family dressed up in multi-hued silks, reserved for rituals, when they came to do puja here. They wore nose-rings, and their necks and arms were loaded with ornaments. When they sat down to do puja adorned like this, it was not just the puja room that glowed with a special radiance, but the entire house. The daily puja was done by Parshuram Bhatji, the family priest. No sooner was the front gate thrown open than he came rushing in like a whirlwind. Puja vessels in hand, *dhoti* hitched knee-high, an old, worn red-bordered shoulder cloth of silk on his shoulder, a round patch of hair with a long tuft dangling from his otherwise shaven, gleaming pate—such was the sight he presented.

All the paraphernalia for the puja would have already been laid out in the puja room before he arrived. The moment he stepped in, his train would start off: '*Shree Ganesha . . . ya . . . namaha . . . Keshava . . . namaha . . . Nara . . . namaha . . . Madh . . . namaha, Damodar . . . namaha . . .*' and so on. Two of his front teeth were missing. And so many words were lost in transit, till all we got to hear was 'namaha',

'namaha'. Then our eldest *kaki*, Kakibaay, would scold, 'What are you doing Bhatji? Do the puja slowly. How he runs!' To this Bhatji would answer while still chanting, 'Fact is Kakibaay, the Dalvis have called me. They've pledged eleven *ekadashi* pujas. That's why I'm in a bit of a rush today.'

He might say 'today', but he was in a rush every day. He would hurtle off the moment he had rung the bell and distributed the candy-sugar offering. Parshuram Bhatji spent his whole life rushing. He had neither infant nor babe. He had a wife for sure, but she was mentally unsound. Why he killed himself rushing around like this was beyond our understanding. With all that, he was a decent and honest soul. There were so many women in the Laud house, strapping young girls too; but not once had he raised his eyes to any of them. All he was concerned with was his work. If he had a problem, he would take it to Kakibaay who was the 'central government' of the Laud house. She was my father's cousin's widow, and though we called her the central government, she was actually very soft-hearted and affectionate.

Kakibaay was short and plump and very fair-skinned. And she was always smiling. Her name was Gulabbaay. Her nature, open and happy, reflected her name. Her nose was like a delicate *champa* bud. Her forehead was high, but stark white, a sign of young hopes and dreams wiped clean by fate. She had devoted her whole life to caring lovingly for the young and old of the Laud family. It was her nature to give generously of her love to everybody. Seeing her you would think she had been part of the house since the beginning of time and would remain so forever. She had two sons—Bhau and Anna. She had handed over their responsibility to the Lauds. They never wanted for anything in the Laud home. As Kakibaay's sons, they were made much of. They were carefully educated. Bhau took a degree in medicine and went to England. Anna became a high-ranking official in the municipality. Kakibaay had little education herself, just enough to read the scriptures. But she managed the huge Laud household with great efficiency. She was in charge of everything. She held the keys to the safe, the storeroom, and the women's jewellery. Her word was law in the house. Nothing moved without her knowledge. She acknowledged the honour done to her with quiet dignity. Family ailments and illnesses, births, marriages, and thread ceremonies, joys and sorrows—she bore the brunt of them all with ease and an unwavering smile.

All my three kakis' favourite seats in the family room were more or less reserved for them. The eldest kaki sat on a bench facing the window. She had her own style of sitting. She would draw up one leg and rest her chin on her knee. From here she would keep an eye on everything that was happening around. She was tall and dusky. A smile was as good as nonexistent on her face. That was because she believed implicitly that nothing was ever done her way. She was constantly muttering complaints under her breath in Konkani. That's why nobody went anywhere near her. Her expression of affection for somebody would be to give his cheek a hard pinch! That was a habit with her. She would help clean and pick rice or wheat only if and when she felt so inclined. Most times she would assert her right as eldest sister-in-law to simply sit around doing nothing.

The middle kaki was fair-skinned, pretty, and clever. Her keen eyes were jet black. She looked at everything with a sharp, fixed stare. She had an edge over the other women because she came from a very wealthy Shenvi caste family of Mumbai. Moreover, she had three sons. In that respect my mother's value was rock bottom. We were three daughters, with only one brother, born as the result of a vow. Our middle kaki was given to making snide, hurtful remarks.

The youngest kaki was very light-skinned and slim. She had four sons and was full of herself on that account. Her favourite pastime was to undo her long hair and sun it. As the youngest sister-in-law, she was our Attya's pet.

Attya herself was light-skinned and big-built. Since she was the only daughter in a family of four sons, her husband had agreed to move in with the Lauds. Attya was made much of in the Laud home. She stood out amongst the others with her fine-textured pastel pink saris, the large vermilion dot on her forehead, and the great big *mangalsutra* round her neck. It was an unwritten law that she was to be waited upon hand and foot by everybody. Taking tea to her was a ritual. A young daughter-in-law, or one of the kakis, would carry it to her in a huge silver tumbler. The kaki had to stand before her, tumbler in hand, till the tea was cool enough to drink. Then Kakibaay would say, 'Do you hear? The tea must be cold.' She would not address Attya by her name because custom forbade daughters-in-law to address daughters of the house by name. Then Attya would cushion the tumbler in the folds of her sari, and drink from it in slow, leisurely sips.

The task of combing and coiling Attya's hair in a bun fell to Kakibaay's lot. Attya would not stand for anybody else doing it. Her bath and hair-washing was a major event. Two large copper vessels of hot water, two brass buckets of cold water, a pan of strained soap-nut water, a pot of chick-pea flour, and large quantities of coconut cream—only when all these things had been placed in the bathroom did Attya rise for her bath. In the bathroom, she would constantly scold the maid, 'Fool! I want hot water and you give me cold.'

We called Attya Akkubai. Akkubai had only one daughter, but mother and daughter never got along. Akkubai couldn't stand girls. She could not stand the three of us at all. In fact, she positively disliked us. She would always pity Papa for having three daughters. 'Poor Pandurang, what a fate,' she would say.

One particular *bhaubeej* turned out to be something of a showdown. All the brothers and male cousins had gathered in the family room for the ceremony. All the women including the three of us—Shalu, Indu, and I—were decked up in our festive best. The first honour of circling the brothers' and cousins' faces with the oil-lamp salver belonged of course to Akkubai. Then came the rest of the platoon. The oil-lamp salver was passed to all the women in turn, and all of them received gifts from their brothers and cousins after the ritual was over. The three of us waited. Nobody gave us the salver. *Pedhas* were distributed. The family scattered, chatting and laughing. We went upstairs fretting. Mummy had everything ready for our own separate bhaubeej. We greeted our brother Manohar with the oil lamp and got a guinea each in return. We were thrilled! The next day Akkubai sent Mummy the gift money due to us from our cousins. Mummy picked up the money as it came, took it downstairs, and put it down in front of Akkubai.

'Dear me, what money is this, Manjulabaay?' Akkubai asked.

'I'm returning the gift money you sent upstairs.'

'Manjulabaay, how can you return auspicious money?'

'Is the ritual auspicious or the money?' Mummy demanded.

Akkubai was suddenly flustered.

'Oh dear! We completely forgot to give the girls the oil-lamp salver,' she said. 'But please take the money now. I'll make sure the girls get their turn next year, all right?'

Mummy said equally sweetly, 'Then next year the girls too will take the money, all right?'

That said, Mummy went upstairs. Akkubai wept and created a scene but Mummy didn't budge from her stand. As a result, the three of us got the first invitation to all family events thereafter!

The family room was surrounded by other rooms, big and small. The most important of them were the confinement room and the storeroom. The confinement room was hardly ever without an occupant. A newborn baby in the house meant a daily treat for us children. We had a share in all the good things that were made for the new mother—semolina *halwa* made in *ghee*, dry fruits, gum *laddoos* stuffed with almonds, poppyseed, coconut and cashews, and almond milk. If the newborn baby was a boy, we also got pedhas, or at least white-gourd halwa everyday, from Mugut the dairyman.

There was a huge, beautifully carved, two-tier blackwood cupboard in the storeroom. The top compartment was filled with heirloom saris and stoles in rich gold-embroidered silk. There were Kashmir shawls and satin saris known as *pilav*, intricately embroidered with gold thread. There was also a large, gold-embroidered parasol with a silver handle for weddings and thread ceremonies, and gold-embroidered back-cloths for horses. The massive cupboard was filled with all this stuff. All of it was considered the joint property of the family. Anybody could ask for any item and use it on special occasions. Before returning it, they would have to air it, fold it as before, wrap it in its cloth, and return it to the storeroom, all under Kakibaay's supervision. All the clothes smelt of *khus*, because small pouches of the fragrant grass were scattered in the cupboard.

The same rules applied to the silverware in the lower compartment. There were dinner plates, bowls, water servers, tumblers, prayer articles, betel-leaf sets, salvers, containers, and a variety of the most beautifully shaped boxes for betel-leaf ingredients, all made of silver. They were meant for everybody's use. It was an inherited treasure, a link that spoke of loving family relationships down the ages.

The storeroom lock was literally the size of a coconut. The key to the lock was also enormously long. An oil lamp hung from the ceiling on a long brass chain in front of the storeroom. Its light fell exactly on the lock. The bowl of the lamp was large and held enough oil to keep its mild flame flickering quietly from dusk to dawn. The flame gave us a feeling of both comfort and company, whatever the hour of night.

The dining hall stood beyond the family room. Lunch sittings began at nine in the morning and went on till two in the afternoon. Tea and snacks were served from three in the afternoon to six in the evening, and dinner from seven in the evening to eleven at night. The place was like a public eatery. It was so overrun by cats that it seemed more like their dining room than ours. They were Kakibaay's pets, all of them. If we ever tried to shoo them away, she would plead tearfully on their behalf, 'Don't, dear, see how hungry the poor darlings are.'

The back verandah was attached to the dining hall. It was a place I detested. That is where beans and pulses were soaked overnight, picked and cleaned. Their strong smell pervaded the air. Beyond that, under the wild almond tree by the wicket gate was Manginbaay's shrine. Lord Ganesha guarded the front entrance to the Laud mansion, while goddess Manginbaay kept a vigil over the back gate, lit by the flame of an oil lamp that burned night and day. All the rites due to her by tradition—coconut offerings, dough-lamps on full moon and new moon nights—were strictly observed. She was the guardian deity of the Laud women. They were expected to use the back gate for their daily comings and goings. Each time they went past the shrine, they would fold their hands to Manginbaay. Custom stipulated that they use the front gate only on special occasions.

My father, Pandurang Shamrao Laud, was the second son of Shamrao Narayan Laud. We used to call our grandfather Babashet. Grandfather was particularly fond of Papa, who had spent most of his youth under Babashet's vigilant eye. Babashet had served as Diwan in the princely state of Khambayat for many years. Papa too had lived with him during that time. Later, relations between the State and Grandfather cooled. His farewell to Khambayat was not very amicable. Papa never talked about it. But there was a prominent scar on Babashet's nose. Somebody had tried to murder him in his sleep. The blow had landed on his nose. When he woke up, the assassin had fled. Babashet had called the doctor himself, bleeding profusely though he was. He had got the wound stitched up there and then, without waiting for chloroform.

There were many beautiful, priceless articles from Khambayat in our Kandewadi house. A velvet rug, silver objects inlaid with precious stones, a four-in-one betel-leaf container of gold and silver, and much, much more. As for *durries*, we had so many of such length and breadth that they would cover the entire floor in our wedding *shamianas*. The blue, yellow, and red checks on them looked like rangoli patterns. Some of the durries were bluish in colour. When they were spread out, they looked like the vast sea.

Among the assortment of things that had come from Khambayat was an incredibly beautiful nine-yard satin sari of the pilav kind. This pilav was purple Surat satin encrusted with intricate gold-thread embroidery. So completely did the embroidery cover the sari that not the tiniest spot of empty space was visible. Every woman in the Laud family had worn the pilav at least once in her lifetime. To wear it was a mark of honour for the matrons, daughters, and new daughters-in-law of the household.

When Grandfather's tenure as Diwan of Khambayat ended, Papa returned with him to Bombay and set up practice as a solicitor. His firm was called Khanderao, Laud and Company. He was very successful in his profession and made his reputation in it. The reason he was able to resolve even the most complicated legal issues with such ease was probably because he had grown familiar with the whole range of legal strategies used in administering a princely state. He was known to be an extremely clever solicitor.

Papa was a very loving man. His kind of love defied description. A noble mind, a sharp intellect, broadness of vision, high principles, and generosity—these were the five sweet and noble virtues that flowed in him. Papa would oblige people around him in untold ways; he would share in their joys and sorrows, but without making a noise about it. Unfortunately, his generosity returned to trouble him in later years. His charity turned out to have been misplaced.

Papa's lifestyle was quiet but expensive and aristocratic. His clothes came from Asquith and Lord. He always wore China-cord or China-silk suits and Bosky-silk shirts with diamond studs. He wore only one ring, but the diamond in it was as large as a tamarind seed. This was how he dressed for office. At home he wore fine Bengali dhotis, hand-sewn shirts of Dhaka muslin, and a pair of traditional, red, padded Pune slippers. Papa did not frequent the club. Social events of every kind bored him. It pleased Mummy no end that he was not a club-going man and that he avoided social events.

Every day, Papa and Mummy spent the time after dinner chatting. This was when Papa gave Mummy a detailed account of everything that had happened during the day. Often this included accounts of High Court hearings. He would describe how he had put some law through the mincer and how a legal point he had raised had tilted the scales in his favour. While narrating these stories to Mummy, he would savour again his High Court victories with childlike joy. Mummy too showed a keen interest in his work and was always responsive. She admired Papa's professional acumen and took pride in it.

Marathi theatre was a passion with Papa. He was particularly partial to the Gandharva Theatre Company's plays. Marathi people are known to be crazy about theatre. But Papa's passion went beyond that. Mummy wasn't too happy with this. Sometimes she even lost her temper over it. Papa had not been trained in any art, but it would have been hard to find a more ardent devotee of theatre than him. When the Gandharva Theatre Company was in residence in Bombay, Laudsaheb was sure to be present at the Elphinstone theatre every Wednesday, Saturday, and Sunday. Two members of his family were regulars. One was Laudsaheb himself and the other was his third daughter Banu—me. There was not a single show of the Company's plays that we did not attend. Even when it moved to Nashik or Pune, Laudsaheb's silver Rolls Royce was sure to head in that direction. We must have seen thousands of shows of their plays. Bal Gandharva was amongst our closest friends. But not once did we see a play without paying for it. Papa had issued strict instructions to us never to step into the theatre without buying our tickets.

Bal Gandharva was so close to Papa that when Ganpatrao Bodas, one of the leading actors of the Company, was about to quit, Papa did everything in his power to save the Company from breaking up. Unfortunately, he could not bring about a compromise. He was deeply pained that this pair of fine actors had parted ways. When the Company was going through bad times, Papa spent not only his time but also his money to free Narayanrao from the creditors' clutches. The Laud and Khote families together saw Gandharva through his worst crisis and kept the Company afloat. Papa did not charge any fee for his legal advice nor did he take a single paisa as interest on the money he had invested. The amount came to more than a lakh of rupees, even in those days.

Despite his involvement in such matters, Papa never neglected Mummy, or us, or the family. Laudsaheb's extended family was large, but his immediate family was small enough to fit into his six-seater car—Laudsaheb himself, his wife Manjulabaay, three daughters Shalu, Indu, and Banu, and the newborn son, Manohar. Laudsaheb's world was contained within this hexagon. Papa and Mummy showered us with all the love that parents could possibly give their children. We were known as Laudsaheb's darlings. Papa's return from the office every evening was something of an event. The moment he stepped out of his car, he would call out: 'Manjul-Shalay-Inday-Banay-Manya.' His hand would already be fishing surprise gifts out of the car like a snake-charmer conjuring things out of his sack. Out came fruits, chocolates, cakes and other goodies, things he thought would make his children happy, things they had asked for in the morning. He would have remembered what each of us had wanted. His car would have scoured the city looking for them before turning homewards. He would enter the house distributing our gifts to us.

Before the era of cars, we owned a two-horse buggy and a couple of mares for us to ride. What handsome creatures they were! The horses were named Tipu and Chand. The moment Tipu was harnessed to the buggy he would begin to paw the ground and prance, while the elegant Chand watched his antics. As soon as Papa climbed in and took the reins, the pair would begin to quiver with excitement. The mere sound of his voice was enough to set their hooves tapping out their beat. Tipu, like his name, was a sultan. Chand took his name from the crescent moon on his forehead. It was difficult to take one's eyes off their lustrous chestnut coats, their large wide-open eyes, their alert ears, and the graceful curves of their necks. Our carriage driver, Devram, and his companion, the *sais*, would look after the pair like their own children. They even performed the ritual of warding off the evil eye every day. We would go to the stable regularly when the sais was grooming the horses. The idea, of course, was to help him with the brushing and massaging; but all we did was get in his way.

All of us, including Mummy, knew how to ride. Mummy looked statuesque seated astride her mare. The mares were not only graceful; but were also very affectionate and docile. One, Jessie, was pure white. The other, Bessie, was sheer black. When we went to the stable, all four horses would nuzzle us affectionately. We would quickly slip the carrots we had smuggled out for them into their mouths. Our excitement on the day our horses had arrived by steamer from Australia had known no bounds. We had gone to the docks with Papa at the crack of dawn and sat through a long and tiresome wait. But no sooner were the horses lowered from the steamer than we drove Papa crazy with our arguments over which ones to choose from that pack of handsome creatures. Finally we had settled on Tipu and Chand.

Trainers from Australia would arrive to train the horses. The horses had to be broken in very gently before they could be harnessed to carriages. They were unused to drawing buggies. One had to be very careful with them on the roads as well, because they were not used to traffic. They had to be patted and stroked all the time while they were getting used to being harnessed.

When motorcars arrived, we acquired a huge Fiat. It was like a veritable steamboat. It had a snub-nosed, red copper bonnet. The car was so enormous that it occupied one half of the Kandewadi lane when it was driven out. Our other car was a Silver Ghost Rolls Royce which became very famous. Its bonnet was pure silver and its aluminium body too was fully coated in silver. When it was on the road it literally shone. Many people coveted it. One customer had been prepared to pay Rs 25,000 for it—quite a sum in those days. We were in Mahabaleshwar at the time. Papa was to follow later. But before he came, we received a telegram from him: 'Silver Ghost offer Rs 25,000. Wire decision.' The moment we read the telegram, we children threw a tantrum. We were not going to let the car be sold to anyone. Not content with that, we camped in the car, afraid that it would be spirited away. We refused to come out even for lunch. Finally Mummy wired back our decision: 'Children want car.' That was that. Papa returned the cheque for Rs 25,000. The customer was very upset. Papa explained to him, 'My children want the car. They don't want me to sell it.'

Such was the extraordinary indulgence we children enjoyed. But that did not mean we were not disciplined. On the contrary, we grew up under the strictest rules. Mummy was exclusively in charge of this department. Homework, tidiness, respect for elders, obedience, punctuality, doing things within the given time—it was like the army, and the British army at that. Mummy laid great store by discipline, because she herself had been brought up that way. People might find it incredible today, but when Mummy entered the Laud home as a bride as Mrs Manjulabaay Laud, she was all of twelve years. But apparently she spoke fluent English even at that young age, and even knew how to ride and swim. She was a daughter of the Sukhthankar family. Her father had sent her to a Christian missionary school and her upbringing had been completely westernized. Mummy had studied at Nikambebai's school. The western ways she had acquired there lingered all her life. Queen Victoria was Nikambebai's ideal! She desired that all her students should emerge stamped with an image from the Queen's own mint and walk into the world bearing that image. So, it was high-heeled shoes, stockings, close-necked and full-sleeved blouses trimmed with lace or frills. Nikambebai deported herself too in similar fashion. When you saw her massive form in a chair you suspected she was fully engrossed in creating an illusion of the Queen's style. Of course it is true that young women from many wealthy families acquired the gilt of western social etiquette from Nikambebai. She was on visiting terms with almost all the rich Marathi homes in the city. Her relations with them were of close friendship.

However, the raft of Miss Manjula Sukhthankar's life suddenly veered in an unexpected direction. Fate had made other plans for her. Her father died suddenly and Manjula descended from the breezy heights of her Malabar Hill home into the narrow alley of Kandewadi. For Papa, it was a 'love marriage'. He was much older than Mummy and it was his second marriage. The story goes that Papa once saw Mummy riding, her thick hair tumbling down her back, and instantly fell in love with the vision. After that he would take a close friend of his with him everyday to gaze upon the apparition from afar. Finally, fate helped him out, and Mummy became a Laud daughter-in-law. Papa admired her immensely. He made her finish the school education she had left halfway. All his life he strove to do everything in his power to make her happy.

When Mummy left the educated, liberal atmosphere of her Malabar Hill home for the narrow alley in Kandewadi, she brought with her the values and ways that had become part of her life. She did her utmost to instil those values in her children. The Lauds of Kandewadi had a different lifestyle. Though they were all very intelligent, generous, large-hearted people and loved life, these virtues were suppressed under the weight of habitual sloth. The Laud family was infected by the idleness of the wealthy, the extravagant pleasures of the rich, and false notions of prestige.

Mummy found this repulsive. Yet, having become a part of the Laud family, she did her best to conform to its daily routine. But she always looked for something beyond the musty, old-fashioned lifestyle and customs of the Lauds. She tried her level best to bring her children up differently, to ensure they would not be trapped in old, orthodox customs. Her children were not to sink into sloth, but advance in life, shine. This was her vision. The Lauds had untold wealth, but that made no difference to Mummy. Their self-indulgence was surely not going to help increase that wealth. On the contrary, the family inheritance would get divided over and over again until the remainder would turn out to be a zero. Then the family would go to seed. With her foresight, Mummy could actually see it happening. That's why she guarded her fledglings against those influences.

Perhaps it was because of this that she had built her nest high, on the top floor of the house. She had drawn an invisible line around it that nobody could cross without her permission. Twenty-five steps separated the lower floor from ours. They helped her keep us away from self-indulgence and idleness. Mummy's nest was beautifully decorated. She used to arrange and re-arrange the settees and chairs in attractively different ways, with colourful cushions and bolsters. Her curtains were soft and sheer, her lamp-stands and lampshades of modern design. She would create attractive flower arrangements everyday. All her ideas of home decor were picked up from *Home*, a foreign magazine.

She was extremely vigilant about our studies too. She took care to inculcate in us the beliefs, customs, and culture of our ancient civilization; but at the same time, she also gave us a modern education. We all learned to dance and sing. We played games like tennis. But along with that she often left the responsibility of the house to us. On occasion she even made us cook. We knew our Shakespeare, Tennyson, and Wordsworth by heart, but we were also made to memorize *slokas* from the Gita and Saint Ramdas, and hymns to Lord Vyankatesh and Lord Shiva by heart. We participated in all the religious rituals and fasts of the Laud household. We would prepare *bel* leaves for Monday offerings in the month of Shravan. We would collect and prepare *tulsi* leaves for the puja and we would also make balsam flower decorations before the image of Ganesha.

The fragrance of incense sticks was all around us then. It wafted over us as we worked. When we served God, we wore short saris called *chirdis*. Mummy had had ours specially woven for us. We girls would mince around in our chirdis holding out vermilion and turmeric powders for the assembled women to dip into and mark their foreheads. We would also smear a little sandalwood paste on them with the leaves of the sweet marjoram. My chirdi was green, shot with magenta, and had a bright red border. Indutai was fair-skinned, so her chirdi was purple. It looked beautiful on her. Shalutai looked regal in her black, silver-starred sari with its flamboyant red *pallu*. For us these occasions were like games of make-believe. But they also taught us about beauty, flowers, and fruit, and the seasonal cycle. They taught us how to cooperate with others and live together in harmony. Mummy was very particular about this. So we imbibed Indian traditions and western modernity simultaneously. But on closer examination, one had to admit that Mummy's personality bore a stronger impression of the West. It was only because she had such a strong sense of discipline that she followed the customs and traditions of the house into which she had come as a daughter-in-law, and saw to it that we did so too. Moreover, deep in her heart there was devotion, faith, and fear of our gods. But she was convinced that to advance in life, to be successful, one had to follow western ideas. The ideals of the westernized section of our society were her ideals too. She observed keenly the leading members of this elite and the stamp of social prestige that marked them. That was the basis on which she planned her children's future. Her children were to reach the top in this society that subscribed to western values, her sons-in-law, among those educated abroad. They would have to belong to the civil service or professions at that social level. Manohar was to occupy the judge's seat in the High Court. She strove and struggled to achieve these dreams. And so she made a point of accepting every invitation that came to her for events at the Governor's residence and dinners at the High Court judge's home. She also worked for the Red Cross Society and the Women's Council.

We always spoke English at home. We dined in western style. The table was laid with knives and forks. The bearer was dressed in well-pressed, starched white livery. He was forbidden to come out without his cap. All this was done to give the children a different kind of upbringing. Papa appreciated the pains she took. He supported her in everything she did. But she never had his active help. He remained a Laud. His mind always hovered in and around the Lauds' Kandewadi home. Also, he was so successful in his profession that nothing else mattered to him.

Though Papa was a Laud in his ways, Mummy stuck to her own lifestyle. Her ideas about when to wear which sari and of what colour, and what and how much jewellery to wear with it, were fixed, like mathematical equations. She expected the same of us. The smallest thing missing or not quite right in our dress would bring a sharp comment from her: 'Bad taste.' Her own saris were extremely fine-textured and expensive. She wore mostly Maheshwari, Chanderi, and Induri saris. She was particularly fond of Irkalis with their flamboyant red pallus. She rarely wore Benaras silks. She used to wear seven-pearl or seven-diamond ear studs, pearl necklaces, and bangles made of large pearls. She disliked clutter and over-ornamentation. The only thing she wore at all times was a 'gipsy' style ring set with a solitaire. She was always so meticulously groomed that even if you woke her up in the middle of the night, she would look as if she had just done her hair.

This then was the Laud home and its melange of cultures.

The house was located in Shenviwadi, on the corner of Kakadwadi, a part of Kandewadi. Twelve of the most well-known Shenvi caste families of the time lived there. They were known then as *Barghar* or twelve homes. The Lauds, Khotes, Dalvis, Telangs, and Dhumes were some of them. A small ditty about them went: 'Dhumes grumble, Wagles are brags, Lauds are hotheads, Telangs are rags.' The Lauds became more famous than the others. But their decline when it came was worse. Except Papa, Anna, Bhau, and Manohar, nobody else made a name for himself, because, except for them, nobody else worked or practised any profession. Consequently, the flow of time swallowed them up.

2

My Marriage

Mummy was greatly relieved once Shalu and Indu were married off. The eldest, Shalu, was married into the Wagle family. Her father-in-law was the Accountant General. His son (Shalu's husband), Balwant Krishnaji Wagle, had followed in his father's footsteps and worked as an accountant with the Bank of India. Indu, the second sister, was married into the Pandit family. Indu's husband Prataprao Pandit came from Rajkot, though the family originated in Bandoday village in Ratnagiri district on the Konkan coast. His father Sitaram Pandit had spent his entire life in Rajkot, acquiring fame and wealth as a lawyer. His son had entered the leather trade and we would jokingly call him our cobbler brother-in-law. He had set up a huge tannery and introduced the white-collar class to the new business of leather curing. Both our brothers-in-law were 'England-returned', that is, educated in England. This had given Manjulabaay greater weightage in the Laud family. Now only Banu remained.

Mummy had already started grooming Banu, me, for the future. The Kandewadi Lauds used to say, 'Now Manjulabai's going to pull the third doll out of her snakecharmer's sack. Let's see which fancy mate she finds for this one.' So far I had worn saris only on special occasions. My normal dress was frocks. But my grooming began with the shedding of frocks for saris. I acquired a whole new wardrobe of saris, puff-sleeved blouses and high-heeled shoes. I was thrilled. So far we three sisters had shared one room. Manohar always had a room for himself. But with the older two sisters gone, I too had a room to myself.

The second step in my advancement was my entry into Cathedral School. When Indutai left school I was given her seat. There was a set quota for non-Christian girls in this school on Outram Road. That quota was never exceeded. Actually, the discrimination wasn't so much between Christian and non-Christian as between white and black. We were even charged double the fees. The atmosphere in the school was *pucca* British. The teaching staff were British too, graduates from Oxford and Cambridge. Since the school was founded by the Scottish Mission, nuns were included in the teaching staff. We were expected to attend chapel service and Scripture was a compulsory subject. No language other than English was heard on the school premises. Even the school servants spoke a pidgin form of it. School lunch was a stylish affair, eaten at tables amidst the clatter of knives and forks. It was the best, the finest school in Bombay and Mummy was most impressed with it. It was exactly her kind of school.

It was indeed an excellent school. It was ahead of all others in everything—academics, sports, cultural events, drama (English plays of course), craft, elocution competitions, Girl Guides. The discipline was strict. It was run like a British public school. It prepared us for the Senior Cambridge examination. Every girl had to participate in every single school event and parents had to agree to this condition before their wards were admitted. Girls were required to be in uniform only for sports and Girl Guides. Otherwise there were no restrictions on dress. And no discrimination either.

Before I entered Cathedral, my English wasn't up to much. In fact it was almost non-existent. My elder sisters used to tease me over this and deliberately spoke to each other in English to keep me out of their conversation. It used to madden me. Furious, I set about learning the language. I would listen to every word and sentence they spoke and learn it by heart. One day they were jabbering away with their school friends in English and at one point one of them made a snide remark about my not knowing the language. That riled me. Till then I hadn't let on that I was teaching myself English. But in the heat of the moment I forgot it was a secret and blurted out, 'Of course I know what you're saying!' Shalutai and Indutai were stunned and could only gape at me.

But this small stock of English was not much use in Cathedral, where English accompanied you at every step. As a measure of self-preservation, I took to learning by heart entire lessons from our reader. I worked very hard to learn the language. That is how I was.

Once I had decided to learn something I had to excel at it and spared no effort to get there. As a result, I soon began winning prizes every year—the class prize, the English prize, and the Bible prize. I became class prefect and captain of the basketball team. Mummy was extremely proud of me. Papa of course would say mischievously, 'The girl has become a brown mem, hasn't she!'

From the time I entered Cathedral, I had become something of a snob. I began to feel that I was different from the other Kandewadi children. Special and superior. When I descended the stairs, my heels tapping smartly on the steps, the others would come crowding out to stare at me curiously, while I got into the car and sat stylishly, slinging one leg over the other! Back home from school, I'd wash up and spend the evening sitting in my room by myself. Now I gave up playing girls' games like five stones, clap-dance, and hand-swirls in the family room, and street games like marbles, kites, and hoppers-and-skippers outdoors. Now my conversation was all about basketball and netball, games that the other children had not even heard of. I spoke English all the time at home, and soon found myself stumbling over Marathi.

My Kandewadi cousins admired me for a while. But since I held myself aloof, they got bored and gave up on me. They decided I was snooty, forgot I existed, and got busy with their own lives. My life was now transformed. A new environment, new friends, new games—these formed my private world, quite independent of any other. Before I knew it, I had lost myself in it. Time passed. I did not know how the next three years flew by. I was so completely submerged in the British atmosphere at school that not a hint of what was happening around me in the country reached me. Nobody at home in Kandewadi bothered much about politics. We read the *Times of India*. If political events were taking place in the country, so be it. Things were bound to be happening all the time somewhere in the world. That was our general philosophy.

But it was precisely during this period, from 1918 to 1919, that a great deal was happening around us. The thunder of political agitation was becoming increasingly audible. The discontent that had been smouldering for years had become a raging fire. Events like the freedom struggle, the non-cooperation and Khilafat movements, and the Punjab massacre had thrown the whole country into turmoil.

Deeply stirred by patriotism, Horniman was writing articles in the *Bombay Chronicle* about the aspirations of the people of India. These articles would be bitterly challenged in the pages of the *Times of India*. Innumerable handbills were distributed, and cyclostyled news sheets circulated. These set off discussions, debates, and arguments amongst the people at large. Politics filled the air to the exclusion of all else. The country resounded to the thunder of Lokmanya Tilak's voice, the reasoned flow of Gandhiji's words, the poetry of Sarojini Naidu's speeches, and the roar of the Ali brothers. Suddenly a whole new breed of orators had sprung up in the country and Mumbai's Chowpatty beach shook with the force of their words. There were more people than grains of sand on Chowpatty beach to attend these public meetings. Early morning processions, bonfires of foreign cloth all over the place, picketing—these programmes were carried out with unprecedented enthusiasm. All communities participated in them as one. The only communities that kept aloof from the mainstream of political activity were the Anglo-Indians and the Parsis. They did not look upon themselves as Indians. Surrounded by patriotism, the consciousness of human values, the sacrifices of great men and women—those were intensely emotional years.

In those days Girgaum was the stronghold of the Marathi people. Processions would wind their way through the alleys of Kandewadi and Kakadwadi, Mugbhat, Borbhat, and Reshim Gully. A short distance away from our house was the compound of Shantaram tenements. This was a regular venue for political meetings. The place was owned by my mother's family, the Sukhthankars. So we had a vantage point from which to observe the meetings held there. The crowds that thronged to hear the speakers were so vast that one wondered where so many people came from. And what persuasive speakers we had! Orators like Pandit Motilal Nehru, C.R. Das, Lala Lajpat Rai, and the Patel brothers held the crowds spellbound with their oratory. Despite myself, my emotions too were stirred. Our family was quite indifferent to the political agitation. But we children were allowed to attend meetings.

Ordinary Marathi women too would be seen walking in processions wearing nine-yard saris made of *khadi* and carrying their toddlers on their hips. The police would charge processions with canes and arrest people but this did not scare the women. Little children would take out early morning processions carrying the tricolour and singing rousing patriotic songs. When I heard them sing '*Saare jahaan se acchha, Hindostan hamara*' ('The best country in the world—that is our Hindustan'), I would ask myself, why then do we sing paeans to the English?

These everyday scenes set my mind in a whirl. I was beginning to feel troubled. The atmosphere in Cathedral School became intolerable to me. I did not want to hear stories of the greatness of British power. I began to have heated arguments with my teachers everyday. I was allowed to continue in school despite this, only because I was good at my work and was doing very well. Every one of my teachers tried his or her best to calm me down, but my mind would not be reined in. Those were times when our national leaders were calling upon students to quit schools and colleges and come out into the streets. My thoughts too began to turn in that direction.

This was 1919–20. One day I was summoned to the office by my class teacher and the headmistress, a nun. I knew a showdown was coming. I was determined to say outright what was on my mind—that I was going to leave school and serve my country. Secretly I was afraid of Papa and Mummy, but I was determined despite that. However, those two approached the problem quite differently. They asked me to sit down and said, 'We admire you. Love you. Your school record is excellent.'

I must admit that I melted. But I still made my statement, 'I want to leave school and serve my country.'

They instantly responded, 'But how can you serve your country if you give up school, and leave your education incomplete? You have only two years left. Why not complete your studies? Also remember, you have taken the Girl Guide oath. You have pledged yourself to being a prefect. Are you going to go back on your commitments? If you break your pledge to your school, how will you keep your pledge to the country?'

Their strategy nonplussed me. They continued, 'Please think about this whole thing calmly. See what your parents have to say. Both your elder sisters studied in this school. You have all done extremely well. Please don't act on impulse.' The school bell rang just then. That is where the argument ended that day.

The heat of politics was touching people at every level. Mummy was a member of the Mahila Samaj. This club for women had so far been involved only with social work. But now, under the leadership of Avantikabai Gokhale, it had turned to political activity. Mummy was not an active participant but a supporter by default. She had taken to wearing khadi saris. That's as far as her role went. Papa on his part was not interested in any of this. However, he was deeply moved by the sacrifices that many men of his profession had made. He had great admiration and love for people like Bhulabhai Desai, Mangaldas Pakvasa, Balasaheb Kher, and Mohammed Ali Jinnah. He looked upon Pandit Motilal Nehru and the others as great national leaders. But he had no interest in politics beyond that. He himself, his family and his profession were his life. When he saw Mummy in her khadi saris, he would say, 'Why are you wearing this sackcloth? Wear something dainty.' 'Dainty' was Papa's favourite word. Mummy had to look 'dainty' at all times. Apart from that he had nothing against khadi and things like that.

Both Papa and Mummy were disturbed by my ideas. How was this girl to be diverted from politics? How was she to be controlled? This was the question that they now faced. We children had been given so much freedom that it wasn't easy for them to rein us in now. We had been free to learn music and dance, participate in sports, go wherever we pleased, spend generously, as long as we followed certain rules of discipline. But if Banu was determined to jump into the political agitation now, the school would have to expel her. What would happen then? Mummy's greatest worry was Manohar. He too was at Cathedral. How would Banu's conduct affect him?

One evening, the two of them gave Banu a talking to. Papa said in an unusually sharp voice, 'Banu, just tell us exactly what you want to do.' I instantly rattled off my little piece. 'I want to leave Cathedral and serve the country.' Papa said, 'What precisely will you do to serve the country?' I had no ready answer to the question. But I told them I would participate in processions.

Then Papa said to me in his legal voice, 'Look here Banu, if you leave Cathedral now, they will not take you back. Without their certificate you will not get admission to any other school. What will you do without an education?' Then he continued, 'And another thing. If you really want to serve the nation, if you want to join the non-cooperation movement, then ask Avantikabai Gokhale to help you get into one of Gandhiji's *ashrams*. Live and work there. Live by the rules of the ashram. You will not be of any use to anybody if you live here in luxury and play armchair politics. But we will not permit you to leave school and wander around aimlessly here and there if that is what you want. If you decide to live in an ashram, we will give you two khadi saris and blouses and a pair of chappals. That is all. Then you cannot expect to have fancy clothes, money, cars, and things like that. Think carefully and then tell me what you want to do.'

Banu had been given a month to think. During this period she had strict orders to attend school regularly and adhere to all its rules. She was free to do anything else she wished to in the mornings and evenings. Though Papa had made everything clear to me, Mummy was still weeping. She said between sobs, 'Banu, if you leave school, what will happen to Manohar's school and education? We want him to become a famous barrister and High Court judge. How will he do that?' I had no answer to her question.

In keeping with Papa's orders, I did a lot of walking around during that month. I tested the ground before making up my mind. I spent as much time as I could in the company of Avantikabai Gokhale, Balasaheb Kher, and Sarojini Naidu. I got to see their hectic life at close quarters. But I did nothing that could be called work. There was no way I could. Nobody told me what work I was expected to do. Nobody was saying a thing about what work students of our age were to do for the nation after giving up school and college. All we seemed to do was crowd round national leaders when they visited, and sit around doing nothing once they were gone. There was no scheme to train youth in serving the nation once they had given up school and college. There was no planning and not even a modicum of discipline. I felt dreadfully confused. I saw many people at close quarters, but very few seemed to be interested in doing real work. The person in front was busy pushing the man behind even further back in order to get ahead himself. Everyone was busy guarding his own position and prestige. There was some self-sacrifice, but there was much service to self too. This was the picture I began to see. As a result, I lost much of the heady fervour I had felt about serving the nation. Then I decided I would not leave school unless I saw clearly what I was going to do instead. Once I had made this decision, I got down to school work again with renewed zest. I appeared for both the Senior Cambridge and Matriculation examinations.

Meanwhile I had had some wonderful experiences during this period spanning more than two years. I met many people, was witness to many events. Of these the memory that remains etched in my mind is of Lokmanya Tilak's death and funeral. The procession began from Sardar Griha at Crawford Market and ended at Chowpatty. I can still see before me the ocean of humanity that had surged out to follow the procession. Every road, street and bylane along the way was bursting with crowds. The trees were alive with people. There were people on every branch of every tree. But there was no sound. No confusion. People walked slowly, raising their voices only to hail Tilak. Every now and then the crowd would heave like the sea at high tide. I was to see many massive parades in later years, in Moscow and Peking. Throngs collected at those places too. But nowhere did I see anything like the crowds that had gathered for Lokmanya Tilak's funeral procession, nor did I ever again sense the intensity of emotion that had swayed the crowd then.

I entered St Xaviers College after matriculating from Cathedral School. I simply could not take my eyes off that Victorian structure when I first entered it. It wasn't all that large. But its carved columns, long corridors, and tall church-like arches created an illusion of grandeur. The minute I stepped into the college, I began to feel grown-up. Girls and boys occupied separate areas. There was a clutch of girls ouside the women's room. The boys were assigned the central hall. The boys would use any pretext to walk by the women's room to check out the girls and make mental notes about them. The percentage of girl students was very small compared to boys. But since Xaviers was a Jesuit college, the girls were given certain privileges over the boys. The first two rows in every classroom were always reserved for girls. That was also the seating arrangement for all college events.

For me, college studies were no burden at all. The standard of the Senior Cambridge syllabus for which Cathedral prepared its students was a little higher than the first year at college. The college hours too were convenient. Other colleges had intermittent lectures spread out over the whole day. But at Xaviers, lectures were scheduled from 10.30 in the morning to 1.30 in the afternoon. The students were free after that. Of course there were numerous extra-curricular activities as well—sports, socials, debates, and picnics. Banu, now Miss Laud, was in the forefront of them all. Miss Laud was quite a big attraction in the college. When I walked into class, the boys on the back benches would make comments like 'Watch that style!' It tickled me pink to hear such comments, but of course I would pretend not to have heard them as I walked haughtily to my seat, heels clicking. At times like these, I felt as if I was making an entry on stage.

College life was tremendous fun. The days flew by in a whirl of activities. Organizing costumes for plays, meeting other girls' parents to coax them into permitting their daughters to participate in college events, collecting subscriptions, running around to sell tickets for our plays and making up for shortfalls in the budget from my pocket. I did all these things without neglecting my studies. My favourite activity in those days was directing plays. I directed some scenes from *The Merchant of Venice. Backward Child*, a playlet I directed for the annual college day, went down so well that the title became my nickname! My elder sister Shalutai and I acted in the play. She had continued with college even after marriage. She had just begun to study law after her graduation. I too dreamt of continuing my education. I was enjoying every moment of college, particularly because so many other things were constantly happening there besides studies. Unfortunately, I was not destined to enjoy it beyond a year. It was the custom in those days to start making inquiries for a suitable match for a girl as soon as she had come of age. I had heard that negotiations were on for my marriage but I took no personal interest in them; it was just something I got teased about. I was much too busy being the stylish Miss Laud at college.

But hardly had the result of my first year college examination been declared than Mr Vishwanath Khote returned from England. He had had to hurry back because his mother, Anandibai, was ill. He was his parents' only child and his mother wished to see him married while she was still alive. The Lauds and the Khotes were social equals and old friends. Apart from the older people, the young people concerned had also known each other well. The match was perfect in every way. And my marriage was fixed. But the prospect of having to give up college upset me.

Papa and Mummy tried their best to console me. It was a fine match, the young man was an only child, the family immensely wealthy, they were as good as family, they had travelled in Europe, I had known Vishwanath from childhood, etc. In addition, Papa said, 'Didn't Shalutai do law after marriage? You too can do that.'

But as things turned out, I had to give up college immediately after marriage. My mother-in-law-to-be announced, 'We do not want to give our daughter-in-law too much education!' A wonderful phase in my life ended abruptly. I was profoundly unhappy.

Mr Vishwanath Khote and I were already acquainted. There was a tradition of alliances between the Khote and the Laud families. Mine would be the third generation of marriage ties with the family. Both families were socially well known and wealthy. My father-in-law, Mr Kashinath Dinanath Khote, generally known as Kaka, had set up business under the name of K.D. Khote and Company after their extended family had been divided. My father made his money in law while my father-in-law raked in profits on contracts during the First World War besides other business ventures. He owned three or four buildings in Mumbai and bungalows in cooler places like Pune, Panchgani, and Lonavala. Four cars stood on call outside their three-storeyed house in Laburnum Road where the family lived. Kaka also had a few more offices in other towns.

My mother-in-law, or Kaki, Anandibai Khote, was Justice Telang's daughter, a fact she was extremely conceited about. Her parental family's prestige was something she never forgot. It was the measure against which she weighed and assessed everybody else. She was a very proud, hard woman. She was always ill. That is why everything ran according to her wishes. The great wealth of K.D. Khote and Company had even allowed her to do a leisurely tour of Europe.

Kaka and Kaki had only one child, Mr Vishwanath Kashinath Khote. Born in an illustrious family, handsome, pampered, raised up in luxury, he was always cheerful, terribly irresponsible, and extremely self-willed. Everybody called him Visha. We had known each other well from childhood. When we went to Lonavala for the summer in those days, Visha would be visiting the Telangs', his maternal grandparents' bungalow there. We loafed around a lot together. We used to have a wonderful time trekking up and down the hills and valleys of Tungarli, picking and eating *karvanda* berries, walking or biking round Valvan Lake, or going on picnics to Karla-Lohgadh.

The state of Visha's education had always been cause for worry. Because he was so pampered and so self-willed, he paid no attention at all to school or studies. Later he went to Benaras. He was sent to the newly established Hindu University school there. The real reason for doing so was the hope that Mr Pandharinath Kashinath Telang, his maternal uncle, who was a patron of the school, would keep an eye on him and Visha would get down to studies. But the hope was misplaced. After barely scraping through his matriculation, he was packed off to study mechanical engineering in England. But it was the same story there. All he did was drive around town in his motor car.

By the time he went away we were well past childhood. The thread of friendship was broken; in fact we had forgotten our earlier acquaintance. The next time we met, it was as betrotheds. We had not had the opportunity to get to know each other anew as young man and woman; all we knew of each other was from our childhood memories of Lonavala. Family tradition forbade us from meeting each other to find out what had happened to each other between then and now and to discuss our ideas for the future. The wedding was set for an early date because of Kakibai's poor health. It is likely that, because of the old friendship between them, neither the Lauds nor the Khotes bothered to weigh the pros and cons of the alliance. The major consideration in finalizing the match seems to have been family tradition and wealth. Nobody thought it was necessary to find out what the groom himself was like.

It was the year 1923. I was seventeen years old. (I was born on Sankranti day on 14 January 1905). On 19 June, Banu became Mrs Durgabai Khote. My name had undergone many transformations earlier. I was first named Vitha after Papa's mother. But since the daughters-in-law of the family were not permitted by custom to take the name of a family elder, the women called me Baby. Later a Parsi friend of Papa's who used to visit us named me Banu. I remained Banu for many years. Then marriage turned me into Durga. Later, when I joined films, I became Durgabai Khote. That completes the list of my names!

I was the first in the Laud family not to be married from the Laud home in Kandewadi. I got married in the spacious compound of the Laxminarayan temple in Madhav Baug, at C.P. Tank. Both families were very large in themselves and each had a huge circle of friends and business associates. That is why the wedding venue had to be spacious. The Laud-Khote wedding became the talk of the town. Newspapers published descriptions of the wedding ceremony. There were write-ups in society columns. The guests included royal families and aristocrats, judges, and barristers and, from the Khote side, wealthy businessmen, industrialists, and municipal corporators. The Madhav Baug neighbourhood was alive with people. Every road leading to C.P. Tank was choked with horse carriages and motor cars. Police were posted from Khetwadi and Kandewadi all the way to Null Bazaar to control the traffic.

The guests were entertained with a music concert by Kesarbai Kerkar. Also Putli, a famous dancer at that time, presented a *mujra* dance. Kaki was ill. So Papa had made a very comfortable seating arrangement for her, complete with bolsters in velvet covers, against which she could recline and watch the events in the *pandal*. Besides the regular gifts that were exchanged between the families, the special gift due to Kaki as mother-in-law was presented to her in a silver winnowing-pan and comprised all the symbols of marriage—a sari, a blouse, a gold kumkum powder-holder and a diamond wedding necklace.

The month following the wedding was spent entertaining guests and in celebratory feasts. It was only after all the post-wedding rituals were over that we were given a room to ourselves. This was two months after the wedding. Once the guests had left, there were only five people in the house—Kaka, Kaki, my husband, I, and Mr Lalnath Khote. Lalnath was my husband's first cousin on his father's side and Mummy's first cousin on her mother's side. He had lost his parents. So Kaka and Kaki had brought up Lalnath and his two sisters. Lalnath lived in our house in Gamdevi. He too had hardly had any education. At no time in his entire life had he either held a job or worked at his own business. He was a bachelor. Much of his time was spent at his sister, Dr Malinibai Sukhthankar's house.

I had spent all my life from childhood in an open, joyous environment. I found the atmosphere in the Khote house utterly alien. There was no laughter, no conversation, no chatting or joking and teasing here. Kaka was always busy with his work. He used to spend all his time with his Khoja community partners. He would leave the house after lunch around eleven in the morning and return only at nine or ten at night. Most times he would have dined out. One was barely aware of Kaka's presence in the house. He hardly spoke at all. Even on his weekly holiday, a stream of visitors came to see him—businessmen, middlemen, and merchants. Kaka took no interest in household matters. The house was exclusively Kaki's domain. She was in charge of everything from the most trivial staff problems to the keys of the safe. She was unfeeling and egoistic and extremely self-willed. But she was also a superb cook and a good housewife. I learned how to run a household under her guidance. She taught me how to cook for fifty people at a time, giving me exact amounts and proportions. She herself never went out because of the poor state of her health, and she did not approve of her daughter-in-law 'gadding around here and there'.

Mr Khote was very fond of playing billiards and had won many trophies in the game. He used to spend most of his time at the Hindu Gymkhana. We met by ourselves only after dinner in our own room. I used to ask him many questions, but never got satisfactory answers. I was keen to discuss our life together, our future, his business. Not only did he not respond, he did not think it necessary even to think about such matters for himself. I was consumed with curiosity about his business. I was quite ignorant about the kind of work people did in a *pedhi* and about the financial transactions that went on there. But Mr Khote was most unconcerned about it. His attitude was, as long as Kaka was looking after the business and it was thriving, and plenty of money was coming in, we did not need to worry.

There was a great difference between this house and the Laud home and its values, where my hopes and aspirations had been nurtured. I found it extremely difficult to adapt. Papa's and Mummy's married life was happy, open, and full of love. I felt I had been cast off far away from it in the Khote house. The Laud and Khote homes were in the same city. There were cars at our door. Yet I felt as if my parents were living beyond the seven seas. Going home to see them was a complex, tortuous operation. Papa would call up Kaka. Kaka would pass on the message to Kaki, and she would tell me about it three or four days later!

The next two or three years were literally like a prison sentence for me. I cannot recall a single moment of happiness. My education had ceased. Kaki had declared quite categorically that there would be no theatre-nonsense, cinema-nonsense, and song-and-dance nonsense in her house. She did not want the Gandharva Theatre Company in her house. So there was no joy in the newly blossoming life of the eighteen year old bride beyond cooking, serving, and clearing up. Not a single servant was willing to stay in that house for long, so I had to do all the chores.

Meanwhile we were blessed with a son. He was called Narayannath after the patriarch of the Khote family. The Khotes added 'nath' to all their sons' names in fulfilment of a vow the family had made to their deity. But since by custom I was not allowed to take a family elder's name, I gave my son a calling name, Bakul. I love the *bakul* flower. It never loses its fragrance, not even after it has faded. Though the Khote home was silent and loveless, Bakul brought fragrance into my life. He was a lovely baby with a fine straight nose, a sweet face, and a high forehead. He had beautiful hands with long tapering fingers—an early sign of how tall he would be when he grew up.

Kaki was overjoyed to have a grandson. She could barely contain her joy. She had been apprehensive that I might bring my mother's tradition of three daughters into the Khote home. She had hinted at this fear on several occasions. She would often say, 'I don't want any girls in my house. Visha must have a son.' So Bakul's arrival made everybody happy. He was placed in a silver winnowing-pan and given a lick of honey off a gold coin. A huge feast was held for the sixth-day prayer. His naming ceremony was a magnificent affair. The Lauds and the Khotes between them left no ritual undone. My grandmother-in-law, Kaka's mother, was still alive. According to custom, she looked upon her great-grandchild's face by the light of a golden oil-lamp.

Nobody in the house knew anything about Kaka's business. Nobody knew when he had begun to speculate in shares and play the market and when his business had begun to slide. Mr Khote, on the other hand, remained under the grand illusion of unlimited family wealth. He would drop in at the office first thing in the morning, assume that business was flourishing, and go off to the Hindu Gymkhana or some other club to spend the day playing billiards or cards till late at night.

It was towards the end of 1925, when we had returned from visiting the temple in Goa, that I became aware of some disturbance in the house. My suspicion was proved right. Kaka had speculated with Lalnath's money too and Lalnath had begun creating scenes in the house. But Mr Khote kept insisting stubbornly that all was well. The bubble finally burst in August 1926. Lalnath left the house to stay with his sister. Creditors began taking charge of properties one by one. By October of that year we were faced with the prospect of handing over the house itself. It was the last Monday of Shravan. I had finished the cooking, made the ritual offering of a fistful of grain to Lord Shiva, regular offerings to the other deities, and returned to my room. Eighteen month old Bakul lay in my lap. Mr Khote was getting ready to go out. He was standing before the large mirror absorbed in buttoning down his collar. In the middle of trying to fix his gold collar-stud, he suddenly stopped and said, 'Banu, we have lost everything.'

'What have you lost now? You're always dropping your collar buttons. It must be lying around somewhere here', I said.

As he continued buttoning his shirt, he turned slightly and said with some irritation, 'Don't be silly Banu! We have lost all our money. Kaka has lost it all on the stock market. We might even have to leave this house in a month.'

I was struck speechless by what he said.

'Are you pulling my leg?' I asked urgently.

'No I'm not. It's true', he replied gravely. He had now tied his bow. Then he added, 'Don't worry. I'll get a lucrative job. Or we'll go into business.'

As he spoke, he put pomade on his hair and combed it neatly. Then he picked up his jacket from off the back of a chair, while I sat rooted to the spot. There was a question mark before me. What was going to happen now? Bakul was being naughty. He was the Khote's pampered first grandson. His mummy was not playing with him, so he pulled her braid. That brought me out of my trance. By then Mr Khote was ready, and on his way out. As he left he said, 'I'm off to the gymkhana. I might be late home. Don't wait for me for dinner.'

Tears gathered in my eyes and spilled over in quick drops. I hugged Bakul hard and sobbed my heart out. Bakul flung his arms around me affectionately. All was lost. But I had my Bakul. Bringing him up, teaching him, making him a responsible human being—I had to do all of that. My mind ran amok. Gripped by such thoughts I held Bakul even tighter. But I couldn't rid my mind of the question: what do we do now? Where had the millionaire Khotes' millions gone? And how? I could not understand it at all. I did not know what to do or whom to turn to. I did not have a clue. But of one thing I was convinced. Though Mr Khote had said he would find a job or go into business, the words were meaningless.

The following day was the last Tuesday of Shravan. Mummy had planned a splendid Mangalagaur for me. It was going to be held at Laud Mansion on Charni Road. I climbed the stairs of the mansion on leaden feet. The liftman stared after me. 'Banubai', he called out, 'The lift is working. Please come.' I handed Bakul over to him and asked him to go up with him. I climbed the stairs very slowly, trying to get a hold of myself. I wanted to buy as much time as I could. I did not have the courage to face Mummy. What would I tell her? If she and Papa got to know what had happened, what would it do to them?

The moment I stepped through the door, my sisters and the others crowded around me. 'What do you mean by coming so late?', they demanded, 'It's ages since the priest came.'

Suddenly I was sobbing. Everyone thought my mother-in-law had probably scolded me. They knew what she was like. Mummy rescued me from the crowd, took me by the hand saying, 'Come Banya. Come and wash up. I've drawn the water', and led me indoors. 'Here's your puja sari. Wear it.' I couldn't utter a word. But Mummy was very understanding. She did not ask me any questions.

I managed somehow to get through that evening. When it was all over, I flung my arms around Mummy and Papa and sobbed my heart out. Papa had already got wind of what had happened. He had asked Kaka about it. Offered legal help. But Kaka had said, 'Everything's fine.' Papa could do nothing after that. Papa tried to console me, saying, 'That's how business is. Things can't be that bad.' I knew Papa was only saying it to make me feel better.

Soon after that, we left our Laburnum Road home. Before that we had had to face innumerable problems. Mr Khote had gone down with typhoid. That in turn had brought on an asthmatic attack. Kaki's health had worsened. With no money in hand, life had become a daily struggle and full of frayed tempers. Kaka took Kaki away to Pune to stay with the Curmallys. Papa gave us a flat in Laud Mansion. I tried very hard to find a small place where we could live independently and fend for ourselves. But Papa would have none of it. He told me very firmly, 'You can do what you please, but I will not permit your children to live in some hole in a pokey alley. I admire your guts Banya. I'm proud of my girl. But I will not allow the children to suffer. We must safeguard their childhood.'

I was convinced by what he said. But I made a decision that I would not burden Papa with any other kind of dependence besides the flat.

Around that time Bakul's brother was born—sweet, lovely, boisterous Harin. Laud Mansion resounded with Bakul's and Harin's games. The house had been built around 1924–5. Papa, Mummy, and Manohar had moved from the Kandewadi house to this place. The other house had been sold off and the family had scattered. Of course Laud Mansion too belonged to the whole family. They lived off the rent that came from it. Papa had kept two flats for himself, crediting the rent to the family account. The rest of the house was rented out to other tenants, a doctor and a hospital. Needless to say, this building too was burdened with debt.

I was constantly on the lookout for some work for myself. But what was I qualified to do? Without a graduate degree I couldn't even get a teaching job at school. There were only two avenues open for women to earn a living in those days—teaching and nursing. It was impossible for me to try for either because of my domestic problems. Quite discouraged, I took on private tuitions. I taught English. But that income was dependent on having students. I had no work that would bring me a good, steady income.

Mr Khote had found himself a small job. But his asthma was making it stressful. He had never worked before in his life. He had never done anything at all, ever. Without a university degree, it was impossible for him to get a better job. It was with the influence and efforts of a highly placed family friend that he had found this small job in the municipality. He was somehow managing to stick with it. His salary was a mere 150 rupees. After deductions, he got Rs 130 in hand. Add to this his habit of staying away from work every now and again; this made me fear constantly that he would lose the job. We were thankful that our influential friend's kindness ensured that he retained it at least as a façade. But the situation was unstable and thoughts of the future filled me with dread. Papa had already helped us so much by letting us stay in such an expensive flat that I was determined not to depend on him for anything else. I was therefore looking out for private tuition opportunities. Some fetched me Rs 15 a month each. But there was one in a wealthy Gujarati family for which I got paid Rs 40. I used to walk everyday from Charni Road to Peddar Road to teach there.

Then one day, at the beginning of 1930, Mr Wadia went to meet my sister Shalutai, unexpectedly. He had been her friend at college. He was making a silent film in partnership with Mr Mohan Bhavnani. But just as the film was on the point of being completed, the talkies had arrived. Mr Bhavnani was a very intelligent film producer. Seeing that talkies were the new thing, he decided to add a ten minute talkie piece to his film, and managed to rake in a decent profit on it by advertising it as 'A 50 per cent walking, talking, dancing, singing film.' The film was called *Farebi Jaal*. Mrs Meenakshi Bhavnani was the heroine of the silent part. But she could not speak Hindi or sing. Messrs Bhavnani and Wadia were therefore on the lookout for an educated woman from a good family. In those days women from good families and films did not go together. Mr Wadia had come to meet Shalutai because of their previous acquaintance. She rejected Mr Wadia's proposal outright but pointed to me. She said, 'I have a crazy sister who is mad about theatre and things like that. Let's try asking her.'

Shalutai brought Mr Wadia to me. I was a woman in need. This was like a straw to a drowning man. So I assented. I had no clue what the film business was all about, what one did in it, where one got costumes and make-up, what lines I would have to speak, how one was supposed to play a role or to sing. I was terrified. I had no idea what I'd got myself into. I literally did not know what I had done. At the same time, I had to find some kind of work. All I had been doing till then was folding my hands before God in prayer, 'Dear God, please look after my children . . . please look after my children.'

Mr Khote returned from the gymkhana in the evening. I told him what had happened. 'You are mad', he said, laughing the whole thing off. But I spent the whole night wide awake, clasping Bakul and Harin close to my heart. Mr Wadia came again the next day. He outlined my work for me. It was a sad scene in which I had to sing a couple of lines. It was to be shot over two nights. Mrs Meenakshi Bhavnani did not like performing before the studio hands. Nights suited me too. The Imperial Studio was located on Kennedy Bridge. We got there at seven o'clock in the evening. The shooting lasted all night. I had no idea what and how it was turning out. But I poured my heart into doing whatever I was asked to do. I wept a lot. Mr and Mrs Bhavnani were very kind to me. But I was petrified. The studio was dank and revolting, full of dark corners and junk. The garbage strewn around the place gave off a stink that made breathing almost impossible. The following night, I pleaded with Indutai to go with me to the studio. The shooting finally ended at five in the morning. They handed me a cheque for Rs 250. I returned home at dawn with it. I put it under my pillow and fell fast asleep, almost lifeless with fatigue. The money I had earned was not much; but even that much helped me face immediate problems.

My role in *Farebi Jaal* was very small. It lasted only ten minutes. I even had a song in it that I had sung myself. Mr Wadia was Mr Bhavnani's associate. He had described only my scene to me. I had no idea what preceded or followed it. Nor did I have any idea about the film medium itself. Mrs Bhavnani was the heroine of the film. I played the role of her older sister. My husband in the film beats me up in a fit of drunkenness and I die of it. My sister runs away and takes shelter in a prostitute's house. Mr Bhavnani had shown all the debauchery that goes on in such a house. Drunkenness, sex, lewd gestures, love games, women smoking, all these things had been shot. The camerawork was abysmal. Everybody looked like ghosts. My singing, my dialogue while I was being beaten, were all done in a weepy voice.

Nobody in my family knew what film acting meant. My sisters thought it was something like what we had done in college plays. *Farebi Jaal* means 'Web of Deceit'. When the film was released, I found myself trapped in that web. The film advertisements had started appearing two months earlier. Mr Bhavnani, shrewd businessman that he was, took full advantage of my name: that is, the name of both my families. The Lauds and the Khotes were highly esteemed families of the time and Mr Bhavnani used that fact. Newspapers carried huge advertisements headlined, 'Introducing the daughter of the famous solicitor Mr Laud and the daughter-in-law of the well-known Khote family.' The film opened at Majestic Cinema, located in a Maharashtrian neighbourhood. It was my misfortune that the film turned out to be the very dregs, worthless in content and in production values. As a result, the Maharashtrian community tore me to shreds. One newspaper played on the names of my families— 'Durgabai, falsely pampered.' (In Marathi 'laud' means pampering and 'khote' false). It became impossible for me to leave the house and go out anywhere in Girgaum. Everyone was pointing fingers at me and saying the nastiest things. I didn't know where to go or what to do. It came to a point where all kinds of people were saying what they pleased about me. The Laud and Khote families began to behave as if they literally wanted to kill me. In their opinion I had brought shame to the good names of the families.

Only Mummy and Papa stood by me. Papa even complimented me. 'I don't care what the rest of the film is like. But you have shown a way for women to earn a living', he said. Even that much was enough to fill my heart with gratitude. But my problems remained unsolved. In fact they became worse. I began to lose my tuitions because I had acted in a film. Pitch black night engulfed me.

Then one day, Prabhat dawned in my life.

3

My Mother's Home

My mother's maiden home, the Sukhthankar house, was as still, silent, and cold as the Laud home was full of life, laughter, and people. The atmosphere in the house was as dry and cold as the black stone on which its three storeys stood. Perched at the very tip of Walkeshwar, its location was utterly lovely—the vast sea before it, a forest of wild berry trees on the right, and a little beyond that, the delightful wooded environs of Government House. The entire city of Bombay lay within its sight. But none of the occupants of that house had the capacity to enjoy the riches offered by nature.

Only two members of the family lived in that huge house: our grandmother Dhaklibai Sukhthankar, whom we called Bai, and her younger son Bhalchandra. The third occupant was not a family member. This was the Hindustani music scholar and theorist, Vishnu Narayan Bhatkhande, popularly known as Anna. Bai was extremely rich, but just as unhappy. She was the only living child of her parents. Naturally she had inherited her father, Mr Shantaram Patkar's, entire estate. That enormous estate included innumerable bungalows, orchards, and tenement houses, as well as Shantaramachi Chaal in Mugbhat Lane, the tenements whose compound had become historically important. All the political meetings for movements like Home Rule, Independence, and Non-cooperation used to be held here. Lokmanya Tilak, Mahatma Gandhi, Annie Besant, Chittaranjan Das, Lala Lajpat Rai, the Ali brothers, and the Patel brothers—all the leaders of the time—had made their thundering speeches there.

But this immense wealth had brought my grandmother nothing but mental stress. She became a widow at a very young age and found herself suddenly responsible for rearing four children single-handedly. She was an extremely intelligent, very well-read woman who even knew English. But in terms of human support, both her parental and her marital families were sources of pain. Wealth became the root of jealousy, envy, and grief. Under the circumstances, Bai's life became very lonely. The whole house came under its shadow. She was plunged into grief on account of her own children too. Her eldest son had stubbornly insisted on going to England to study when he was only sixteen, and didn't return during her lifetime. She never saw him again. This pained Bai deeply. Her younger son, uncle Bhalu, was very bright but self-willed, whimsical, and crabby. Though he had studied law and set up his own solicitors' firm called Gupte-Sukthankar Solicitors, he did not do too well. His wife Dr Malini Sukthankar was a municipal corporator.

My aunt Lalita also had an unhappy life. She was very fair-skinned and had long raven-black hair which she spent a great deal of time caring for: oiling it regularly, sunning it and brushing it. She was married into the Laud home, to a cousin of Papa's. She used to live in the Kandewadi house. Unfortunately, she never had a happy family life. All her four children died in infancy. Living in the same house as her sister, she must surely have felt acutely the sharp contrast between her own circumstances and her sister's. All in all, the only joy in Bai's life came from my mother. Bai's daily routine included four or five hours of prayer, some time spent managing the estate, and the rest reading.

Bai was passionately fond of music. But it was unthinkable for women to learn any art in those days. However, she made an enormous if indirect contribution to the codification of Hindustani classical music by offering all possible support to Mr Anna Bhatkhande. Bai spent thousands of rupees to help him in his project of evolving a notation system to teach Hindustani music. She paid honoraria to all the musicians who assisted him in his work, and housed them. She enabled him to travel all over India to collect the information he required. The teaching methodology for Hindustani music that he evolved was built on the strength of her support. Yet, the house where this was happening was itself musically mute. How unfortunate that not a single member of Bai's family benefited from the presence of so much music in the house. Bai herself loved music.

Uncle Bhalu loved playing the harmonium and the violin. Bai's son-in-law, Papa, was extremely fond of the arts. I, from the next generation, spent a lifetime with art. Yet not a single note was ever heard in that place which should have been a surging sea of music.

We children were always excited about going to Grandma's. But once there, we felt imprisoned. There were no shouts of excitement and no laughter. In fact there was no sound of any kind. The only sound was of the sea, and of uncle Bhalu's cockatoos—the one solemn, the other shrill. In that three-storeyed house, Bai moved around alone on the third floor. She would sit on the verandah for hours looking at the bottomless ocean with blank eyes. She came downstairs only if she had to. Otherwise she descended only at mealtimes and to go for a drive in her closed car in the evenings. That was her sole contact with people.

Uncle Bhalu occupied the middle storey. He lived his life between his study and the cot on the verandah. It was an untidy, chaotic place, covered in dust. Nobody was allowed to enter it or touch a single object, not even to dust it. That was the law. Attached to his room were an enormous hall and a library. Their windows were always kept closed, as if the sea breeze was disagreeable to the inmates. This was where the office of the Hindustani Music Research Project was located. All their administrative work was conducted from here. The place was like one of those old, musty museums. A pair of beautiful *tanpuras* stood dejectedly, facing the wall. The room was arranged as if for a private concert. Mattresses, bolsters, and cushions covered the floor. But no tanpura had ever been strummed nor a singer's voice ever heard in the place. All musical knowledge was locked up in books, gramophone records, and a huge old gramophone horn. This was Anna's space.

Anna Bhatkhande was an erudite musicologist who had once enjoyed the reputation of being a fine singer. But we had never heard him sing. At some point, fearing a heart condition, he had put his tanpura down, never to pick it up again. The pen took the place of the tanpura and he threw himself into his work on the Hinduatani classical music system. Nobody was allowed to approach the subject of music, his domain. If you did venture to ask him a question about it, you received a disdainful look and no answer. Anna was by nature disinclined to explain or to persuade. Perhaps it angered him to be asked trivial, superficial questions about a subject that he considered profound. Perhaps his anger was a manifestation of the inner pain that an artist, forced to give up practising his art, feels. But on the whole he appeared to believe that music was not meant for 'you people'.

An extremely important part of his research project was conducted in these rooms. Musicians from all over the country were invited for recording on 'Cylinders'. This was a very old system of recording. Anna would make his notes on the scales, structures, contours, and categories of existing Hindustani ragas from these recorded samples. This formed the basis of his volumes on the Hindustani music system.

An elderly musician once came to Anna, accompanied by his young son. The music recording went on for a very long time. When the old musician finally emerged, he was wiping his eyes. Covering his face he muttered, 'I've been robbed, I've been robbed', and broke into uncontrollable sobs. On hearing the recording he had realized that he had parted with all the knowledge he had ever possessed. The fee in his hand must then have seemed like a paltry price for a lifetime's work.

The atmosphere on the ground floor of the house was a complete contrast to the upper floors. The household shrine, the kitchen, the dining room, were all located on this floor. It was a huge airy space buzzing with servants. When we visited Granny's place, it was here that we spent all our time, laughing and playing. All the fun of being in the Walkeshwar house was here. This is where Balkrishna the clerk stammered and bustled about; the two maids, Anni and Jamni, told tales about their village near Sawantwadi; the north-Indian servants made us laugh with their broken Marathi; and Waman the water-server narrated children's stories. Waman also sang an amusing song about bed-bugs which went something like this:

> Lord these bed-bugs are driving me crazy!
> Had my bath, said my prayers, cooked myself some rice
> Scooped it up and found in there a bed-bug fat and nice.
> Ten o'clock, late for work, I hurried to the office
> Opened my book and found there was a bed-bug in the pages.

The song continued this way through the events of the whole day. We split our sides laughing. The servants were very affectionate towards us. Chandrabai always said that the house became a home when Manjula's children visited. Chandrabai was a widow from a good family who had arrived at Bai's place years ago to cook and keep house. She had spent all her life there and had no other place or people she could call her own. She fed us and looked after us with a lot of care.

Going down to the basement from the kitchen was very exciting. This *budav*, as we called it, was in fact a huge tunnel carved out of massive stone. The huge rocks that jutted from the ground had been leveled to make the floor. Even the steps leading into the tunnel were hewn out of stone. Perhaps the house was founded on this very stone. They said smugglers used the tunnel to come and go. Maybe the story was meant to put fear into us children. It was a large airy place, bright with sunshine pouring in through tall stone windows. There were hollows in the tunnel which sent back echoes. A tombstone stood against the outer wall of the budav. Many people lit oil lamps there every evening.

Bai hardly ever visited anybody. But she never failed to visit Kandewadi during festivals and on each of our birthdays, carrying baskets of fruit and flowers and large salvers of milk sweets. She loved us and was very fond of Papa too, but she never fondled us or held us close. She would give us the gifts, put a gold guinea in the birthday-child's hand, and leave instantly, as if she wished to distance herself from all human bonds. Bai, with her white *mull* sari, dried up skin, Kashmir shawl draped over the shoulders, Parsi style velvet slippers, and eyes brimming over with sorrow, was a monument of grief. One day when she was praying, her sari caught fire from a silver oil-lamp. She was alone upstairs in her quarters. By the time she could quench the fire single-handed, her entire body was blistered. She never recovered from the accident. Finally she died of consumption.

Bai left all her estate to Bhalu uncle. She had given up hope of her elder son Gulab ever returning. They never met. He returned to India with his family many years after she died. He was a very handsome man. His general style was very German. He had a fair complexion, dreamy eyes, and a medium length beard. He always had a pipe or cigar in his mouth. He spoke little and that too in a clipped manner. He had moved to Germany after squandering a whole lot of money and much of his youth in England. He was strongly influenced by the German people and their culture. A huge change overcame him now. He plunged into a serious study of Hindu philosophy, and acquired a doctorate in the subject. Back in India, he settled in Pune and continued with his research work in Sanskrit at the Bhandarkar Institute. He became a Sanskrit scholar. His translation of the Sanskrit play *Swapnavasavadattam* into German was held in high regard in Germany.

One day after his return to India in 1917, he discussed cinema at great length with Mummy and Papa. In the course of this conversation, he touched on all its aspects. He spoke of the medium, its development, its wide-ranging usefulness, and its potential as a link in international relations. We listened to him in awed silence. Finally Gulab uncle said to Papa, 'Pandurangbhai, cinema is not merely a medium of entertainment. It is going to touch and influence every part of life—education, science, the arts. Nothing will remain outside its orbit.'

Today, fifty odd years later, uncle Gulab's prediction would appear to have come true.

4

Memories of the Marathi Stage: 1910–26

I had inherited Papa's love of the arts. Appreciation of the arts was in his very bones. It was he who fed me my first sips of theatre madness. I saw plays continuously for twenty years from the time I was five, mostly Marathi plays, both prose and musical. Gujarati and Urdu plays too. The first play I saw was Gandharva Natak Mandali's *Manapaman*. It was an extremely important event in my life. Little five-year-old Banu who had to be lifted into her seat. But I was drawn to theatre from that very moment and am still flailing around in its powerful current today. Banu saw plays like *Manapaman*, *Swayamvar*, *Ekach Pyala*, *Draupadi*, *Saubhadra*, and *Mricchhakatik* thousands of times. Besides these there was the intermittent bonus of other plays like *Mookanayak*, *Shapasambrahm*, *Shakuntal*, and *Sharada*. The memories of Gandharva's plays had left layers and layers of permanent impressions on her mind. She knew entire plays by heart. Musical phrases and trills from the songs echoed constantly in her ears. She would identify intimately with all the characters on stage and be carried away by them. She became one with the joys and sorrows of the heroines. She laughed and cried with them all. She lived their emotions not only in the auditorium, but outside it too.

The memories of that era of Marathi theatre are so vividly etched in my mind that even today when I hear Narayanrao's—Bal Gandharva's—recorded songs, the sounds and sights of that era of theatre return to me in every detail. Elphinstone Theatre, its broken, slithery wooden chairs, the enraptured audience, swaying in sheer bliss for hours on end to the sound of music, spellbound by the flow of emotions, grown one with the stage. These scenes unspool before my eyes like a film. They seduce me yet again with their magic. But theatre turned out in the end to be just a pastime. I regret now that I took nothing from it, neither an understanding of music nor the art of drama. I did not have the vision then.

I can never forget seeing Narayanrao as Bhamini that day. Papa took me backstage at the end of the first act. Narayanrao stood before an enormous mirror, straightening his ornaments and sari, ready for his next entry. I stood there staring at him. Papa asked me, 'Do you recognise him?' Instead of answering his question, I said to Narayanrao, 'Are you the lady who visits us?' I think Narayanrao was momentarily taken aback. Then he said, 'Do I visit you in these clothes?' I merely shook my head, but my eyes would not budge from his face. His sari, his jewellery, the rich stole over his shoulders, none of these made any sense to my child's mind. But I was certain, even then, that I was looking upon a most beauteous sight. I honestly do feel, even now, that such natural beauty and such sweet charm are rare things to behold.

Narayanrao's body had a softness that made it perfect for female roles. His movements were so graceful and attractive that even the most beautiful women of the time attempted to model themselves on him. There was not a trace of theatricality or affectation in the way Narayanrao carried himself. His movements were absolutely natural. Off-stage he looked tall and was of medium build, with not a hint of effeminacy. There was only one exception, his long hair, which was knotted and pushed under his black fur cap. He did not go anywhere without the cap. Apart from this, he did not affect any physical gestures or mannerisms of the kind displayed by other actors who played female roles. His female roles were his profession. A very attractive profession, certainly, but just that. I do not remember his profession ever crossing the dazzle of stage lights. We visited him often and he came over to our house just as often. His behaviour was extremely informal. He would give concerts at night in our Lonavala house during our Christmas parties. Naturally, he would always come prepared to stay overnight. But nothing he did or said on these occasions made anybody feel uncomfortable or embarrassed. His behaviour was always straightforward and modest.

There was a *parijatak* tree in our garden. He would sit under it and chat with us like one of the family. He would talk at length about the stage, about make-up, costume, hairstyles. He had great respect for artists like Dhurandhar and Anandrao Painter, brother of the famous Baburao Painter. After all, it was their ideal of female beauty that he had internalized for his roles. He and Mummy used to have long discussions about these subjects. On one such occasion he said to her, 'Akka, our Banu is dark-skinned. One of these days I'll make her up lightly to show you. You won't even notice the make-up. But you'll see what a difference it will make to her face.' This was around 1918, a time when nobody wore make-up everyday. At most you plastered your face generously with chalk-white Cashmere Bouquet talcum powder and that was that. It is remarkable that Narayanrao should have, in those days, talked about enhancing the beauty of a face with make-up.

Narayanrao was not very educated, but he had a keen aesthetic sense. He visited the Italian hairdresser, Fucille, with Mummy to get his opinion on which hairstyle would suit his face best and to have a wig made in that style. We once took Narayanrao to Excelsior Theatre to see Anna Pavlova dance. He was spellbound by her performance. I still remember the remark he made at the end of it. 'This is beautiful. Beautiful beyond imagination. But there's something mechanical about it. Their idea of beauty is very different from ours.' At a time when the Marathi stage was influenced by western ideas of set design, his set designer, Baburao Painter, and he took their inspiration from the Ajanta Caves and the Hampi ruins for Draupadi's Palace of Illusions and for the stage set of *Swayamvar*.

Narayanrao was an attractive man. He had an alluring face, a well-proportioned body, a light-coloured complexion, and expressive eyes—natural endowments that were perfect for his profession. But the beauty of his hands and gestures lay beyond description. You couldn't help but notice them, whether they were Bhamini's hands wielding a rapier; Rukmini's holding the garland for her chosen bridegroom's neck; Sindhu's turning the thick peg of the grindstone; Draupadi's held out to Krishna in tearful supplication, or even a courtesan's seductively offering paan. From shoulder to wrist his arms glowed with a soft lustre, almost like ivory in their fairness. Supple, delicately formed, and rounded though they were, they could also suggest steely strength on occasion. His fingers were the epitome of natural grace when they twisted and untwisted the end of a sari in maidenly coyness.

Many heated debates have taken place to date on the subject of males playing female roles. People have argued that men playing women amounts to dishonouring women. But one thing is indubitably true, that there was nothing even remotely perverse or unnatural in the way Narayanrao played his heroines. In deportment, costume, jewellery and every other detail, his female characters were imbued with the grace and dignity of women from upper-class families.

He wore rich, finely woven saris and stoles for his female lead roles. He strictly eschewed cheap colours and gaudy, flashy over-embroidered fabrics. He only wore textures that moulded themselves to the body and draped well. The Indore and Maheshwar saris he wore in his plays on social themes, became trendsetters for the fashionable, upper-class women of Maharashtra. Narayanrao took a keen personal interest in the overall look of his productions, bringing to them his fine sense of aesthetics. When Sindhu, the heroine of *Ekach Pyala* falls on bad times, he wore saris that looked like faded versions of the ones she had worn in happier times. She could not have afforded to buy new saris then. So he combed the whole of Chor Bazar till he found the saris he was looking for. His ornaments in mythological plays were replicas of what he had seen in reproductions of the Ajanta Cave paintings or traditional, gem-studded designs worn for generations by women from princely families. Mummy possessed a pair of dangling gem-studded earrings from Jaipur. Narayanrao used to call her Akka, elder sister. He fully exploited the rights of this relationship by demanding the earrings from her to wear in his first scene as Draupadi. They stayed with him for many years. By a strange coincidence, I demanded them back from him with equal insistence when I needed to wear precisely that design of earrings years later when I acted in *Ayodhyecha Raja*. They were perfect for my role as Taramati, adding a special touch of grace to her costume.

Narayanrao's acting style was sheer enchantment. In those days the audience did not observe performances in great detail. It was enough for them that the dialogue suited the situation and mood, that the actor spoke it clearly, imbued it with strong emotional expression, and had a voice that projected it well. Even then, Narayanrao maintained the strong contours of every character he played with such consistency that he left his mark on the roles for all time. Every future actor who played Bhamini, or Revati, or Sindhu was compared to Narayanrao, whether the actor was a woman or a man. Once, when he saw my acting in a film, he said, 'This is one actress who has never imitated me.' I was naturally thrilled to hear this. For, by the time I entered films, Narayanrao's acting style had changed drastically. Gone were his modest deportment and chaste gestures. They had been replaced now by a charade of vulgar mannerisms. He would stand on tiptoe, jump about, move his neck coyly this way and that, giggle frivolously, and stress the wrong words to pervert the meanings of lines. Such tricks brought his acting down to a vulgar level. The pity of it is that the next generation of actors not only emulated all these tricks, but also made their own contributions to the repertoire. This became the standard acting style. This was theatre. This is what the audience applauded.

By this time Narayanrao, and indeed all the actors of the Gandharva Natak Mandali, had become flabby, ungainly, and obese. When Narayanrao, Master Krishna, and Ranade stood together on the stage in Amritsiddhi, you could not see anything around or beyond them! The stage was tightly packed! Their tasteless multi-coloured costumes and ugly wigs made a travesty of the saintly Mira. Narayanrao's heroines had become pathetic. His fall began around 1926. Papa talked to him about it once. His answer was heart-rending. 'Sir, when the entertainer grows old, he must resort to such tricks.' He was fully conscious of his condition. He had lost his self-confidence. Around this time he played a male role, Pundarik, in Shapasambhram. I asked him, 'Narayanrao, what did you think of your performance?' He said, 'What can I say Banutai? I stopped just short of reaching for my pallu. I did everything else.' Prabhat Films presented him very effectively in the film Dharamatma in which he played the male lead. But he was not happy. He said, 'My wife says, what awful home-spun costumes you've worn in this film. Where's the splendour of your silk saris and stoles in this role?' Prabhat Films instantly cancelled his contracts for future films. Later, he produced a film with Mr Baburao Painter in which he played a female role. It would be best not to describe it.

I used to literally plead with Narayanrao to give me just one chance to act on stage. It didn't matter how small the role was. I was even prepared to play the heroine's slave-girl. But he would say with genuine concern, 'Please don't, Banutai. Once this grease paint goes on the face, it never comes off. Don't you get into this messy business.' I would have loved to play the slave-girl in one particular scene in *Swayamvar* in which she sings, '*Ati anand phulavi kalika*'. The boy who played the role had sung the song beautifully and won loud applause. Later his voice had broken and he had disappeared who knows where. Yet my dream remained unfulfilled. Narayanrao refused to give in to my plea. But that did not stop destiny from taking its course.

BAL GANDHARVA'S MUSIC

The spell that Narayanrao's music cast on the Maharashtrian mind continues to be as powerful today as it was in his heydey, sixty years ago. There must be thousands of people like me who listen to his records with their hearts in their ears. His voice was a divine gift. All its natural qualities, unique virtues, and greatness were contained in the four syllables, Bal Gandharva. The title had been bestowed on him by Lokmanya Bal Gangadhar Tilak. The great vocalist Alladiya Khan Saheb once said, 'What emerges from his throat is the true musical note.' Khansaheb was often seen at the Elphinstone Theatre. That solemn imposing figure in a pink turban and blue tinted glasses, with his pure white hair, beard, moustache, and side whiskers, swayed for hours to Bal Gandharva's music. A great maestro himself, he would sit completely absorbed, for ten hours at a time, carried away by the flow of the music. When Bal Gandharva hit a particularly fine note, or a rapid *taan* burbled by in a spontaneous stream of crystal clear drops, Khansaheb's fingers would gently wipe away the tears flowing from his eyes.

Narayanrao never betrayed his music. He used to pour his heart and soul into it. He always sang the songs exactly as Annasaheb Kirloskar, the late Bakhalebuwa, or Master Krishnarao had composed them. Why, he did not change even the *ghazal*-like tunes that Sunderabai had given to the songs in *Ekach Pyala*. He would never add ornamental twists and turns of musical phrases to the original melodies against their nature, just to win the applause of his audience. With age, his voice lost its purity. It tired easily and he could not hold his breath for too long. Yet with all that, his singing remained as sweet as ever. I once asked him in my usual way, 'Narayanrao, how do you always sing so sweetly, beautifully, and effortlessly? Who taught you?' He said, 'I had an aunt. She used to sing very beautifully, sweetly, and effortlessly. I took my first lessons in singing at her feet.'

Producers of contemporary plays claim that songs in plays harm the drama, interrupt the flow of narrative, sound artificial, and are quite unnecessary. But the singer-actors of those days were accomplished in integrating song and speech. Song would start where speech ended in a smoothly blended, continuous flow. This allowed the audience's emotions too, to move uninterruptedly from the prosaic to the lyrical. The link between the two was always appropriately made. If I remember right, the singer-actors began their songs without waiting for the orchestra to start, taking off smoothly from the emotional pitch that their speech had hit. To do this, they must have had to carry that basic note in their heads. The accompanying instruments would then pick up the note and blend in with the song. One thing is certain. One never sensed even a moment's gap between speech and song. They formed a continuum that carried the audience along on a rising wave of emotion. Gandharva's plays were full of such instances. In *Ekach Pyala*, for example, Sindhu's speech ended with, 'Don't look at me like that my baby', leading most naturally into the song which began, 'Don't look at me with those pleading eyes.' The pitch and emotion of Draupadi's prayer, 'Lord Madhava, today though I . . .' would emerge from the line, 'How often do I burden you, my Lord. . . .'

GANDHARVA NATAK MANDALI

The moment advertisements went up on the walls of the city announcing the imminent arrival in town of the Gandharva Natak Mandali, Mumbai's theatre lovers would begin to hover eagerly around the premises of the Sunkersett temple. For years, the Mandali had stayed in the house adjoining the temple whenever they came to Mumbai. The Gandharva Natak Mandali had grown into something of a princely state. Wherever they went, three or four rail wagons full of stuff went with them. Curtains, wings, flats, trunks, beddings, kitchen stuff—it was like a moving township.

Along with this came a herd of cows and buffalo- complete with cowherds, to supply the company with milk and milk products. Leading the troupe of actors was the company manager, Balasaheb Pandit. Dressed in a long coat, always unbuttoned, a black cap and patent leather pumps, one hand holding up the pleats of his finely woven dhoti, he would get busy ordering his soldiers around. Dadasaheb Katdare was always beside him like his right hand. Large crowds of theatre lovers stood about with requests for advance reservations. Katdare was a master at making promises. Having promised everybody what they wanted, he would give them the slip and escape unscathed. Once the Gandharva Natak Mandali was known to be in town, people came thronging to see their plays. The company was formed after breaking away from the famed Kirloskar Company. It had some of the finest talents of the time in its fold— Narayanrao Rajhans, Ganpatrao Bodas, Govindrao Tembe, and Jogalekar were all leading stars of the Marathi stage. But chiefly, it was Bal Gandharva's name that was on everybody's lips.

The way the Gandharva Natak Mandali established itself from the very start was like an invitation to the evil eye. Every step it took until 1926 carried it to the summit of success. Many events took place in between, but none of them harmed the Company's progress in any way. But when Govindrao Tembe and Ganpatrao Bodas quit, the Company became a one-pole tent around Bal Gandharva. But he still had with him extremely talented writers, actors, and musicians who enhanced the company's glory and impact. The Company's music was first in the hands of the late Bukhlebuwa, and then Master Krishnarao. Thirakhwa Khansaheb for tabla and Majid Khansaheb for sarangi were an important part of the Company's splendour. Pandharpurkarbuwa, Madhavrao Joshi, Master Krishna, Ranade, and Devdhar (Taliram) all made an enduring impact on the audience in their roles. Every actor had an understudy who was also selected with the greatest care.

Stage sets, costumes, jewellery, curtains—everything received detailed attention. There was an abundance of all things, but not a trace of loudness or vulgarity touched anything. Baburao Painter and his brother Anandrao supervised these departments. Of course, wings and curtains were used. Modern ideas of stage design did not exist then. But colours and lighting were chosen to reflect the character and mood of each scene. The velvet front curtain too was the Painter brothers' idea. The dressing rooms and make-up rooms were neat and well-equipped. The men in charge of them were also skilled workers.

The master playwright, Kakasaheb Khadilkar, was the rock that supported the Gandharva Company. He had added his own trump cards like *Manapaman*, *Swayamvar*, and *Draupadi* to the successful productions of the old Kirloskar Company. Gadkari's *Ekach Pyala* was a thundering success. All these things put together made the Gandharva Company's coffers overflow. Every play, old and new, became popular. The main factor was unbdoubtedly Bal Gandharva and his music. All new plays were written for him, were designed to suit him, keeping his strengths in mind. The Company's income regularly exceeded ten thousand rupees a month. Wednesdays, Saturdays, and Sundays were the main days for performance, plus holidays. Charity shows and all other shows were packed. The crowds would not decrease even after the Company had been in residence for six months. Plans would fill up two months in advance. The rising arc of collections—Rs 1200–1400 on Wednesdays, Rs 1500–1700 on Saturdays, and Rs 1900–2100 on Sundays remained unchanged for years. In addition, there were patronage fees from the Baroda Court, sundry gifts, and royalties from gramophone companies. The Company's itinerary included halts only in Mumbai, Pune, and Baroda, and occasionally Nashik. Each time they moved on, the audience would ask eagerly, 'When will you come back?'

But even in those days of prosperity and huge earnings, the Gandharva Natak Mandali was never able to make income meet expenditure. The art direction and stage settings were princely, and always beyond its means. The cost of mounting *Draupadi* exceeded a lakh-and-a-half. There were velvet-covered bolsters and cushions, carpets heavy with gold work, silver crowns and maces gilded with gold, footwear covered with silver thread embroidery, a bounty of Benaras saris and stoles and, to top it all, a variety of *attars* from Kanauj, worth Rs 5000 and more, for the actors to wear so that a strong whiff of perfume reached every member of the audience with each entry! This was the royal splendour of *Draupadi*. Finally, all of this fragrant treasure had to be given away because the attars were affecting actors' voices.

This was more or less the order of expenditure for all productions. Narayanrao's well-wishers spoke out strongly against this extravagance, but by now the heady intoxication of success had trapped him completely. Debts kept mounting. Some of the later plays did not do as well as expected. Expenses could not be curbed. The IOU's to Multani creditors amounted to far larger sums than income figures. The Gandharva Company's magic began to wane. In 1930, the Marathi stage did not have the strength to withstand the onslaught of cinema. Narayanrao was crushed under the burden of debts. Finally, the celestial community of the Gandharva Company went into a tragic decline.

THE MARATHI STAGE

The Marathi stage was at the height of its glory in those days. Wealthy businessmen, eminent citizens, reputed orators, and political leaders were patrons of theatre. As lovers and well-wishers of the arts, they also acted as its advisors. They were consulted at every stage from the time the theme of a play was discussed to its final staging. When the playscript was ready, it was read before a small group of cognoscenti. Rehearsals would begin only after it had been discussed threadbare. These were unique celebratory occasions.

I can still vividly recall the reading of *Ekach Pyala*. The listeners came together at Mr Laud's house at ten in the night. Present on the occasion were the pillars of the Bal Gandharva Company like Narayanrao, Ganpatrao Bodas, and Balasaheb Pandit, while Papa, Mummy, Solicitor Vaidya, and Mr Kunte represented the audience. Ganpatrao's chaste reading brought tears to the listeners' eyes at the end of every scene. The reading ended at four in the morning. And then began the discussion.

There were major disagreements over the ending of the play. Should the end remain tragic, or should Sudhakar give up alcohol and reform to make the end sweet? One view was that people would simply not accept a tragic end, that nobody would come to see a tragedy. But Narayanrao flatly refused to change the end. The argument was still raging when morning broke. So it was carried over to the following day when the same group gathered again. Once again Narayanrao stuck to his guns. Finally, the play was presented to the public with only a few scenes dropped, but not a word changed. Narayanrao's hunch proved correct. *Ekach Pyala* brought untold profits, not only to the Gandharva Company but other theatre companies too.

On another such occasion, when *Draupadi* was discussed, Mummy had objected to the word 'naked'. This occurred in Duryodhan's line, 'Pull off her sari. Let's see her naked.' She had suggested the word 'disrobed' or at most 'stripped bare'. But the word 'naked' was retained to show Duryodhan's coarseness and to underline the brutal manner in which Draupadi was dishonoured. But it was unanimously agreed that the word would not be emphasized in the speech.

Marathi plays were popular not only because they provided high quality entertainment but also because, prominently at the root of their writing, lay two preoccupations—social concerns and political issues. The language and narrative outlines of many mythological and historical plays were very clearly those of the political movements of the time. The British were shaken by the general import and impact of these plays. Some of them were even banned. The plays came from the powerful pens of people like Khadilkar the master playwright, Kelkar the king of literature, and Veer Vamanrao Joshi the political leader. These plays still hold their position in the canon of Marathi literature. Marathi theatre was blessed by Lokmanya Tilak's support, N. C. Kelkar's encouragement and the good wishes of several honourable leaders. Theatre companies also served the Motherland in their own way through their art. In 1912 two leading theatre companies, the Gandharva and the Lalitkaladarsha, buried their rivalry to come together for the most glorious productions of *Manapaman* and *Saubhadra* that the Marathi stage had ever seen. The ticket rates ranged from Rs 25 to Rs 500. It was a unique celebration of Marathi drama. The amount earned from the two shows was handed over in its entirety to the Tilak Fund. The Baliwala theatre was filled to overflowing. People stood packed together at the back. Both shows were painstakingly presented in a spirit of intense competition. Whether this was done out of the urge to serve the nation or in compliance with a request from popular leaders, the fact remains that theatre lovers were granted this unheard of and unbelievable opportunity to see Bal Gandharva and Keshavrao Bhosle perform together on one stage. The event will remain inscribed forever in letters of gold in the history of Marathi theatre. Unfortunately, Keshavrao Bhosle died soon after.

From 1922 onwards, Marathi theatre began to slide gradually from its position of glory. Not a single production of any company became popular in the old way after that. Nobody's financial condition was satisfactory. The more a drowning man struggles the further he sinks—this would aptly describe their circumstances. There were many reasons why this happened. But chiefly, it was the arrival of cinema that set Marathi theatre on the path to oblivion.

THE MARATHI STAGE OF THE TIME

Those were undoubtedly days of glory and prosperity for Marathi theatre. Drama was the only medium of entertainment. It is true that the educated middle-class in Maharashtra was very eager to see plays. The literary and musical value of Marathi plays being very high, they offered the white-collar class the combined pleasure of chaste entertainment and intellectual satisfaction. Love of theatre is embedded in the very bones of Maharashtrians, and politics runs in their blood. That is why they felt so close to plays that dealt with history, burning social issues of the day and current political events. The most significant plays of the time focused on these themes. Further, because tickets were reasonably priced, people could afford the luxury of seeing plays with their families. Theatres were always filled to bursting whether the play was straight prose or a musical. The Elphinstone and the Bombay Theatres stood opposite each other, and both overflowed with spectators. The audience took a friendly personal interest in the rivalry between their favourite actors. There were theatre companies besides the Gandharva Natak Company that also toured in style—Lalitkaladarsha, Balwant, Maharashtra, Shahunagarwasi, and Shivraj were some of the reputed companies which also had very popular and much-discussed productions in their repertoire. There were other theatre companies too besides these, some big, some small. There was a children's theatre company and one run by women. All of them were dedicated to serving the public and bringing entertainment into their lives. They adorned the Marathi stage like a garland of gems around the neck. Each jewel had its own lustre, its own facets, its own shine. It would have been difficult to find a Marathi theatre-goer who was not captivated by the range of Keshavrao Bhosle's voice, the late Dinanath's quick-spinning *taans*, the nightingale sweetness of Sarnaik's voice, Ganpatrao Bodas's impressive speeches, Pandharpurkarbuwa's sonorous *alaaps*, and the lyrical spell of each note Master Krishna sang.

In performance too, the actors of those times left their stamp on the characters they played. Ganpatrao Bodas's comic roles became just as popular as his serious roles. If Lakshmidhar, Shakar, Shashidhar, and Phalgunrao made viewers laugh, the pathos of Sudhakar's plight brought them to tears. Pandharpurkarbuwa left an enduring impression on people's minds with his Duryodhan in *Draupadi*, and Ramlal in *Ekach Pyala*. Datey's Aurangzeb was so cunning and fanatical that he drove viewers to fury, almost causing Hindu-Muslim riots. Dinkar Kamanna's Kannadi Appa in *Bhavbandhan* carried the whole burden of the play on his frail shoulders. Theatre lovers who lived during that era of Marathi theatre must be considered exceptionally lucky. Theatre in those days was an integral part of people's lives. It was an active element in social and political progress. The most eminent leaders, orators, and citizens, and the wealtthiest merchants were not only patrons of theatre but lovers of art and were looked upon as well-wishers and advisors of theatre companies. Being patrons of theatre companies was a mark of honour for kings and princes. Playwrights of those times were popular leaders and suffered grave hardships on account of the political agitations of the day.

5

The Dawn of Prabhat

Farebi Jaal brought me much notoriety. 'That godawful film and that woman Durga Khote who acts in it' became the favourite topic for malicious gossip. Since Mr Khote felt some of the heat in the Hindu Gymkhana, I got to hear recitations of my stupidity everyday. I wanted to die. Around this time, V. Shantaram, the well-known director of Prabhat Films, came to Bombay to scout for actors and actresses for their first Marathi-Hindi film. The news of *Farebi Jaal* had already reached his ears. Keen to know what Solicitor Laud's daughter had gone and done in the film, he went to see it.

My scenes were confined to the first ten minutes of the film and he liked my work. But he was furious with the rest of the film. Apparently he spoke with extreme disgust about educated women from respectable families being asked to act in such films. After making several inquiries, Shantarambapu came to see me with Prabhat's music composer Govindrao Tembe. I was still living in Laud Mansion. Govindrao had known Papa from his Gandharva Natak Mandali days, but I didn't recall having seen him.

Govindrao introduced Shantarambapu and asked if I would act for Prabhat. I couldn't believe my ears. I just about managed to mumble a faint 'No'. But Shantarambapu asked me why not in an understanding way. I said, 'I have disgraced myself so badly that my father will never allow me to act again. I wouldn't even have the courage to ask him.' There was a catch in my throat as I spoke. I continued, 'My people have faced a lot of trouble because of me.'

Shantarambapu said, 'That film was awful, but I liked your work. There's no reason why you can't act in good films. Think it over. See how you feel.' Trying to keep my vacillating mind under control, I said, 'I'll ask Papa and call you tomorrow.' They were staying in Madhavashram. I spent the whole day struggling with my innermost wish to say yes to Prabhat. I rushed to Papa in the evening. Papa, Mummy, and Manohar had rented out their entire floor in Laud Mansion and gone to live on Nepean Sea Road. Papa had just got back from work. He gave me an affectionate hug. 'Why have you come alone?' he asked. 'Come. Sit down. I hope you're all right.' I found I couldn't utter a single word, faced with this shower of love. 'Papa,' I blurted out, 'don't be angry but I need to tell you something.' Papa looked worried. God only knew what further calamity had befallen his child. But he said, 'Tell me what it is. Don't be afraid.' I gulped and said, 'Papa, please let me act in another film.'

Papa flew into an instant rage. 'Idiot. Isn't the disgrace you've already earned enough? I've told you to come and stay with us but you won't. I'll have to chain you now if you get up to any more mischief. Don't you dare do any such thing.'

I don't know which devil suddenly got into me then. I shouted back with equal anger, 'Why did you pat my back then for showing women a new way to stand on their own feet? I don't want to be a permanent burden on you. I'll do what I am capable of. I'm going.' I was on my way out when Papa sprang up from his armchair and hugged me tight. 'My little lion cub. You'll never eat grass. Sit down here. Don't torment yourself my child. Now tell me what this is all about.'

Mummy and the others had come running out when they heard our shouting. Papa was laughing and wiping my eyes. Then he wiped his own and promptly ordered the servants to bring in tea and snacks. I told Papa the whole story and fell at his feet, 'Give me your permission this once. If things don't work out, I'll do anything you tell me to,' I promised. 'Give me one chance Papa. Give me an opportunity to erase my disgrace. Please Papa.' Finally Papa gave in. 'But I'll look into everything before agreeing. You will not rush into anything,' he warned. It was decided that I would bring the Prabhat people to meet Papa the following day.

The next morning I rushed through my chores as fast as I could and, even before it was eight-thirty, I was ready to go to Madhavashram. I took five rupees out of my meagre savings of 250 and tied them tight in a handkerchief. I left Bakul and Harin in the care of a neighbour and stepped forth to test my luck. I rushed all the way to Madhavashram and sent word of my arrival to Shantarambapu's room with a hotel boy. They were stunned to see me there. 'Papa has the time now. It would be so good if we went over right away.' To fill in the time between Madhavashram and Nepean Sea Road, I kept up an incessant chatter in English. Shantarambapu was listening quietly. But it seemed to me that he looked worried. To make an even better impression on him I now blabbered on in even classier English. Finally, just as the taxi neared Papa's house, Shantarambapu asked Govindrao in an undertone, 'Tell me, can this lady speak Marathi? Otherwise she'll be no use in a Marathi-Hindi film.' I am sure Govindrao suppressed his laughter before nodding affirmatively. The taxi pulled up at Papa's house. My blabbering had stopped in shame. Papa led them into the drawing room and took me inside. He warned me, 'You will shut up. You will not say a word. I'll do all the talking and deciding.' Tea was over, small talk was over, and now the conversation turned to the main subject. Papa came out with a long list of conditions couched in typical legalese. Costumes, make-up, story, the standard of accommodation, my colleagues' behaviour with me—it was a very long list.

Shantarambapu heard him out quietly. Then he said, 'Mr Laud, it makes good business sense in our profession to get the best work out of our artists. But Durgabai will also have to put her mind to it. To work hard. You can make any arrangements you like for a companion to ensure her comfort. It is unfortunate that Durgabai's first encounter did not turn out well. But we give you an assurance that she will not have any problems with us. We will treat her like one of the family.'

Papa thought what he said was proper, reasonable, and to the point. For me the suspense was unbearable. I was just waiting for the interview to be over. At the end of further negotiations over niggly points, it was finally decided that I would work for Prabhat. I signed a three-month contract. My salary was to be Rs 2250 for the entire period. I was to bear my own travel expenses there and back. But all other arrangements were to be made by them, because we knew nothing about Kolhapur. And I had heard many rumours about it!

6

Departure for Kolhapur

I had to prepare immediately for my departure to Kolhapur. Indutai was to go with me to settle me in. Others in the family would later take turns to stay with me. Bakul and Harin were to stay with Papa and Mummy. Kaka and Kaki had settled down in Bombay. Mr Khote, who now had a 150 rupees-a-month job in the municipality, was to stay with them. If and when I got time off from work I would visit Bombay. When he got time off, he would come down to Kolhapur. Everybody had worked out this plan to help reduce the pressure on my mind. But Mr Khote insisted that he would take three months' leave and come to stay with me in Kolhapur. This was not at all right in view of his job. Moreover, we could not afford it financially. But we could do nothing. We were obliged to change our plans. We left Bakul and Harin with Papa and Mummy for three months and Mr Khote and I left for Kolhapur. Although Mr Khote came with me to Kolhapur, he frittered away all his time there gossiping with people in the town. Talkies had just begun and he had a good opportunity, which he lost, of learning the art of recording from scratch. In those early days, even Prabhat was learning the technique of recording, and I am certain they would have gladly and respectfully taught it to him. I felt sorry it did not happen, that is all.

The owners of Prabhat had rented a cosy little bungalow for us in the cantonment area and furnished it beautifully. The studio was close by, but even then a car was arranged to take me there and back. Mummy had sent an old retainer with me to do the housework, and a cook. Both she and Papa urged me repeatedly not to allow anything else to worry me but to give all my attention to work.

There was undoubtedly a lot of hard work at Prabhat. But it was interesting and inspiring. It never felt like work. I had to learn everything from scratch. Prabhat's first rule for me was—the lady will not speak a word of English during her three months' stay in Kolhapur. Especially in the studio, not a word will be uttered in any language except Marathi and Hindi. Prabhat had thought up this idea to make my language more chaste, my diction clearer and emotionally expressive. My Marathi was 'impure' because I spoke it with a Goan accent. The words were drawn out in a lilt. As for Hindi, I had to learn it from scratch. Prabhat's plan succeeded one hundred per cent in ensuring that I was able to memorize my dialogue in both languages by the time the shoot started.

Shantarambapu was a strict teacher. Nothing was allowed to pass on the basis of 'It will do'. He took immense pains, observed my walk, speech, gestures, posture, the way I moved before the camera, and every other such detail with a minute eye to get exactly what he wanted out of me. He placed two mirrors opposite each other in front of me and told me to make a mental note of all my movements. My second lesson in cinema—acting! Acting had to be natural but attractive at the same time—Shantarambapu taught me this lesson. I wept copiously in one scene in *Ayodhyecha Raja* but the impact of that entire footage was reduced to some extent by my lack of control over the flow of tears. How to control emotions, how to make them look attractive—this guru of mine taught me painstakingly. I salute him a hundred times for it.

How to make my rather shapeless figure look better before the camera was something the late Sahebmama Fattelal got me to understand. Sahebmama used to look after the wardrobe and jewellery departments personally. He was a very fine artist. He would have dozens of photographs taken of all the actors in the cast, paint on the constumes and jewellery designed for them and only then order them to be made according to those designs. It was during this exercise that the Prabhat people found my Jaipur earrings most suitable. The figure, the shape of the face, the character to be played—all these were taken into consideration in Sahebmama's art department.

The Company's cameraman, the late Mr Dhaibar, showed me with the help of several experiments, which angles of my face looked best, which hairstyles would enhance and lend charm to my performance, and how to skilfully camouflage my natural flaws and shortcomings. Damle Mama taught me during our recording sessions how to control my voice so that it didn't sound screechy in emotional scenes. The credit for my success in *Ayodhyecha Raja* belongs to the owners of Prabhat. They got that performance of Taramati out of me with their commitment and warm personal rapport. It was their training that ensured that this step I had taken in the film industry proved successful in the end and became the foundation for my future development. Govindrao Tembe looked after the music. Though I loved music, I was not a trained musician. So my singing was nothing to write home about. But he somehow managed to make my songs more or less acceptable; that was about all. The fact that they became popular was undoubtedly on account of their melodious tunes, their beautiful picturization and their perfect placement in the scene.

I was busy almost twelve hours a day in Kolhapur, working on something or the other connected with the film. There was no electricity in Kolhapur in those days. We had to be in the studio at the crack of dawn because all the shooting had to be done in natural light. Make-up, costume, hairstyles had to be completed by half past seven when the shooting began. It went on till about five o'clock, when the last rays of the sun were fading. There was a one-hour break for lunch in between. After my make-up was removed and by the time rehearsals for dialogue and songs, the narration of the following day's scenes, and so on were over, and I was on my way home, it would be seven o'clock in the evening. Then I did my exercises to lose weight and gave myself a massage to take away the day's fatigue. By the time I was through with the massage and bath and had had dinner at nine o'clock, I was totally exhausted. With loving memories of the boys came the tears that I hid in my pillow, praying to the goddess of sleep to come as I lay still. The next morning the day's routine would start again from five o'clock onwards.

The days flew by in this way, packed tight with work. Shooting gave me the chance to see Kolhapur and the beautiful sights surrounding it. A darshan of the goddess Ambabai always gave me great solace. We shot in some lovely locations. We shot for an entire day in a boat, on the banks of the Krishna, and in Narsobachi Wadi. Prabhat organized a huge puja for Dattaguru. I asked sincerely for

God's blessings and some *prasad* and requested a small puja to be said for us. The entire scene was indescribably lovely. To see beautiful places like the *ghats* of the Panchganga, the Kushira plain, and Jotiba Hill was to shed all the accumulated stress of the mind and body.

The shooting and every other part of the work were done in such a warm and congenial atmosphere that one was filled with sadness when it was over. It was not the owners of Prabhat alone, but also their families and the Company workers in general who had treated me and looked after me with great respect and love. They would inquire solicitously after my food, health, and other arrangements. They would send me sweets on festivals. When Bakul and Harin visited Kolhapur, they made much of them. With what words can I express my gratitude to them all?

With all that, I was still filled with trepidation when I thought of my work. It was the old question once again—what next? My three-month stay in Kolhapur had been very satisfactory for me. This was the first happy time that had fallen to my lot in eight years. I had to wait and see now how people responded to the new path I was treading. The die had been cast—my future depended on which way it fell.

7

After the Dawn

The Bombay Mail left Kolhapur for Bombay as the sun was setting. My eyes were fixed on the west where the sky was a blaze of orange-yellow. I turned right only once, to fill my heart with the sight of the Tembhlai temple. Mr Khote bought fruits and dinner at Miraj Station, but I had no desire to eat. I only had some coffee and stuck my head in my pillow to try and sleep. I fell asleep with the thought that my two sunrays, Bakul and Harin, would light up my dawn the next day.

Papa was at Boribunder station with the boys to receive us. Both of them shouted out 'Mummy! Papa!' and clung to my neck. This was 1932. Bakul was eight and Harin six. Bakul said, 'Mummy, you mustn't go away anywhere again.' Harin said something very funny. 'Chee! How black you've become, Mummy!' We couldn't stop laughing at that. I hadn't realized what a tan I had acquired working in the sun everyday. Papa and Mummy inquired after Mr Khote and told the servants to put our luggage in the car. The boys pounced on the prasad we had brought—*kavath* fruit *barfi* from Wadi and roasted gram and pedhas from the Ambabai temple. They were stuffing their mouths and chattering away non-stop at the same time.

Mummy had had our Laud Mansion flat cleaned up and put in some flowers. Bakul and Harin asked me to close my eyes and lovingly put two rose blossoms in my hand. Oh the joy and the celebration of coming home after three months.

Ayodhyecha Raja was released at the Majestic cinema in Bombay. The Marathi version became very popular. Two Hindi versions of the Harishchandra story had already been released before the Prabhat film came out. One was Madan's and the other was Krishna Film

Company's. Both were of average quality. Both were stuffed with fifteen or twenty songs each, and their plots and dances were typical of the Urdu theatre style. The main actors were stars from the Urdu stage, acting in the style characteristic of that theatre. The sets were painted curtains depicting palaces, jungles, and roads, and you could actually see the palace curtain flapping in the wind. But the public put up with all this because talkie films were a new thing then. Both films made very good money.

Kajjanbai and Nissar, from the Madan Film Company of Calcutta, was an extremely popular singer-actor pair on the Urdu stage and in Hindi cinema. They sang mostly in the ghazal-*qawwali* style. Their films like *Laila-Majnu* and *Shireen-Farhad* had become very popular. Agha Hashra a famous contemporary Urdu writer wrote most of the screenplays. His mythological screenplays too—*Sati Savitri, Indrasabha,* and *Bilvamangal*—were notable for the money they earned. The writing was in Urdu and the dialogue was sprinkled with couplets. In every film, the lead pair sang ten to fifteen songs. There were sixty songs in *Indrasabha.* Whatever the story, whether myth, history, or fantasy, the characters were always dressed in gold-encrusted gypsy-style costumes.

Krishna Film Company's pair of Neelambai and Ashrafkhan was particularly popular in Bombay and Gujarat. The Krishna Film Company's emphasis was mainly on opulent costumes and jewellery. Their Taramati wore diaphanous gold-embroidered saris and loads of jewellery even when she was wandering in the jungles starving and suffering great hardships. Yet, the fact remains that both companies made plenty of money at the time. But when *Ayodhyecha Raja* was released, audience taste and the way they looked at films changed overnight. The realistic sets and locations of the Prabhat film, the magnificent palaces, real jungles, real rivers, and the wonderful shots taken on the steps leading to them thrilled and awed the audience. The Marathi film became very successful. Now people began to shower me with praise, accolades, and admiration. The public granted me success and acceptance.

Papa was emotionally overwhelmed by *Ayodhyecha Raja.* He attended the eight o'clock show everyday without fail. He knew exactly at what point a particular scene would come, which lines would be said when and when my song would start. He would begin rushing dinner at seven-thirty every night, nagging Mummy constantly. 'See, I'll miss that line. The song will start. Hurry.' But Papa paid for his ticket everyday to see the show. The Prabhat people joked, 'Mr Laud is returning to us all the money we paid his daughter!'

Kaka and Kaki had now disowned me. Mr Khote's reaction was exactly the opposite. He saw the Hindi version and criticized our Hindi to his heart's content. He did not see the Marathi version at all. The film's success had given me great hope that Prabhat would broach the subject of their next film with me. But it was not their way to depend on established film stars for their films. They always explored new subjects for each film and groomed suitable actors for it. In fact, they had already started shooting for their next film. Papa made many roundabout inquiries about my working with them again. Their answer was extremely courteous and frank. 'Sir, we cannot make "star films". Each of our films is made on a different theme. If we have a suitable role for Bai, we will certainly call her back with the greatest pleasure.'

But what was I going to do till their next call came? This was the big question facing me. Although the film and my performance had won resounding public praise, this question still remained. I would have found it difficult to fit in with the way films were handled in the Bombay film industry. A twenty-six year old woman, mother of two, a housewife with a home and family to run—such a woman would hardly be considered suitable for the heroine's role in Bombay. Also I was very scared of taking on any old work now. I had seen that a film turned out well only when its various parts worked together perfectly. The Prabhat people had shown their genuine concern for me when they courteously suggested that we give due thought to my age, the story, the appropriateness of the role, the people involved in the project, and my co-actors, before accepting work. That was all very well; but when was I going to find the magical confluence of a company like Prabhat, a director like Shantarambapu and a lead role like the gentle and chaste Taramati again?

A storm of doubts was raging within me. But I decided to break through the vicious cycle of thoughts that kept spinning around in my mind, hand 'Durga Khote' over to the Majestic cinema for some time, and submerge myself in the daily routine of household chores and children. As the run of the film at the Majestic theatre grew longer, so too did the line of film producers at my door. But I could find no logic or coherence in their scripts, dialogue, or characterization. I did not know what to do. I decided to force myself to be patient, sit still, and wait. There was of course the warm feeling of having money, though it was not much. Producers soon decided Durgabai was a Prabhat star. She would not work for anybody else. Only the Lord knew the inside story!

8

Maya Machhindra and After

It was 1932–3. One day, I received a letter from Prabhat. They had a suitable role for me in their next film, *Maya Machhindra*. I would have to work hard to prepare for it. The letter suggested I would have to go to Kolhapur well before the actual shoot. The role of the princess Kilotala in *Maya Machhindra* was completely different from Taramati's. The film was about a kingdom ruled by women and the heroine's dominant expression had to be warrior-like. Naturally, she had to be trained in fencing, wielding the *dandpatta*, riding, and other martial skills. I was thrilled. I left Bakul and Harin in Mummy's charge, Mr Khote went to stay with Kaka and Kaki, I took a woman with me as companion and housekeeper, and left for Kolhapur.

Maya Machhindra was full of entertaining features like songs, dances, and special effects created with technical and mechanical devices, which made the picturization very appealing. Incomparable sets, elaborate costumes, hairstyles and jewellery, eye-catching outdoor scenes of the spring festival—all these together made the film visually striking. Another novel feature had been introduced in the film to attract the audience. Rani Kilotala was given a pet female cheetah. Her name too suited her perfectly—Sundari. Sundari would follow me around like a faithful dog, flicking her proud upright tail gracefully. When I sat down, she would sit at my feet, her elegant head held high, looking around haughtily. For the audience it was like something from another world. The presence of this dumb creature added hugely to Rani Kilotala's style, glory, and ferocity. The cameraman Keshavrao Dhaiber would often jokingly ask, 'Shantarambapu, which tigress's close-up do you want—Durgabai's or Sundaribai's?'

While we were shooting the spring festival for *Maya Macchindra*, a huge vehicle as large as a truck, painted orange and flying an orange flag, turned up on location. It carried a large group of young women and a few men, about twenty-five people in all. Judging by the men's turbans, I decided they must have come from the palace. Suddenly, members of our crew were running helter-skelter, holding on to their own caps and turbans, rushing to make their salutations. The Queen Mother and Princess Akkasaheb, Chhatrapati Rajaram Maharaj's sister, and her family were in the vehicle. They expressed to Mr Dhaiber their desire to see the shooting. Shantarambapu stepped forward and had some chairs fetched to organize their seating. I was sitting under a tree, observing everything from a distance. Soon Govindrao came over and said that the palace party would like to meet me. I went over and pressed my palms together. Just then Shantarambapu called me for my shot. The royal party stayed till the end of the shoot. Afterwards they sent me an invitation through Kale Mama, asking me to visit the palace. I formally accepted the invitation and took my leave of Kale Mama. Kale Mama was one of Akkasaheb's most favoured people. As her secretary he handled her finances and all other matters. In those days, it was the custom to add 'Mama' after people's names as an honorific like 'Mr' or 'Shree'. So we had Patil Mama, Ghorpade Mama, Pendse Mama, Damle Mama, Saheb Mama, etc. Kale Mama had played the male lead in Shalini Cinetone's film *Usha Swapna*.

I had had no occasion to meet the royal family when I was shooting for *Ayodhyecha Raja*. Nobody knew me in Kolhapur then. Nobody had noticed the shooting because most of it had been done in Kushirawadi and other such locations. But this time, invitations kept pouring in from the palace. I would find some pretext or the other to avoid going there. The work was so strenuous that all I wanted to do in the evenings was go home and lay my back down in bed. But by and by my relations with the palace grew closer. It was clear that the people around the Maharaja were keen that he should start a film production company like Prabhat. But I was too preoccupied with thoughts of my children and home. I had no desire to get involved in the business complications of any production project. Meanwhile, the shooting for the film was done, and I went to Bombay and from there to Calcutta for my films there. In the following two years, two new film companies were started in Kolhapur, one by the Chhatrapati himself and the other by Akkasaheb.

Prabhat made good profits from both the Marathi and Hindi versions of *Maya Machhindra* (1932–3). Their business grew rapidly after that. They soon shifted base from Kolhapur to the expansive Prabhatnagar in Pune. *Maya Macchindra* established me pretty well in the Hindi film industry. New Theatres called me to Calcutta for their film *Rajrani Meera*. Their *Puranbhakt* had received a lot of attention and the director Debaki Bose had become quite a name. Bosebabu's way of working and the Calcutta studio's functioning were very different from Kolhapur. The sets were smaller, recording was in natural voices, and the film's pace generally very slow. The working hours were also irregular. One felt a lot of time was being needlessly wasted. The exuberant atmosphere of Kolhapur was missing. But minute nuances of acting, emotional dialogue, and an emphasis on the eyes and facial expression, were the hallmark of Bengali films. The intellectual and technical levels of the films were also very high. But the visualization, sets, and costumes were heavy-handed and slipshod.

Music was not based only on classical melodies but composed to suit the situation. The Ravindra sangeet style of music entered the film industry through Calcutta. Instead of having the lead pair sing the songs, the songs were given to characters like mendicants or blind men and the like, who were included in the script for that purpose. The lead actors sang only if they were playing professional singer characters. Though the songs were full of sentiment, they were not the kind people could croon and grow to love.

In the course of my visits to Calcutta, I made four films in all—*Rajrani Meera*, *Sita*, *Inquilab*, and *Jeevan Natak*. Though *Rajrani Meera* and *Sita* were better films, they were not commercially successful. The other two fared no better and were also weak as films. Prithviraj Kapoor and I co-starred in all four films. Prithviraj's performance as Rama in *Sita* was incomparable. On Rakshabandhan day, he asked me to tie a *rakhi* on him, honouring me by making me his adopted sister.

During my time in Calcutta I was able to see several Bengali plays and meet many well-known artists of the Bengali stage. I did not have the opportunity to work with people like Shishir Bhaduri,

Durgadas Bannerji, the great dancer Uday Shankar, the famous singer Indubala, and the producer-director of *Devdas*, P.C. Barua, I met all of them at various tea parties. They were all well-known names in theatre as well as cinema.

One of the most celebrated actor-singers of cinema, Kundanlal Saigal, played a role in *Rajrani Meera*. His song in the last scene was so profoundly moving that its haunting strains would make the audience forget the rest of the film. Saigal was a person of great generosity of heart and joyousness of spirit. The way he spoke, his wit, and his clever mimicry would keep everyone on the set entertained. Saigal always carried his harmonium with him. If anybody, at any time, anywhere, requested him to sing, he would begin without a moment's hesitation, pouring his heart into the song. His favourite song was '*Babul mora naihar chhooto jaye*'. As if the raft of life was slipping away from his hands ... sadly, he died at the very height of his powers....

Mr Birendra Nath Sircar, the owner of New Theatres, was a very kind and courteous man, a qualified engineer from an illustrious family. He had stepped into the film industry with high hopes, thinking of it as an artistic business. But unfortunately, he failed financially. He made *Yehudi ki Ladki*, *Vidyapati*, *Rajrani Meera*, *Chandidas*, *Devdas*, *President*—films that covered a wide range of themes. They fetched him countrywide acclaim. But New Theatres suffered losses because its directors formed cliques. Finally, the company went into financial decline. Mr Sircar loved billiards. When Mr Khote visited Calcutta during this period, they played several rounds of the game together.

I learned Bengali as a challenge. This is how it happened. *Rajrani Meera* was made in Hindi and Bengali. There were two casts for the two versions. The Hindi film had Prithviraj and me. The Bengali had Chandravati and Durgadas Bannerji. I would feel very embarrassed during the shooting. There was one set. Each shot was taken first in Hindi, then in Bengali. As soon as the Hindi shot was over, a buzz would fill the studio. Everybody would be saying something urgently to Chandravati. I used to think, I'm sure these people are discussing and criticizing my performance. Prithviraj, too, did not know Bengali. But in his Punjabi couldn't-care-less way, he kept on working regardless. He was a veteran of silent movies, but this was only my third film. I used to be very nervous. Our director Mr Debakikumar Bose was very caustic. He would use the harshest words for the smallest mistake—English of course. But I did not understand what he said to the others in Bengali. I would feel very uneasy. Finally, my desperate need to understand what he was saying drove me to learn Bengali. First, I learned the entire Bengali dialogue of *Rajrani Meera* by heart. Though I could not pronounce the words, I began to understand what they meant because of the Hindi dialogue. Then I actually engaged a Bengali gentleman to tutor me, and within three months I was speaking Bengali. Only then did I realize what the unit members had been saying. They had been urging Chandravati to copy my performance. In a sense, the way I learned Bengali was a repetition of the way I had learnt English.

I had some unforgettable experiences during my stay in Calcutta. The minute I got three or four days off between schedules, I would make a trip to some nearby place. I knew nobody apart from the people at the studio. So this was an excellent opportunity to see different places. I got a chance to visit Santiniketan and even spend a little time with Gurudev Rabindranath. He was full of appreciation for my ability to converse with him in Bengali though I was a Maharashtrian. He urged me affectionately to spend a few days there. But I had only two days to spare from my shooting and had to return that same day. So I regretfully declined his invitation. Gurudev asked one of his women students to look after my lunch and show me as much of Santiniketan as was possible and explain how it worked.

Santiniketan appeared to me like a beautiful, sprawling village. School classes were held under trees. Several subjects were taught, but the emphasis was on music, dance, art, craft, and language. There were beautifully proportioned cottages, fully equipped for comfortable living. Everything fitted the rural lifestyle. Life was simple and filled with natural beauty. How much could I have seen in such a short time? But however briefly, I did experience the joy of a simple, well-regulated life. I was served a lunch that consisted of vegetarian as well as non-vegetarian preparations cooked in the Bengali way. Returning by train from Bolpur station, I wondered how useful, in practical terms, it was to be educated in Santiniketan. What purpose would it serve in the daily grind of life? Santiniketan was after all an *ashram*.

I decided to go to Darjeeling during the Puja holidays, but how wonderful it would have been if all of us, Mr Khote, Bakul, Harin, and I could have visited this picturesque place together. That was the thought that kept nagging me. But I decided to lock away all such thoughts in my mind as I took my reserved seat in the ladies compartment of the train at Sealdah station at eight-thirty in the evening. Some girls from a Calcutta college were travelling in the same compartment. Watching them chatting, laughing, and ragging each other in that wonderfully carefree way of youth, I was reminded of my own college days. Noticing that I was quiet, the girls started talking to me. I told them I was also a college student from Bombay on my way to Darjeeling to see the place. I would have felt embarrassed to refer to my work in films. Only two films of mine had been released. People were not as crazy about films in those days as they are today. The girls offered me some of their food. I too placed before them the dinner that I had got Firpo's restaurant to pack for me. Dinner was fun. The girls were wonderful company. We hired two taxis the next morning from the station and reached Darjeeling. The girls gave me their addresses and told me where to stay and what to see in Darjeeling. One of the things they urged me not to miss seeing was the sunrise over Mount Everest from Tiger Hill.

Darjeeling was crowded with Puja holiday-makers. Not a single room was available in any of the hotels. Some people recognized me. They expressed regret at not having a room for me. It had not occurred to me to book my hotel room in advance. After trudging around for a long time, I managed to find a room in a small hotel. It was September, and drizzling continuously. The weather was very cold. The Pahadi coolie who had accompanied me, carrying my luggage around on my search, looked like a good, reliable, clean sort of fellow. I fixed him up as a guide to go around with me the whole day and show me the sights. I arranged for him to have his tea and breakfast while I had my bath, and then we left. I felt quite safe with the Pahadi walking a few paces behind me like a bodyguard.

We went first to the botanical garden. With the recent drizzle, everything looked fresh and green. Tall trees, dense creepers, a light mist floating above, the mixed fragrance of wet earth and flowers—

with what words can I describe this paradise at the foot of the Himalayas! As we walked around, I suddenly got a whiff of a sweet and heady scent. As I looked around to see which tree the fragrance came from, I noticed a middle-aged man coming towards us. He was carrying an object as large as a medium-sized coconut, shaped and coloured like an egg. Its long leaves resembled the leaves of the *kavathi-chafa*. As the man came closer, the scent became stronger. I kept staring fixedly at the flower. The man greeted me with a *namaskar* and said, 'You will be surprised to know that this is indeed a particularly large kavathi-chafa.' I asked him in astonishment, 'Where is it available? I want to buy one.' He laughed and said, 'You need not buy one. Take this. It's from this garden itself and I'm in charge here.'

He paused for a few seconds, then asked, 'Are you Durga Khote by any chance?' I was flabbergasted. He praised my performance in *Rajrani Meera* and *Sita* to the skies. He had seen the films four or five times and remembered all the dialogues. He then inquired where I was staying, etc. He gave strict instructions to my bodyguard to look after me well. He did more than that. He made several arrangements to ensure that my stay in the hotel would be comfortable. I made only one request. He should not reveal to anybody who I was, because I was there alone. Nobody should be put to incovenience on my account. Even then he wrote out, on a page torn out of his diary, a list of sights I should visit. He explained how to get there and drew maps for me. He also wrote down a few phone numbers in case I needed them. He himself was going to Calcutta that afternoon, otherwise he would have liked to offer me the hospitality of his home, he said. I thanked him profusely. What else could I have done?

I had lunch at a restaurant and went to see the racecourse. The short, sturdy mountain ponies there were very cute. I thought instantly of Harin and Bakul. The ponies were swift runners. The boys too loved riding. It would have been impossible to rein them in here. I smiled at the thought. My Pahadi bodyguard thought I was smiling because I was pleased with the place. I was keen to see the race. I put five rupees in his hand for him to put on any horse he fancied, in case he wanted to. I would sit there and watch the fun. He ran off and was back half an hour later jumping with joy. He had made fifteen rupees on the five he had taken! I was amused to see how happy he was.

I had trudged around a lot that day. I decided I should rest now. And so I turned back towards the hotel. The Pahadi man took me back by another route, through the nearby Mall Road. All sorts of articles made of agate and other semi-precious stones were on sale in the small shops that lined the road. I bought quite a few things and became so absorbed in looking at the Pahadi women's costumes that I lost all sense of time. Before I knew it, evening had fallen.

The following day I saw different 'Points', gardens, and Pahadi temples. The Tibetan Buddha temple was particularly interesting. The monks took turns to circumambulate the temple, carrying their prayer wheels and chanting mantras continuously. What I now yearned to see was Tiger Hill. I returned to the hotel early and got the manager to arrange for a rented car. The first faint rays of the sun could generally be seen from Tiger Hill around three o'clock in the morning. One had to get to the bottom of the hill by two o'clock. I was told that the climb would take at least half an hour. Naturally, I was a little worried about going out at that time of the night, but my Pahadi bodyguard was all set with lantern and all. The main problem was the rain. It still hadn't stopped completely. There's always a heavy mist during the rains. Everybody doubted whether the sun would be visible at all. The snow-clad mountain tops were already hidden by mist anyway. But my eagerness to see the sunrise was intense.

We left the hotel at one o'clock and reached Tiger Hill by car. It was pitch dark. The footpath leading up the hill was well made. It was bitterly cold. But I managed to reach the top of the hill, walking behind the Pahadi, guided by the dim light of his lantern. Once there, I saw that all four quarters were shrouded in mist. Doubt fluttered in my heart. Was I not going to get a glimpse of Kanchenjunga and see the sunrise after all? But what a miracle! ... I had to hold my breath. In five minutes the mist began to lift. Pink rays appeared in the sky. I stopped breathing for a moment. I could not contain so much joy in my heart. Soon, before my very eyes, the entire sky was suffused with red. In front of me was the white snow-clad peak of Kanchenjunga, and behind it the golden dawn. My eyes were dazzled. The Sun God rose slowly like a painter tinting the sky with a delicate hand. Then suddenly, as if somebody had tipped an enormous cauldron of molten gold, golden light poured over that glistening white snowy peak and flowed down it like a golden Ganga. Here indeed was Kanchenjunga! My simple-hearted Pahadi broke spontaneously into a loud cry of 'Shambho! ... Hargange!'. The call from that pure heart must surely have reached the Lord of Mount Kailash.

I sat on a rock, absolutely still, and who knows for how long. But however long I sat, trying to store the beauty of that vision in my eyes, it was still not enough to satiate me. All the quarters were now flooded with light. The raindrops and dewdrops falling from the trees sparkled gemlike in the sun's rays, like tears of joy. And then the profound silence of the place and our trance were rudely shattered by the driver waiting in the car below, blowing his horn. When I looked at my watch I saw it was past eight. We hurried down. But my spirit was still high, intoxicated by the beauty of nature. On the way down we visited the Buddha Dhoom Monastery. All these wondrous places that had existed here for millennia—it was impossible to even think of storing them all in my memory. Only some images of what I saw remain etched in my mind.

Back in the hotel everybody congratulated us. Sunrise was rarely seen during the rains. I spent the rest of the day savouring that morning's magical experience. That evening nature gave me an opportunity to see another miracle. I went in the opposite direction from Tiger Hill with the idea of seeing the Raja of Coochbehar's palace. I was acquainted with Bhaiyyaji, the Raja, and the Queen Mother. Even if they were not in residence, I had decided to see the palace and its famous surroundings from the outside. So I set off with my Pahadi bodyguard. Just as we reached the gates of the palace, I saw the white peak of Mount Everest before me gilded by the golden rays of the setting sun. This beauty was very different from the morning's vision of the sunrise. I stood watching the sight for a long time in complete silence. The Himalayan peaks, big and small, seemed to sit astride the blue clouds like proud riders, flying their golden pennants. The entire day had been one of rare good fortune for me.

When I met the hotel manager the following morning to ask him to arrange a taxi for me, he gave me a piece of astonishing information. Every morning at eight o'clock, a railway carriage attached to a small engine—a trolley-like mini-train like the Matheran train—left Darjeeling for Siliguri. There was a connecting train to Calcutta from there. If you paid first class fare to Siliguri and back, you could book the whole carriage. The train stopped at all the stations on the way, however small. Its route, winding around hills, was breathtakingly beautiful. If the line was clear you could stop the train anywhere to enjoy the beauty of nature. It was like having a fairy's magic wand thrust into my hand. I quickly paid the hotel bill and train fare, packed my bags, and got ready to leave. The manager had made excellent arrangements. The journey was like a glorious dream. The only sign that I was awake was that I was thinking of the boys all the time.

The little train wound its pretty way round bright green hillocks and hills. It chugged along at a leisurely pace through beautiful countryside flanked by tea plantations, thick woods, lush creepers, and, occasionally, emerald green fields—as if she was a guide showing me all the marvels of nature. Occasionally one saw an astonishingly lovely sight of wild flowers blooming on trees that rose to touch the sky. At times the track crossed a motorable road. Short, sturdy Pahadis could be seen walking on the road, carrying their plump, red-cheeked babies in baskets slung on their backs. The tiny hamlets and little shops on either side of the track appeared close enough to touch. Arriving at Siliguri station was like waking up from a dream. This rare experience, so full of joy, was over before I knew it. I planned that I would return here one day for sure, with Mr Khote and the boys. But the plan never materialized.

Sita was shot in Calcutta's Botanical Garden. It was so beautiful and so quiet that Sita's forest could not have been any different. It was spread over miles. The trees rose to touch the sky. We were told that botanical treasures comprising thousands of species of trees, shrubs, and creepers from the Himalayas and its foothills had been planted here. We were stunned to see those sky-scraping trees with their enormous trunks. There was a very famous banyan tree there. It must have been at least 1000 feet round its girth and over 100 feet tall. Its aerial roots alone numbered more than 300. Prithviraj and I challenged each other to run round the tree. But we would have to run back each time our shot was called, and it took us at least fifteen minutes to catch our breath. Finally, the director scolded us for wasting valuable shooting time. And that is where our bet ended.

Calcutta has innumerable places worth seeing. Your stay in Bengal will remain incomplete if you have not visited the Kalimata Mandir on Kalighat which houses the divine image of the avenging goddess Durga, as slayer of the demon Mahishasur. Its precincts resound to the call of 'Maa Lakhi! Maa Lakhi!', particularly on Thursdays and Fridays. The days of the Navaratra puja are like an epiphany of religious passion. Day and night, flocks of devotees pray to the power of the Mother Goddess, invoking the blessings of Kalimata with recitation of divine names, prayers, and hymns, *aartis*, ritual sacrifices, and offerings. On Dussera day, huge images of Kalimata are immersed the way Ganapati images are immersed in Maharashtra. It is like watching two seas coming together—the human sea and the mighty ocean itself.

The Dakshineshwar Kali temple and the Belur Math opposite on the banks of the Hooghly are centres of peace. However large the number of pilgrims, there is absolutely no disorder, noise, or chaos here. The prayers and sermons are conducted quietly. The prayers that each person says in his own heart are more important. This form of Kalimata is completely different from the Mahishasur Mardini of Kalighat.

Towards the end of the *Sita* shoot, we were in a location a short distance away from the city for a small scene. I was in the car reading, waiting for my shot to be called. Suddenly I felt as if somebody was pushing the car back and forth. Soon I felt it heaving up and down. I thought the village children were playing pranks. But just then I noticed that the members of our unit were running. When I opened the car door to see what had happened, I thought I saw the ground shudder. There was a lake nearby. The water in it suddenly surged high. Noises churned out of the ground like the rumbling of some monstrous machine. There was noise everywhere. People were shouting different things from different directions. The trees were shaking so violently you thought they would be torn up by their roots any moment. I have no idea how long this terrible time lasted before things gradually quietened down.

Later we came to know that it was an earthquake. It was as if mother earth were opening up to receive Sita into her womb. My role as Sita would have ended there and then. The film *Sita* ended in the same way. The following day we heard that a powerful earthquake had rocked Monghyr and the entire village had been razed to the ground. The destruction of life and property could not be measured. Every newspaper headline told us of the horrifying power of the earthquake.

During 1934 and 1935, I acted in four films that were made in Calcutta. I signed a four-month contract for each one of them and was paid Rs 2500 per month. At the end of every shooting schedule, I would return to Bombay. I earned Rs 40,000 during that period.

9

Dongersey Road: A New Life

During 1934–5, after completing the Calcutta films, I decided to work only in and around Bombay and turned down offers from Calcutta and Lahore. Bakul was now ten and Harin seven. They needed a secure home and family life. I too had had enough of this frenzied running around. I had been waiting for the day I could bring enough stability to my home and family life to allow the boys and us to live together. The boys were now old enough to understand things. They longed for a home of their own. They were fed-up with our unsettled life, here one day, there another.

Both were in the Cathedral Boys' School. It was very important now to keep an eye on their studies, general conduct, and health. Harin's rowdiness worried me. He was very affectionate and sensitive. He needed a lot of warmth and understanding. Unfortunately, from the time he was small, the problems and circumstances of my life had made it impossible for me to give him any time at all. The guilt of this still pricks my conscience. Bakul was quiet, reasonable, and mature beyond his years. But the minute they heard I was going out of Bombay, they would both cling to me. I used to feel terrible, but I too was helpless. They wished Mummy would not go away anywhere, that we would be together all the time.

Mr Khote's health had not been too good. His cough and asthma had become worse. He did not take his medicines regularly and was careless about his diet. That had affected his general health badly. I had bought a Morris Minor car for him so that travelling to work and back was not a problem. But then I began worrying about his driving. He drove so fast that he had narrowly escaped accidents on a couple of occasions. His expenditure on the club, food, and racing had also mounted. We had somehow managed to scrape through in these difficult times. But things were looking up now. I was well established in the film industry. Everybody was happy to hear of my decision. The boys in particular were thrilled.

We rented part of a large bungalow on Dongersey Road. It was an independent house with a small garden. There were two fruit trees in the garden. The boys instantly adopted them, one each. The *chikoo* tree was Bakul's, the custard apple tree Harin's. It was decided that the two would take turns to look after them. We bought new furniture and decorated the house beautifully. The boys' room was huge. There was enough space there for their bicycles, cricket gear, Meccano set, carpentry toolbox, and toys. All the rooms opened on to a broad verandah large enough to seat twenty-five people for a meal. That, and its highly polished floor, reminded me intensely of our house in Kandewadi.

I had silver dinner sets—plates, bowls, and tumblers—made for the four of us. I loved using silverware. I had the boys' names engraved on their plates. This thrilled them no end. Every mealtime, they would make sure they were eating from their own plates. If the plates got mixed up by mistake, there would be a great scramble to claim their own back. They took turns to sit next to me, and, when Mr Khote was at home, next to him as well. That became a fun routine. The boys were experts at pinching a piece of fish or a puri off my plate when I was not looking. They would then catch each other out. How often do these sweet sights reappear before my eyes! How happy were those days!

Fortunately, I was soon offered a role that suited me. It was a Bombay-style film, a mythological one like *Sita*, sentimental, with appropriate sets. I had now come to terms with my work. This was my profession and I would try as hard as possible to do justice to whatever role I was offered. This decision took much of the weight off my mind. I was now in command of the characters I was playing. Though they all fell into the same mould, I found ways to play them a shade differently each time. Groping to find a way for myself, I was soon able to put my individual stamp on my roles. Unlike Prabhat and Calcutta, the Bombay studios had no tradition of training or guiding actors. We were given the bare outline of stories, and things would be regularly dropped or added ad hoc during the shoot. The birth certificates of the dialogue fell into our hands only when we arrived on the sets.

Back home from the studio, the house would be ringing with laughter, with the happy noises of the boys' games, their shouting, telling on each other, and reciting to me the day's happenings in school. One day Harin came and stood before me with a very serious expression. 'What's the matter, Harya?' I asked. Without saying a word he held out a letter imprinted with Prabhat's *tutari* logo. I opened the letter quickly. Shantarambapu was offering me a role in *Amarjyoti*. I was overjoyed. I was so engrossed in my own happiness that I did not notice Harin's expression. His eyes were fixed on my face. When I did look at him, he said in a voice heavy with tears, 'Mummy, are you going away again for work? I thought you were going to stay here forever and work.' I was very moved. I held him close to me and said, 'I'm only going to Pune, Harya. That's not too far away. We have a car now. You can easily come down to Pune for the weekend, or I will come up. I'll only go when there's work, and it won't be a long stay.'

He clung to my neck and said, 'Mummy, promise?' And I said, 'Promise.' Harin's face brightened instantly and he skipped away to give Bakul the news. I was surprised and moved by his love. It is my misfortune that the events destiny had in store for me did not allow me to nurture these delicate bonds of love the way they should have been.

My family's reactions to my work were very amusing. Bakul would say, 'Mummy, please don't cry in your films. It makes me very sad. Why do they make you cry? You look so beautiful when you smile. Look at your dimples.'

Papa would say, 'Banu, you look best with a sword in your hand. You should always play that kind of role.'

One day I had to punish Harin for something naughty he had done. When the punishment was over, he said to me sniffling, nostrils flared in anger, 'You only love the children in your films. But you're always beating me.' I burst out laughing and said, 'Why do you do naughty things then?' To which he retorted, 'Aren't the children in your films naughty? Are they always good?' Poor Harin. He had to take a lot of disciplining from me.

Mummy's attention was forever on my weight. 'Banu, don't eat rice. See how fat your arms look. You must exercise everyday.'

Durga Khote as Jijabai in *Sambhaji*

As Rani Taramati in *Ayodhyecha Raja*

Mubarak and
Durga Khote in
Saugadi (Marathi)
produced by the
actress

As Rani Kilotala
in *Maya
Macchindra*
(Marathi)

As Rani Taramati
in *Ayodhyecha
Raja* (Marathi)

Durga Khote in *Pratibha* (Marathi)

Durga Khote with Nargis, Jawahar Lal Nehru, and Raj Kapoor

At the Peking Language School, as member of the Indian delegation which visited China in 1954

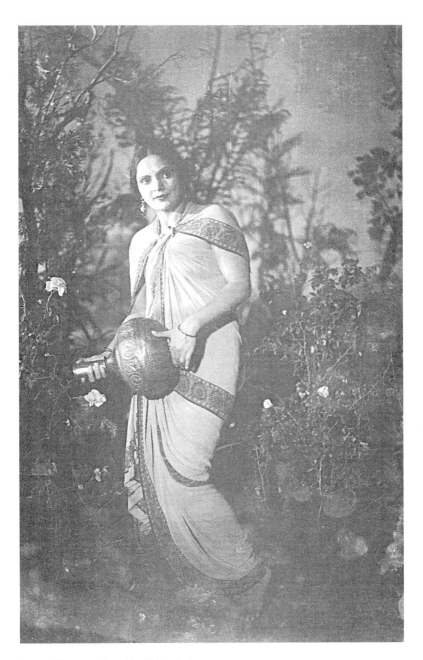

Durga Khote in *Pratibha* (Marathi)

As Rani Kilotala, with a cheetah at her feet, in *Maya Macchindra*

Durga Khote in the palace with attendants—as Jodhabai in *Mughal-e-Azam*

A studio shot

Durga Khote and her family
Front row (L to R) Mangesh Wagle, Gokul Pandit, Viju Wagle, Sharada Pandit, Bakul; Middle row (L to R) Shalini Wagle, Saraswati Pandit (sisters), Manjula Laud (mother), Vasant Pandit, Pandurang Laud (father), Durga Khote with Harin; Back row (L to R) Balwantrao Wagle (brother-in-law), Prataprao Pandit, Manohar Laud (brother), Vishwanath Khote (husband), Ratan Laud (sister-in-law)

With Yeshwantrao Chavan and Indira Gandhi

Durga Khote with Nargis, Jawahar Lal Nehru, and Raj Kapoor

At the Peking Language School, as member of the Indian delegation which visited China in 1954

Mr Khote was also angry all the time. 'Good God! I just can't take your Hindi,' he would say. His own Hindi had been honed at Benaras Hindu University. When a new film was released it was this censor in the house that I feared most. Luckily, my viewers tolerated everything.

A film like *Amarjyoti*, an imaginary story and beautiful in every respect, happens only once in a rare while. The cinematography, sets, costumes, jewellery, songs, and backgrounds were so perfectly attuned, that the audience went crazy with every scene. Every element, whether it was shots of ships, surging waves and enormous rocks, or the casting and performances with minute shades of expression, heroism, self-sacrifice, and extreme tyranny—was striking in itself, and in complete harmony with every other element of the complicated plot. Shanta Apte's songs became very popular. Vasanti's lovable charm, the harsh anger that I, as Saudamini, expressed against injustice, Chandramohan's impressive performance, light eyes flashing—were all wonderfully effective. The costumes of the smugglers, their lifestyle, the weapons they carried, were all imaginary, and yet they came through so convincingly on screen. Every costume was so precisely selected that it fitted in its place perfectly, as if carved for that space.

Prabhat had taken great pains in the making of *Amarjyoti* and they got the success they deserved. Stories and legends about *Amarjyoti* still circulate in the film world. I too received my share of benefit from its success just like everybody else. I was offered a string of roles in Bombay films after it was released. I accepted two contracts from amongst them and returned to Bombay for four months.

During these four months I realized that the condition of both our homes was worrisome. Papa looked very tired and disturbed. The problems of the Laud family were multiplying. The family had expanded but nobody was earning anything. They had decided to sell off the house in Kandewadi along with the land they owned in the Mahim-Worli areas, and to extend the Charni Road houses with extra construction. In principle it was a good idea. There was no other way to support the growing family and its expenses. Not a single creature in the family was earning his bread. Everyone was busy having a good time. And now the Laud family began seeing dreams of a magnificent mansion on Queen's Road. But the time and money spent on building Laud Mansion went way beyond all estimates. Everybody wanted a mansion of his dreams. The family was fragmented into small rival, whispering groups. There was no control over expenses in the Laud family, at home or outside. The burden of supporting the whole family fell on poor Papa. He was at the end of his tether and under great strain. It was Papa they came running to in every crisis.

Mummy had always protested against the lifestyle of the Lauds. Family responsibility and tension was all Papa got out of it. So Mummy's anger was justified. Now it had grown sharper. After Manohar's marriage, Mummy had shifted her home to Nepean Sea Road. She never returned to Kandewadi after that. Naturally, Manohar's life was affected by all these goings-on. Mummy could not bear that. The atmosphere in Papa and Mummy's home had turned turbid. All of Mummy's ambitions had been pinned on Manohar. She had hoped that once he qualified as a barrister, he would take over the family firm and do even better than his father. She had done her best to give him all the support she could, but nothing had come of it. In reality, Manohar was a second-class student. Though he went to Britain and qualified as a barrister, it took him years to establish himself in his profession. His married life, too, was in a shambles. The daughter-in-law Mummy had brought home with such hopes turned out to be too difficult to handle. Both problems wounded Mummy's ego deeply.

The atmosphere in our own home in Dongersey Road had also become depressing. I just could not see where and how I could control Mr Khote's extravagant lifestyle. I had fervently hoped that once my career and home had stabilized everything would sort itself out. But I hoped in vain. I was at my wit's end. Mr Khote was adding new addictions to the old. He did not go to work regularly. He kept company with wastrels. He gave no thought to home, children, money, or life. His behaviour was completely irresponsible. He never once took the boys out for a drive. It was as if the car had been bought for his friends. The poor boys would ask me to take them out somewhere when I returned from work. Then we would go out for ice-cream. Papa would often take them for a spin too. But they wanted a car of their own. Finally I bought them a Lancia. Their joy knew no bounds. Harin said to his father, 'We won't let you come in our car now.' That made Mr Khote smart.

10

Kolhapur: Shalini Studio

In 1936, after my work with the Bombay film *Kal Ki Baat* was over, I went to Kolhapur to work at Shalini Studio owned by Her Royal Highness Akkasaheb. They had started shooting for two films, *Ushaswapna* and *Savakari Pash*. A third script, *Pratibha*, had also been written specially for me. All three films were to be directed by Baburao Painter. Rajaram Maharaj had arranged for me to stay at the palace. I used to go to Bombay every Friday and return on Monday if I was required. The studio had conceded to this condition. The boys too would come to Kolhapur for a few days now and again. Mr Khote also came down once. Maharaj and Akkasaheb treated us with much affection and warmth. The boys loved Kolhapur. They loved the royal life and all the wonderful things they could do there like horse-riding, deer and cheetah hunting with the Maharaj, and occasional forays on the back of a canopied elephant.

The work at Shalini Studio was also regal in style and pace, and governed by whim. Baburao Painter the director would spend most of his time painting. He had designed very simple but attractive costumes for *Pratibha*. They had appeared as photographs and also in several calendars. But the pace of shooting was very slow. We would shoot alternately for *Ushaswapna* and *Savakari Pash*. Only rarely was the *Pratibha* set put up. I had a talk with Baburao about this. Later, a slight coldness developed between us over this. I hated sitting around doing nothing, or going out with my royal hosts just because there was no work. At last, however haltingly, the film got made. But it did not run.

Around this time some people in Bombay suggested that I should enter the film production business. I myself had been wondering how much longer I could expect to get roles that were suitable for me and which were worth doing. I was thirty-one then and had eight films behind me. The idea of setting up a company was good provided I did not have to invest money. The person who had broached the subject with me was a reputed solicitor, Mr Natwarlal. He and a wealthy friend of his from Jaipur were planning to set up a company called Associated Productions which would finance and distribute films. Examining the proposal from all angles, they appeared to be the right people to do business with. After lengthy discussions with Papa, we established a company called Nataraj Films. There were five partners in the Company—director Parshwanath Altekar, music director Govindrao Tembe, production manager and main actor was Mubarak Merchant, manager Mr Peshkar, and Durgabai Khote. Associated Productions was to handle all finances and remit agreed sums of money in instalments to the account of Nataraj Productions. The most important clause was that we would not bear any financial responsibility. Further, the people who were investing the money would not meddle in any aspect of the filmmaking process. Production was to be handled entirely by Nataraj Productions. Our responsibility was to complete the Hindi-Marathi versions of a given film within the given time and budget. Naturally, Associated Productions would reserve the right to inspect our accounts from time to time. In accordance with the agreement, over and above our salaries, Nataraj Productions would get twenty-five per cent of the profits for overseeing and handling the production, but they would bear no responsibility for losses. In addition to this, I was granted the right to act in films produced by other companies besides Nataraj. Natwarlal and his associates had accepted all these conditions.

Nobody in the film world had ever heard of such a one-way contract. The first instalment from Associated Productions was soon credited to our account and we set to work in high spirits. Mr Altekar got Mama Warerkar to write the Marathi story for *Soungadi*, which was adapted into Hindi as *Sathi* by Pandit Anandkumar. We decided to shoot the film in Pune because it would be less expensive than Bombay. There was also another reason. Mr Keshavrao Dhaibar had left Prabhat after some misunderstanding and set up a production company of his own called Jayashree Films. His first film *Nandkumar* was being distributed by Associated Productions. Mr Dhaibar and Natwarlal were both very keen that I should do the role of Yashoda in it. I agreed instantly. Since both Jayashree's *Nandkumar* and Nataraj's *Soungadi* were going to be shot in the same studio in Pune, it was going to save us a lot of running around, and make it easier for me to work in both films. All these plans fell into place so smoothly that none of us could have imagined that a calamity was waiting to strike.

11

Fate Strikes Again

We had begun shooting for *Soungadi*, and work was going according to plan. The film was proceeding in leisurely style, allowing me time to make frequent trips to Bombay. I used to go on Saturday mornings, spend the weekend with the boys and Mr Khote, and return to Pune on Monday.

One of these Saturdays happened to be the Coconut Festival. The whole crew had been given the day off. So we were shooting on Sunday instead. I had planned to return to Pune on Saturday evening, but the boys were very keen on going for the Coconut Day fair. Then Mummy and Papa insisted we have dinner with them that evening and catch the night train later. After dinner, Mr Khote drove us to the Victoria Terminus station to see us off on the 10 o'clock train to Pune. Bakul had holidays so he was going with me. Harin was staying back with Mummy because he had a cricket match. As we left, Mr Khote told our servant that he would go to Dadar to Kaki's place from the station, and directly from there to work on Monday. He ordered lunch to be kept ready for him on Monday.

When I went to the studio on Sunday, I was told they had not been able to put up the set because the shops had been closed the previous day and they could not buy several things they needed for it. Anyway, since I was in charge of office work, I spent all of Sunday answering letters and checking accounts.

We were sitting in the office on Monday morning waiting for the set to go up and, in the meantime, discussing the next scene, when a telephone call came to the studio from Bombay. The studio sent word to say that there was an urgent call for Mr Altekar or Mubarak. The studio and office were just across the road from each other.

Since it was an unexpected and urgent call, both left immediately. Neither came back for almost fifteen minutes. I was on the point of sending a peon to find out what had happened when they came back and sat before me with lowered heads, not saying a word. I could not understand what was wrong. I said to them, 'Has our negative been damaged in the laboratory?' I received no answer.

I suddenly realized that a deathly silence had fallen over the office. After a moment's pause, Altekar said, 'Bai please leave for Bombay on the three o'clock train this afternoon. We've sent Peshkar to book the tickets.' I was taken aback. 'But I've only just come from there. If the set was going to take longer to put up, you could have called me. Saved all this needless coming and going.' Mr Altekar said nothing to that. Mubarak said, 'Bai, there's been an accident. Mr Khote is seriously injured. You must go immediately.'

I screamed, 'What happened?' and began to rush out of the office. They both held me and put me into the car standing outside and took me to my Pune home. The house was very close to the studio. I kept asking, 'What's happened?' But all they said was, 'Mr Wagle (my brothert-in-law) said only this much—there has been an accident.' Mubarak took Bakul's help to lock up our cupboards and other things. They put Bakul and me on the train. All of us left for Bombay by the Poona Express.

During the four hours in the train, the whole world spun around me. Poor Bakul sat huddled close to me. At Byculla, Altekar and Mubarak got ready to get off. I said, 'Why are you getting off here?' Just then I saw Mummy and Papa as the train entered the station. Bakul was still clinging to me. Altekar and Mubarak both held me. Papa came to the door of the compartment and he and Mummy helped me down. I clung to Papa and said, 'Why are we getting off here Papa? Let's go home quickly.' Papa said, 'Banay, we are going to the hospital. Come. Hold my hand.'

How brave Papa was! His face had darkened, but he did not for a moment allow his grip on my hand to loosen. Papa and Mummy held me and led me out from a small side gate of the station. They practically pushed me into the car parked outside. Mummy and Papa sat on either side of me holding me tight while Mubarak sat in front with Bakul. The car was speeding ahead. I was asking all the time, 'Where are you taking me? To which hospital?' When we got to a less crowded street, Papa held me close and said, 'Banu, Visha is no more. You must understand this. It was a heart attack. You must be brave for the sake of your children. Now we'll go to your place on Dongersey Road.' I have no idea when and how we got to the Dongersey Road house. My place ...?

When I came to, I was in Papa's house, lying on Mummy's bed. Gradually I came to know what had happened. Mr Khote had gone to Kaki's place in Dadar after seeing us off. On the following day, Sunday, he had lunch at Dadar and left, saying, 'I'll probably go home to Dongersey Road tonight.' Nobody knew what happened after that. On Monday morning some municipal employees noticed his car parked by the side of the road at Grant Road market. He was seated in it with his head resting on the steering wheel. They informed their superior immediately. He was the health officer and one of our kin. He instantly arranged to have our family fetched to the place. That was it. Everything was over.

My world was now a void. I knew nothing. Understood nothing. Two days later Tai brought Bakul and Harin to me. Bakul seemed to have grown up overnight. He had lost his childhood and was suddenly an adult. Harin looked completely bewildered. The two brothers came hand in hand and stood very close to me. My two little cubs— one thirteen, the other ten. Day followed upon day. A month passed. I was facing an old question after twelve years—what next?

One day Papa came and sat beside me. Holding my hands tight in his, he said, 'Banu, we're going to Pune tomorrow.'

I burst out sobbing uncontrollably. 'Why to Pune?' Stroking my face he said, 'To complete the two films my pet. The sets are ready.' Then Papa went on, 'We've blocked some people's money. I've assured Natwarlal that my daughter will not cause losses to anybody; she will complete your work. We'll decide what to do after that. You will stay here with your sons. I will not let you stay alone with them. We've locked up the Dongersey Road flat.' He found it difficult to say anything more.

That evening Papa went to meet Kaka and Kaki. Kaka was staying in Dadar and working with Prabhawalkar Contractors. Papa tried to console them by saying that they still had their grandsons to look to. But he got no response. Instead they heaped all kinds of accusations on me, saying I and the boys had been responsible for all their misfortunes and wounded Papa deeply with the other bitter things they said. There was no need to drag the poor boys into our misfortune. Actually Kaka and Kaki had not even inquired after us from the time we left Laburnum Road. Also, they were furious with me for having chosen to become a professional film actress. There was no denying that the poor old couple's life too had become terribly sad and pathetic. Natwarlal on the other hand had very decently promised, on behalf of his company, to release me from our contract without demanding compensation for losses.

The following day Papa took me to Pune. The set was ready in the studio. Papa took me to the make-up room and sat on a chair outside while I got ready. When I was fully ready, he handed me over to Altekar and the others saying, 'Take care of her.' He stroked my back and said, 'I will always be there, standing beside you. Don't be afraid.' Papa left for Bombay by the afternoon Express. As soon as I finished the Nataraj set, I completed work on the Nandkumar set too. While the next Nataraj set was being put up, the Company, instead of sending me back to Bombay, arranged for Mummy and me to go to Mahabaleshwar for eight days.

Though the Nataraj shoot began all right, more unexpected disasters befell us. The financier-partner of Associated Productions died suddenly of a heart attack in Jaipur. This second shock rocked the Nataraj Company to its foundations. Mr Natwarlal also came under great financial stress. Shooting had to be stopped for some time. Meanwhile the boys and I came down with malaria. Bakul became very ill indeed. The house I had rented in Pune was on the bank of a canal. The location was beautiful, thickly wooded. But we had no idea that it was infested with malarial mosquitoes. Finally we shifted residence to the cantonment area. We managed to complete the two films in the end, and I returned to Bombay sometime in 1938.

In Bombay, too, the cycle of misfortune continued to spin around us. Harin had become very disturbed after we left the Dongersey Road house. He had never had a sense of security in all his young life. It had made him very ill-tempered and obstinate. He would not listen to anybody. He would cling to Papa or me all the time. Meanwhile Mummy's nature had changed a lot because of their circumstances. She did not even attempt to understand Harin. Her harsh Victorian discipline seemed to surge up only where the boys were concerned. She had only one goal now—Manohar. She even seemed to have cast Papa aside. Manohar had to have everything—cars, club memberships, going out—all the external show required for his business. Manohar was a barrister. He took a long time to establish himself. But the entire household revolved around him even in those days.

My dear brother took full advantage of Mummy's obsession with him. Manohar did not give a thought to anybody apart from himself. That year passed in acute mental stress and confusion. Hardly had 1939 dawned than Papa also left us. This was the third stroke of fate in two years. For me it was like being buffeted around in a cyclone. Living with Mummy became very difficult now. The boys were utterly fed-up. Harin had been very fond of Papa. He simply could not be controlled. To make things worse, it was Bakul's Senior Cambridge year and I was out working day and night. The boys were being neglected. Neither Mummy nor Manohar gave them any attention. I wondered if this transformation in Mummy had happened because Manohar's marriage had broken up. I wished I could move out to live by myself with the boys. But when Papa had been in financial straits I had promised Mummy that I would help her as much as my circumstances would allow. It was my duty after all. But now I felt trapped by my own promise.

The entire burden of running the household and Manohar's personal expenditure was thrust on my shoulders. Soon it was more than I could afford. Even the boys felt the effects of this. However much one tried to hide the rifts in the home from them, they were now old enough to understand everything. Bakul put up silently with Mummy's discrimination even in the matter of food, but it became difficult to control Harin. He could not get on even for a moment at home. He began defying Mummy openly, saying, 'It is Mummy's money. Why should we get less? Why does uncle get more than us? Why is everything for uncle? Why not for Mummy?' This was seen as unforgivable rudeness and everyday I was presented with a long list of complaints about him. I would get upset and punish him. He felt deeply aggrieved by the insult and injustice.

Everything was spinning beyond my control. Harin obstinately refused to study. He managed to pass only because he was intelligent.

He loved cricket. But at home, the most trivial reason was good enough for his bat to be confiscated as punishment. Poor Harin. Because of all the restrictions put on him as a child, his temper became unstable. He would suddenly explode like a volcano. But he was equally affectionate and sensitive. He was proud but just as generous. He loved me with all his heart. But I was destined not to be able to do anything for him. Circumstances always kept the two of us far apart. Luckily, Bakul passed his Senior Cambridge examination with flying colours. He got a First Grade with honours—at the young age of fifteen.

12

The Boys' Future

Bakul's excellent performance at the Senior Cambridge examination, his First Grade honours and second rank at school made Harin, more than anybody else, exult. He threw his arms around my neck that night and said, 'Our Dada is going to be a big man isn't he?' I said, 'And what about you?' 'I? I'm going to captain the Khote eleven. I'm going to tell my wife to give me twelve men for the team.' We had a good laugh over his plan. It was a very long time since we had had such moments of happiness and laughter.

Bakul's school principal congratulated him and gave him a good certificate of recommendation. I had begun to make inquiries about which college to send him to and which profession he should prepare for. I discussed this with several people. An arts degree would take four years and lead to nothing better than clerkship. Degrees in engineering and medicine would mean supporting him for ten years. How could I afford that? There was Harin's education to take care of too. It was only just beginning. My income was going three ways. There was the Dongersey Road flat to maintain, Kaka and Kaki's financial problems to take care of, and now the burden of the Nepean Sea Road household!

Bakul was still not old enough to enter college. He would be eligible only after a year and a half. That is why we decided that he should attend Davar's College of Commerce in the meantime and see what openings that would offer. I had asked several people close to us for some assurance that they would take him on as an apprentice so that he could acquire a skill. But I was fobbed off with hollow, insincere promises like, 'We'll see after he finishes college.' If I had received a firm assurance from even one of them, I would have liked to send Bakul to Xaviers or Elphinstone College. Finally Bakul enrolled at Davar's for secretarial training.

A number of people close to me, including my brother-in-law Mr Wagle, had been urging me to put my grief behind me and come out into the world, meet acquaintances, friends, and relatives whenever I could spare time from my work. Apart from anything else, meeting people might throw up ideas for work opportunities for the boys. Mr Wagle and my sister Tai began taking me out regularly to Willingdon Club. I met a number of old friends there and received warm invitations to visit their homes.

It happened around 1940–1. I met Mr Anthony D'Mello at one of these parties. He was a founder member of the Cricket Club of India, Advisor to the Maharaja of Gwalior, and a director on the boards of several companies. His wife Rita who was also there was a very old friend of mine. They were staying at the Taj Mahal Hotel where they invited me to visit them. They inquired after the boys and me. Then Mr D'Mello said, 'Durga, why don't you place Bakul in Caltex as an apprentice? American companies are not enamoured of Indian graduate degrees. They are looking for young men from good families. Two years there will take him a long way. I know the Caltex people very well. Bring Bakul to Delhi. I'll take him to Caltex. I'm sure it'll work out. He'll get just seventy-five rupees as spending money for the first six months. After that he will be paid a salary, determined on the basis of how well he works.' Then he added, 'Anyway he's only fifteen. If things don't work out there, he can always come back after two years and go to college.'

I was convinced by what he said. I took Bakul to Delhi. Mr D'Mello had booked a room for us in Western Court. Bakul's interview went off very well and he was taken on. I arranged for him to stay with an Anglo-Indian family in Canning Street as a paying guest. A very affectionate Parsi woman lived next door to them with her two children. Her husband Jehangir, was in the Railways. He had taken a commission in the army. The Second World War was going on and he was serving on the Burma front. She looked after Bakul like her own son. Some Maharashtrian families in Delhi had also agreed, most willingly, to keep an eye on him. They included highly-placed people like top army officers and bankers. Bakul was very good-looking and very young. That is why I was anxious. As it turned out, it was Bakul who determined the future course of his life and prepared for it with hard work, unfailing courtesy, and a sweet disposition. I would visit him every six weeks or so. My heart would fill with joy and all of life's pain would melt away when I heard glowing reports of how he was conducting himself.

With Bakul gone, Harin was left alone at home. My sister's children avoided coming to Nepean Sea Road. They complained that Uncle said nasty things and harassed them. They could not tolerate the way Mummy glossed over Manohar's utter disdain of everybody. I was now consciously careful about how I behaved with Harin. Even then he had to face a lot of problems at home in my absence. I was running in three directions—shooting, Delhi, and Bombay. In the midst of all this, I did not realize exactly how deeply hurt and depressed he was feeling. I told myself he was still young. He would calm down in time. But my judgement proved completely wrong. Because of his frustration, Harin's temper became uncontrollable. I was worried about him and, at the same time, afraid for him. I tried hard to find someone who would advise me, help me in this. But nobody came forward to help. Nobody bothered with how the two of us were coping. If I could have found an understanding companion for him, to take care of him, to handle him sensitively, to give him affection, it would have made things easier for him. He refused outright to go to boarding school. I myself did not have the courage to send him away either. I wished I could give up my work, stay home, and just hold him close to me! But what would we do if I stopped working?

When he appeared for his matriculation examination, I was away on location and he really suffered during that time. It is a wonder that he got through at all. His teacher told me later that he would have done much better if he had been emotionally stable. As a result he could not find a place in Elphinstone College. We enrolled him in Wilson College. That upset him dreadfully. All his friends were at Elphinstone. As a result, Harin simply refused to study the whole of the following year. He spent all his time in rowdiness. Doubts stormed my mind now. I wondered in which direction the drifting raft of Harin's life would take him from here.

13

From the Frying Pan into the Fire

It happened during the shooting of *Prithvi Vallabh*. The set was to take a while longer to get ready. Still in a disturbed state of mind, I went to Delhi to meet Bakul. I didn't want to upset him by telling him about Harin. I put his mind at rest by saying, 'He's become a little self-willed. But it'll pass. He's still a boy.'

I did not stay in a hotel that time, but with Bakul. A single woman and an actress to boot, alone in a hotel! People were constantly hovering around actors. There was also the bustle of war. The Second World War was going on. There was a menacing presence of khaki everywhere. People were falling over themselves to join the army and notch up a 'war record' that would ingratiate them with the government later. So there were invitations and parties all the time. I was like Papa in this respect. The social whirl held no interest for me. But I forced myself to go once in a while so that Bakul could meet more people and get to know those who mattered in Delhi.

It was at one of these parties that I met Nawabzada Mohammad Rashid. We exchanged the usual formalities and Bakul and I returned home. That night I came down with very high fever. Poor Bakul got terribly scared. At the end of four days the fever had still not subsided. The doctor diagnosed it as an acute attack of malignant malaria and advised complete bed rest for at least eight or ten days. This meant extending my stay in Delhi. People made solicitous inquiries after me and helped Bakul a lot. Many friends came to see me. Amongst them was Mr Rashid who kept up a stream of visits *mijajpursi ke liye*—to inquire after my health. He always came with flowers, fruits, or chocolates. I was beginning to feel quite embarrassed. We talked about many things in the course of conversation. We discussed the film industry and my work in it; he asked about my family in Bombay and about Bakul's plans for the future.

Then he began saying things like if Bakul needed anything done for him in Caltex I should not hesitate to tell him because he knew people there. Everything Mr Rashid said and did bore the mark of pedigree, breeding, and style. He came from Muradabad and was related to the royal house of Mehmoodabad. He had spent many years in Europe and America. You could see the mark of western ways and ideas on his lifestyle. Before he joined the Air Force, he had served the Prince of Mysore as Comptroller of the Household. His ties and close friendships ranged from kings and princes to government officials and the Viceroy himself.

One day Bakul said casually, 'I would love to be in the Air Force.' Instantly Mr Rashid offered to try to get him in. 'I'll make an appointment with the Air Vice-Marshal in a couple of days and take you to meet him. It'll give you a war record which will open up chances for promotions later. Now even America has joined the war and Caltex is an American company.'

The very next day he called to say he had made the appointment. 'You'll meet the Air Vice-Marshal tomorrow.' Instantly I felt afraid. The Air Force? But I thought to myself, let us see what happens, and refused to allow fear to invade my mind. Bakul failed the Air Force test because his eyesight was not good enough, and that is where the matter ended.

Soon I was feeling better and returned to Bombay. Mr Rashid booked my ticket and made all other arrangements for my journey through his office. It was not so easy to get reservations in those days. Rashid insisted on seeing me off at the station. It was awkward for me to refuse. At the station, even before I could look for my compartment and seat, an Air Force cadet came out of nowhere, saluted me and led me to it. Rashid had booked an entire coupe for me. When I entered, I saw flowers, fruit, magazines, and newspapers, all neatly arranged to make my journey comfortable. Even my bedding had been spread out on one berth. I was sure I had entered the wrong compartment. Mr Rashid was standing outside on the platform. I put my head out of the window and said, 'What is all this?' He replied, 'You are not well. You should travel in comfort.' Before I could respond Mr Rashid had merged with the crowd of passengers. I had been on the point of saying something like thank you, but you shouldn't have taken the trouble, when the Frontier Mail began to move.

A little later a railway employee came with a tray loaded with breakfast, saying that the *sahib* had ordered it for me. To be quite honest, I was confused and deeply touched. Nobody had ever shown me so much concern and courtesy. More importantly, while doing all this, the man had not once made a show of it or been over-familiar or brash. Normally, people who hover around film actors are inquisitive and glamour-struck. Mr Rashid's behaviour, on the other hand, was so different and so well-bred that I could honestly not fathom what it implied. But it did set me thinking.

I was still staying at Nepean Sea Road. My Bombay routine had begun. Shooting, anxiety about Harin, and arguments at home. Discussions about Rashid became an additional feature. There was a reason for it. Parcels of flowers, fresh fruit, and dry fruit began arriving from Delhi by the Air Vice-Marshal's airplane. The Air Vice-Marshal and Rashid were close friends. The discussions came to a head when Rashid started making trips to Bombay on one pretext or another.

One day Rashid took me to the Taj for dinner. That evening he almost pleaded with me to marry him. This was not altogether unexpected in the context of the four months we had known each other. But there were certain things about which my mind was made up. I told Rashid frankly there and then that I was not interested in anything beyond my children's future. I needed help. I needed guidance. If marriage were the price I had to pay for it, I would pay it. I was going into this with eyes wide open. But I would not take on any financial responsibility and I would not give up my work in films. I was offering something like a contract. Rashid accepted all my conditions. 'Now think about it,' he said and left it at that.

Though Rashid had not got Bakul into the Air Force, he got him an army commission with a posting in Karachi. He also began to make efforts to get to know Harin. He would call to inquire after him even when I was away shooting. And when he was in Bombay, he would take him out to dinner or to see a film. Harin loved spending time with him, listening to his stories about the Air Force and his days in England. He began to get very attached to Rashid. I too felt more reassured about him. I pushed away the last shred of doubt, steadied my vacillating mind, and came to a decision. I was forty years old at this time and Rashid must have been fifty. He had divorced his European wife. We got married in Bulandshahr on 10 October 1943. There was no question of my changing my religion. It was a civil marriage. Rashid's brother-in-law was Chief Engineer of the Canal department of the government of the United Provinces. He organized everything quietly without creating a fuss. We returned to Delhi the following day. In Delhi I completed all the formalities such as getting an Air Force identity card, ration card, travel pass, and other documents, and returned to Bombay.

The atmosphere at Nepean Sea Road was expectedly tense. But I had decided not to let it worry me now. The only thing I did was to assure Mummy that there would be no change in the present arrangement, that Harin and I would continue staying there for the time being, and that she should not worry about household expenses. She needed this reassurance because Manohar had still not found a foothold in his practice. He was still considered a junior. This hurt her a lot. A junior did not get paid and was made to work very hard. Manohar did work hard and gained a lot of experience, but the rewards were late in coming.

Nothing of what people in the film industry might be saying about me came to my ears because I was not close enough to anybody for such things to be reported to me. I simply continued to do my work as of old. But one thing was certain. Many people were very upset that I had married a Muslim. Their sentiments towards me were hurt by this act. The Hindu-Muslim enmity was then entering a particularly bitter phase and the heat of it soon began to affect me. Meanwhile Rashid, in his usual way, pulled strings to get himself transferred to Bombay. The Air Force gave us a big flat. But it was in the security zone where Harin could not stay with us. He had to stay on in Nepean Sea Road. He would come over to the flat in the evenings, have dinner with us, and return. I felt terrible about it, but there was no way out until we found another flat. I had also signed a contract with Mr Bhalji Pendharkar to play Kunti in his *Maharathi Karna* for which I had to go to Kolhapur. Harin was in his pre-university degree year at the time. So I decided it was best to leave things as they were till Harin finished his examinations.

In Kolhapur, a distinguished, extremely well-known, and eminent local family whom I had become acquainted with in Delhi, insisted on my staying with them. They had gone out of their way to take care of Bakul. We had grown so close that they were like family now. I felt perfectly at home staying with them. Bhalji's wife Leelabai and I had been very close friends from the Prabhat days. Finally, after many years, Prithviraj was going to be my co-star once again. I could not have asked for a better, more friendly set-up. The shooting was proceeding in a congenial atmosphere. One day, out of the blue, I received an urgent letter from Rashid saying that Manohar had thrown Harin out of the Nepean Sea Road house at nine o'clock in the night.

Some sharp object that Harin had been playing with had landed on Mummy's bed. Mummy had gone into hysterics. Manohar had instantly called up Rashid, asking him to take Harin away at once. Rashid had tried his best to reason with them. He said we could take a decision after I returned from Kolhapur. But it was no use. Finally Rashid packed Harin's things and drove him to the Air Force quarters. He got permission from the Air Vice-Marshal to allow him to stay with us. I was stunned to read this. I could not return to Bombay in the middle of my shoot. I managed to get through that schedule somehow and returned to Bombay two weeks later.

Harin's exams were over. The college was closed. The big question now was how to keep him occupied for two months. Finally we took him to Muradabad to visit Rashid's sister who had invited us. Harin enjoyed his two months there, rowing, hunting, and picnicking with the family. He grew calmer too. But he failed his exam that year. Of course, this was not totally unexpected. We enrolled him now in Ismail Yusuf College at Jogeshwari under the principal, Dr Rehman's eye. Dr Rehman took personal interest in him and brought him back on track. Harin studied really hard that year and did very well in his examination. As soon as the results were out, Rashid pulled strings to get him into the Aeronautic School in Reading, UK. Harin was admitted to the three-year course in mechanical and electrical engineering.

Many events, good and bad, took place in my life in the next three years. We left our Malabar Hill house and moved into the Taj

Mahal Hotel for two years. I began to feel suffocated in that closed circle. The place was filled with the old rich and the new rich. It was always the same people, the same food and the same superficial smiles and chatter. Everything was shallow, flippant, formal, devoid of real feeling. But for Rashid, this life was like his life in Europe years ago. I grew restless.

As soon as the war was over, Rashid's commission in the Air Force came to an end. I expected him now to look for other work. But things began to take quite a different turn. The jobs he should have got because of his war record never materialized. The men on whom Rashid had relied were either Americans or Europeans. They had returned to their respective countries. Princes and rajahs were tottering. With the tension between Hindus and Muslims and the power that the new rich wielded in society, there seemed little chance of Rashid finding a job to suit his aristocratic ideas.

He started many ventures in the name of business. Many companies were formed. His ideas were good, he was a persuasive talker and he spoke with a certain style. But given his extravagant lifestyle and complete ignorance of business, nothing worked. There was no count of the businesses he started—import-export, a chain of luxury shops, retailing redundant wartime jeeps and trucks—nor of the amount of money he squandered in the name of business. But not a single idea bore fruit. Rashid had gone as far as to buy a pair of aeroplanes for joyrides. He had poured 30,000 rupees into it. One of them crashed at Juhu airport from a height of 250 feet. I was in the plane. God knows how I survived. The poor pilot suffered a serious back injury and he was in bed for six months. I had a lot of bruises on my head and lost a lot of blood. There was consternation in the film industry, because I had four films on hand, including *Mughal-e-Azam*. Fortunately I was able to return to work within a month and nobody suffered losses. But a huge amount of money went down the drain in these abortive business projects.

I bought a flat in Goolestan on Cuffe Parade for a huge price, only to try and bring some semblence of order into this chaotic life. But I simply wasn't destined to have a quiet family life. There was no Bakul and no Harin in Goolestan. It became a haunt for the Taj Mahal Hotel crowd. When I came home from shoots, thoroughly exhausted, they would all be there, eating and drinking late into the night. Old cronies from Muradabad would land up under the pretext of business, and camp for days at Rashidsaheb's place in Goolestan. Finally I declared outright that I would have nothing to do with any of Rashid's businesses and enterprises. We were drifting apart in our personal relations; this became amply clear to people with inquisitive eyes. Suddenly all 'business' games stopped. Fortunately, Rashid found himself a job around this time as secretary to a wealthy Parsi gentleman. This individual was a proper wheeler-dealer with many business interests. Amongst them was an airline he was planning to start. Rashid scored a hit here. His old Air Force friends came in useful and the job was right up his street, because it involved trips to England, something he longed for.

I went with him to England to meet Harin. It was my first trip out of India and I was very excited. I made time for it by quickly completing the assignments in hand and postponing others by two months. I promised myself that I would travel as much as I could and see everything possible in that time. But the future began to look problematic with the general circumstances of Rashid's job. I made my own plans then to see London. I spent a lot of time seeing plays, films, places of interest, museums, zoos, and parks. As soon as Harin could spare time from his work, I left for Reading to be with him. We were meeting after months. He got very emotional on seeing me. He was very perceptive; he said just one sentence. 'Where is my dimpled Mummy? You are not happy.'

I laughed and said, 'It's the weather. I don't care much for it,' to which he instantly responded with, 'Ah! My *ghati* mother!' And we both laughed. But Harin's expression was worried. He had grown to be very understanding. His earlier rowdiness had vanished. He was quiet, sensitive, mature, almost too old for his years. I began to miss his boyishness. Why had my child grown up so fast? The silly thought kept disturbing me. I longed for my little babykins, my Harya.

Those ten or twelve days with Harin went by much too fast. We travelled to our heart's content. We saw Oxford and Cambridge, the boat races, cricket matches. We loafed around aimlessly in Reading, travelled on Greenline buses to see the picturesque English countryside. We saw Hampton Court Palace, ate in small inns, and gambolled through meadows and fields like little children. Returning home at nine in the late twilight of the English summer, Harin sang new songs for me. He had a lovely, supple voice and an innate sense of rhythm. He loved western music and dance. Much later, after he got married, what he loved doing most when he got back from work was to pick up his son Ravi and dance to a gramophone record with the little fellow in his arms. Ravi too would respond with all his little heart to the beat. I am certain Ravi's later fascination for western music was inherited from his father.

During the fortnight I spent with Harin, I felt completely liberated, as if I had tossed off the burden of twenty-five years of living. Meanwhile many calls started coming to our Green Street flat from the High Commissioner's office for me. The High Commissioner, Mr Krishna Menon, wished to meet me and so did many other Indians. It was his wish to host a small get-together for which the office wanted to know my schedule. The calls were a huge nuisance for Rashid. He started calling us in Reading all the time. He insisted I return to London immediately. I had decided to escape the whole thing by planning to go to Switzerland. Rashid was flummoxed when he heard of my plan. He made Harin promise over the phone to send me to London at all costs. He also gave Harin an assurance that he would personally make all the arrangements required for Banu to go to Europe. Harin assumed an elder's voice and air to bring me around. 'We are an independent nation now,' he said. 'The High Commissioner's office belongs to us. Their invitation is a mark of honour. You are a popular public figure. You must meet the High Commissioner for the honour of our country. You must pay a courtesy call.' He said much more in this vein. I was greatly amused by what he said and also admired him for it. I was particularly struck by the fact that he did not mention Rashid's name even once throughout. I left for London the next day to honour his word.

The High Commissioner's office showered me with attention. Mr Krishna Menon prepared a long list of things I should see and do in London. He insisted that I attend the first post-war international film festival in Venice. He gave me a diplomatic visa to allow me to visit countries like Czechoslovakia to see places that had been devastated by the war, and to travel freely around cities like Prague. He ordered our offices in these places to make all the necessary arrangements for my visits. Rashid tried his best to acquire a similar diplomatic visa for himself. He dropped many direct and indirect hints, but to no avail. He was told that Durgabai was a well-known artist. Only she could be awarded such honours and facilities. Naturally, this upset Rashid, but outwardly he was obliged to gloss over the whole thing.

Mr Krishna Menon had called the world-renowned film director Alexander Korda, asking him to meet me and show me around his studio. In the course of the long conversation I had with him, we spoke at length about my expreiences of working in the Hindi film industry. He was keen to make a film in India but I heard later that he had dropped the idea. Frederic March was shooting for *Christopher Columbus*. Mr Korda arranged for me to attend the shoot. I had a long, informal chat with Mr March. Shooting and production of films in the West was quite similar to the way it was done in India. Though they were technologically far ahead of us and had many more facilities and conveniences, there was very little difference in things like delays in putting up sets and time lost between shots, and the general work atmosphere. The two of us shared a good laugh over it. The studio gave me lunch in the canteen. I met a number of people informally there. It made me happy just to be in the familiar atmosphere of a studio. Rashid had told me that he had made travel arrangements for us to go to Switzerland and had booked us into the Beau Rivage in Lausanne. But I now decided to go to Switzerland only after I had completed my new programme.

14

Europe: The First Encounter

I left London for Paris. Even as a child I had longed to see Europe rather than England. This yearning had much to do with Uncle Gulab's evocative descriptions of it. He could not stand England: 'Dry, ugly, inelegant, hypocritical people', he would always say. 'Drab grey and dreary brown are their favourite colours.' He was angry with the British also for enslaving us. I now began to visualize the stories he had told us about France, Italy, Switzerland and, most importantly, Germany. I could not wait to see Paris, Rome, and that western paradise upon earth, Switzerland. Even the speed of the plane struck me as too slow. I had to laugh at myself. What and how much could I see in two weeks? How was a greedy mind to be satisfied with sights seen superficially?

That is where my chain of thoughts broke. Suddenly a dazzling light became visible some distance away in the dark of the night. 'Paris', the airhostess announced in three languages. That splendid sight was Paris. Even as we watched it from the aeroplane, the distant view drew closer every moment. It was as if we were looking at the abode of the gandharvas. Sparkling multi-coloured lights, looming forms of buildings and light that spread for miles around—the sight dazzled the eyes. The pilot brought the plane down gently but my mind was still floating in space. An official from Thomas Cook was at the airport to receive me. He took care of all the irksome customs formalities on my behalf, put me in a car in fifteen minutes, and told me that arrangements for my stay had been made at the hotel Royal Monceau. Before that, he urged me to drive around and see the night-life of Paris. I drove for almost two hours through the bright lights of the Champs Elysees and its neighbourhood. I even caught a glimpse of the Eiffel Tower.

As I observed the liveliness, brisk movements, neat clothes, careful make-up, and enjoyment of every moment of life that marked the crowds of men and women on the streets; and as I took in the chattering, laughing, joking, and animatedly-gesturing people lounging in the multi-coloured chairs of tiny pavement cafes, I wondered how these people could be so optimistic about life when they had just emerged from a harrowing war.

The Royal Monceau was truly very beautiful. It had every kind of convenience, excellent service, a very quiet, clean environment, and heavy red velvet drapes that muffled all noises from outside. But then all 'A' grade hotels in Europe were like that, as I learnt later.

The hotel had booked me tickets to the ballet in the Opera House, the Folies Bergeres, and a nightclub. They had drawn up a full four-day programme for me. My reservation for Venice had also been made. Along with all these tickets came a bunch of papers consisting of city guides to Paris, maps of Paris, and information about hotels. With them also came a huge bouquet of flowers from the hotel manager. Rashid was not with me on this trip. He was not the least bit interested in this kind of travelling. Now were there any illusions about it. I decided that unless I walked around, I would not be able to register and retain what I was going to see in the next four days. All the programmes were for the evenings. So the next day I left in the morning, armed with a map of Paris, street names noted down, and started walking. The place did not look as attractive by day as it had done at night. The buildings looked old and patchy. The shadow of war still lingered on them. The people on the streets too looked tired. The tense, cheerless faces of women under the mask of make-up gave a clue to the general condition of the country. The highlight of Paris is its shops, dominated by shops for women. Paris is the home of world fashion. The streets were lined on both sides with shop upon shop of goods for women—dresses, hats, parasols, shoes, gloves, stockings, and coats for all seasons—summer, winter, and rain. Every shop was tastefully decorated and every article was designed to catch the eye. There was a continuous stream of shoppers going in and out of the shops. Besides that, the streets were full of people simply looking, since window-shopping has been granted a place in the West as a legitimate pastime and source of entertainment. It is a clever way to feed your eyes on things that your pocket cannot afford. And walking around for miles in a daze is good exercise!

That night I saw a ballet in the Opera House. The stairs of the Opera House are majestic, like a set. The ballet was beautiful. The audience loved my sari and Benaras cloak. They kept coming up to me and saying nice things about them. They would touch and feel them. I was still acknowledging compliments at every step on my way out, till I finally got into my car and returned to the hotel.

The next day some of us from the hotel accompanied a group of Americans who were going in a tourist bus to see Paris and its outskirts. The tour gave us a brief view of country life, an old palace, some picturesque woods, and most of the well known city sights. But these were just quick glimpses. That night I went to an American nightclub with a fellow woman resident of the hotel. It was not a large place. It was filled to bursting. Our seats were close to the dance floor. The performers were dancing in the nude. But their bodies were so well-formed and beautiful that what you chiefly saw and admired was nature's art. They were like living works of art. There was nothing obscene or lewd in their body movements and gestures. They seemed to be floating on air. Their white skin made them look as if they were carved out of alabaster. There was one African woman, Josephine Baker. Her lustrous, black skin gave her the look of a live figure carved in ebony.

After the first two dances, the planks of the floor parted automatically and a tree-like form rose slowly from the depths. The tree was hung with myriad lights. The lights were shaped like fruits. In the middle of this arrangement, two figures, a man and a woman, were entwined around the tree like serpents. The figures were so still as the tree rose that, till they started slithering down, you thought they were inanimate figurines stuck to the tree. The tableau represented the Adam and Eve story. The performance was so sensitively done that the audience sat absolutely enthralled, hardly breathing. But all through the show I was scared because the artists were moving around with all those electric wires trailing around them. I wondered what would happen if there was a short circuit.

It is a mark of great honour and friendship to be invited to attend a play rehearsal. I had never imagined this opportunity would come my way in Paris. I got a call from the hotel management to say arrangements could be made for me to see a rehearsal of the Folies Bergeres in the afternoon if I so wished. Of course I 'so wished' and promptly said yes and thanked them. I could not believe it. I was so impatient that I ordered a car immediately after lunch and went to the theatre. There was only a handful of people at the door of the theatre. I showed my card and went in. The auditorium was almost empty. The stage curtain was up. A few stagehands and music accompanists were on the stage. The usher presented me with a printed programme and showed me to my seat.

As I sat looking around at the theatre, a bell rang and the curtain came down. Five minutes later another bell rang and the curtain went up. The show started exactly at three as printed in the programme. The musical instruments were placed in an aesthetic manner to blend in with the stage design. The artists went on stage from the auditorium, their otherwise bare bodies covered with diaphanous robes. They handed the robes down to the women standing below and took their places. The setting, lighting, and music were exactly as they would be for the real show. Without a single unnecessary word, and no stumbling, the act came to an end, the curtain fell, and a ten-minute discussion followed. The second act started immediately after. All three acts were completed in this fashion. The last act was thrilling. Once the preliminary dances were over, flames seemed to leap from beneath the stage out of a square pit set into the right-hand corner of the stage. The lighting made the sight awe-inspiring and unforgettable. In the finale of the act, young girls came leaping and running like deer out of the opposite wing and jumped into the fire. When the curtain came down, the handful of spectators present sat rooted to their seats. When the curtain went up again and the performers came out from the wings, we congratulated them from the bottom of our hearts by breaking into repeated applause. The Folies Bergeres show was performed that night to a packed auditorium, and looked even more spectacular.

The very mention of Venice brings Shakespeare's poetic plays to mind. Venice doesn't appear to have changed since his times. It is a cluster of small islands linked by canals. All the transactions, business, and traffic between the islands, is taken care of by gondolas plying on the canals. Tall smiling young men row them, singing Italian love songs as they work. On either side of the canals stand old palaces and large squares and piazzas. The piazzas, like the pavements of Paris, are dotted with small open cafes with their colourful chairs and huge canopy-like shades. Apart from tea, coffee, and snacks, wine flows freely here. Some of the palaces display old artefacts for the benefit of tourists, but no information about them is available. Most of the objects are in a state of disrepair. I was staying in a beautiful hotel in the precincts of one such palace. It had an old-time atmosphere. Even the staff wore colourful, traditional livery. For a moment, the whole place gave me a feeling of being on stage.

We heard that the venue for the International Film Festival was on an island a small distance away from ours. An American tourist and I fixed up a gondola and decided to leave a little early, ride along the coast of the canal for a while, and then go to the festival. We were carrying a packed dinner with us. Because of the festival there was quite a bit of traffic heading in that direction. The gondoliers challenged and teased each other through songs, filling the air with merriment. The evening sun lay like a wash of gold on the water. The long shadows of the gondolas played hide-and-seek with the waves, dipping, melting, and splintering. It was a captivating sight.

We were welcomed ashore at the festival venue with great honour. Our invitation cards were taken from us and we were given our seat numbers and bouquets of flowers. The usher led us to our seats. The theatre was choc-a-bloc with famous artists from all over the world. The women's outfits, hairstyles, and jewellery were designed to outdo each other. Yet they reflected the wearers' individuality. The whole gathering looked like a fashion parade. Many of the films were black and white. Colour had not arrived in cinema in a big way yet. It was nearly daybreak by the time the evening's programme ended. When the audience emerged, the sun's rays were already lighting up the eastern sky. Back in the hotel I rushed through my bath and went out once again for breakfast and to see the sights of Venice. As I left Venice, I wished I could have taken the same gondola all the way to meet Bakul and Harin!

Czechoslovakia presented a completely different picture from Venice. Its houses devastated by war, its countless cemeteries, and its vast, deserted tracts of land made a terrifying sight. It was harrowing to see how war had ruined human life. Yet, despite the terrible destruction, the people had already begun working at rebuilding their nation. A factory to manufacture Czechoslovakia's famed glassware had been set up in a dilapidated building. Elsewhere preparations were afoot to erect a studio dedicated to making animation films. Everywhere small businesses were struggling to find a foothold. Prague was equally depressing. The streets were crowded with crippled war victims. Citizens were crushed under the burden of post-war hardships like shortage of food. Only the buildings in Prague remained standing. The huge universities, music academies, and their invaluable libraries had fortunately escaped destruction. Prague was considered the home of western culture.

Before landing at Geneva airport, the pilot of the Swissair plane circled around to give us a glimpse of Switzerland's beauty. We saw green fields, plump cattle grazing in them, tall trees standing erect against a background of snow-capped mountains, small cottages hugging the mountain slopes, and burbling brooks. It was like an idyllic picture created entirely from imagination by a skilled painter. Switzerland must be the only country in the world where nature and industry co-exist in a state of perfect harmony. There was no chimney in sight; no square, grime-blackened buildings to destroy the beauty of nature; no ugly factories belching smoke. Yet plenty of trade and industry, factories and warehouses existed. It struck me as a rich and happy country, a laughter-filled paradise, peaceful, clean, and bursting with vitality. This was not an illusion. I visited a factory and saw how attractively designed it was. Both sides of the approach road were lined with tall trees, flower beds, and vegetable patches. The canteens were neat and bright and the workers were housed in pretty cottages.

The Indian Ambassador to Switzerland, Mr Dhirubhai Desai, was an old friend of the family. In the short time I had in Geneva, he arranged for me to see the main sights. When I left, he urged me to see Interlaken and Jungfrau without fail. I went to Interlaken from Zurich. It is a pretty little town, famous as a tourist resort. I stayed in a cosy little hotel there. It served excellent food. There was a plentiful supply of warm bread rolls, fresh butter, cheese, thick milk, and cocoa. I went the very next morning to Jungfrau. A mini-gauge electric train, like the one in Matheran, carries tourists up to the Jungfrau peak. It passes two tiny stations on the way. You can have coffee, chocolate rolls, and other refreshments here. The surrounding hills are covered in snow. It was bitterly cold. The bright white light of snow on all sides dazzled the eyes. You can hire dog-drawn sledges from Jungfrau station to take you around. But I could not do that because my time was short and the waiting crowds too large. I engaged a guide instead and went around on foot. I returned to the station only when my feet were on the point of turning to ice. I sat by the fireplace, soaking in the radiant white splendour of the surroundings. In Darjeeling, I had seen the Kanchenjunga and other snow-clad Himalayan peaks from a distance. But the excitement actually being on a snowy peak was another thing altogether!

Every town in Switzerland had its own special sights. The Beau Rivage hotel in Lausanne was located on the bank of a river on top of a tall hill. The place is very popular for rowing and swimming. A funicular—an electric elevator—was installed to take people up to the hotel.

There is a melange of three regional cultures in Switzerland— German, Italian, and French. The unique character and language of each culture is retained, but the three co-exist perfectly in practical life. I got to see the Swiss National day celebrations in Zurich. All three cultures were represented by their distinctive costumes and folk dances, in which everybody, men and women, young and old, participated. At night, the flames of the bonfires lit on distant mountains leapt skywards. Intermittent bursts of fireworks and myriad fairy lights strung on trees seemed to rival the stars in the sky. The most impressive sight of all was the Swiss Guard Parade. The tall, strapping guards, dressed in red, black, and white uniforms, wore sprays of white feathers tucked jauntily into their tall hats, which bobbed up and down as they marched in time. The whole show was unique, joyful, and breathtaking.

We travelled from Switzerland to Italy by train and car. I wanted to see the country around Lake Como. This highway was famed for its beauty. The region is an attractive blend of Swiss and Italian culture. Everything in Rome was gigantic, whether it was historic monuments, churches, or the Pope's palace. The Grand Hotel where we stayed was in the heart of the city. Here again I walked around the streets to see the sights. The enormous fountains, the huge and beautiful marble statues that stood in them, the massive, carved marble columns of its buildings, its art galleries, large and small, bore witness to the historic importance of the ancient Roman Empire.

My stay there coincided with Rome's summer opera season. The operas are staged in an enormous open-air theatre. I saw a historic performance. The audience was packed tight under a cloudless sky. The stars twinkled above. The soft, dim lighting on the stage created a magical atmosphere. The stage was enormous. For one scene there were something like a hundred actors present, plus horse and camel riders moving around in the background. Since this was an opera, the dialogue was in the form of songs. The audience had thronged to the theatre to hear the famous singers in the cast. These performances continue for a whole month. It reminded me of Sahitya Sangh Mandir's open-air theatre festival on Marine Drive.

Mr Syed Hussain, our Ambassador in Rome, persuaded us strongly to stop over in Cairo on our way back to Bombay. This gave us the unexpected opportunity to see the world-famous pyramids. Those gigantic structures still stand unchanged in the desert thousands of years after they were built. Their unique form and construction make you marvel at human genius. The inside walls of the pyramids are smooth and cool to the touch like cowdung-plastered floors. Some of the tombs are open. Artefacts from them like jewellery, pots, and weapons are arranged for display. But when one walked about in them, one had a frightening sense of harshness.

From Cairo we travelled through 150 miles of desert to Alexandria. It was fascinating to travel through a desert on a moonlit night. Everywhere nightclubs stood open in luxury hotels. Alexandria is a beautiful seaside town. Miles and miles of sandy desert stretch along its magnificent seabord—an extended Bombay Chowpatty. Again like Marine Drive, the beautiful homes of the rich line the seaside. The aristocratic Pashas of Egypt come here to enjoy the air. They own extensive vineyards and apple and pear orchards. Their fruit exports to Europe are worth crores of rupees. They also own the extremely lucrative cotton trade. I spent four days in the home of Yahya Pasha before returning to Cairo for my flight back to Bombay.

Meanwhile Rashid had lingered on in Europe!

15

Bakul and Harin

Bakul had settled down well in Karachi. People were very kind and affectionate towards him. He didn't have much work. But army life with its strict discipline provided good training for him. He also met educated people in high places. And found friends. In their company, the seeds of a new, liberal view of life were sown in his young mind. He learned from them how to conduct himself in the world and developed the capacity to think about and plan the course of his life in a mature, responsible way.

A Muslim judge's family took him into their home as their son and gave him all the kindly care and guidance that he needed. He won instant affection, being a good-looking, hard-working, and promising young man.

As soon as the war was over, Tata Airlines recruited Bakul for their Karachi office. He was appointed to a good post and soon became the station director. He was given charge of the entire business of the Karachi office during the extremely difficult time of Partition. He was barely twenty-four when he took over, but he handled all his responsibilities with perfect efficiency. He dealt with visitors, flight charts, passenger permissions, and lawful distribution of tickets while running an office at the same time, with all its administrative problems. People spoke of how efficiently he had dealt with all his responsibilities, of how he had worked day and night, and how courteous and helpful he had been to everybody in the midst of all the rioting and chaos. Many people who returned to Mumbai from Karachi sought me out to tell me, with tears in their eyes, how grateful they were to Bakul.

In the course of his work, Bakul often had to travel at all hours of the day or night to the airport, miles away from the city. At such times, one or two members of the Muslim family unfailingly accompanied him there and back, never letting him go alone. I will be eternally grateful to them for this. Bakul's work continued in this fashion for two years in those chaotic conditions. It would be impossible for me to describe the state of my mind during that period.

Soon afterwards, Tata Airlines became Air India International and Bakul was posted to Bombay. In the new company, Bakul's responsibilities expanded immensely and England, Europe, America, Canada, Japan, Hong Kong, and Bangkok became everyday destinations. He was constantly on tour. Bakul had a hand in setting up every single branch of his company abroad. It was his practice, wherever he went, to observe minutely the history, culture, art, and industry of the place, spending all the time he could spare from his work to study them. He brought back with him to his home in Goolestan handcrafted objects, paintings, glassware, and metalwork from all these places. His job gave him the opportunity to meet well known personalities from different walks of life during his foreign trips—journalists, western music scholars, artists, scientists, painters, bankers, businessmen. Many of these acquaintances became lifelong friends. They continue to corrrespond with him to this day. When one of them visited Bombay and made a point of inquiring after and meeting 'Mr Khote of Air India' in Goolestan, I felt deeply gratified. In 1960, Air India made Bakul their commercial manager. The new Boeing 707s were inducted under his supervision.

My Harya had calmed down considerably after he went to England. He would always say to me jocularly, 'Don't you call me Harya now. I'm a grown man.' He had learnt from experience and had worked very hard to complete his three-year course with good grades. The post-war years in England were tough. Even daily necessities like soap and butter were in short supply. Chocolates and cakes were not even to be thought of. Everything was rationed. But Harin endured it all without complaining. Not once did he ask me for anything that would make life easier for him. He never wrote asking me to send him this or that. He lived like everybody else did. He spent thriftily and managed to survive on his stipend. He did not ask me for a single paisa. Of course I looked after his major expenses. He had stated clearly in a letter to me when he reached England, 'I don't want to be a burden on anybody now.' I was very happy to read of his decision and to see the change in his attitude. I thought he was doing the right thing. His letters from England were always happy and full of jokes about the current situation. But you could see how hard his daily life was, despite which he managed to pursue his twin passions, cricket and western music, quite happily.

The Indian company Telco, located in Jamshedpur, was then in the process of selecting young Indians for training with the Mercedes Benz company in Germany. Harin was overjoyed when he was selected. He had a wonderful time in Germany. By the end of his stay, he was speaking German so fluently it could have been his mother tongue. He worked in the factory for three years and got along famously with the Germans. At the end of the three years, he returned to India and immediately joined duty in Jamshedpur. The German officers working in Jamshedpur also adored him. He had many close friends in Jamshedpur's Parsi community as well. His jocular nature made him popular with everybody. Harin had an innate gift for picking up languages fast. Within no time of his arrival in Jamshedpur he was speaking the local Bihari language like a native. This endeared him to the Bihari employees and to the local people as well. He also represented the company in the Ranji Trophy cricket tournament. Harin's jokes and general ribbing used to send us into splits. He had a soft spot for children. When he visited Goolestan, Bakul's children would cling to him. They would not let go off him for a single minute. Harin stayed in Jamshedpur for three years. He decided to return to Bombay after he got married. We used to think Jamshedpur was too out of the way for the family. They came to Bombay around the time Ravi was expected. Harin joined API (Automobile Products of India). The Jamshedpur people were heartbroken. They did everything in their power to persuade him not to leave Telco. The German officers in particular were very insistent. His Indian seniors were also no exception to this. But Harin's argument was that he could not break the word he had given API. As a matter of fact his contract with API was only verbal. But in view of the tragic events that were to follow, it was good that they left Jamshedpur and came to Bombay. That way we got at least four years together. It was many years since Harin had stayed with me. He had an independent place of course. It was a beautiful flat on Nepean Sea Road.

Harin was extremely intelligent, but he had been deeply scarred by the unsettled conditions of our life during his childhood. He was very affectionate, sensitive, and generous. He only had to hear of someone being in trouble, and you could be sure he would make it his personal mission to help the person. He couldn't bear injustice. But he was stubborn too. His temper would explode like a volcano but would cool down just as quickly. He had a boundless love for children, whoever they belonged to. In Khandala he would regularly pack his car with children, buy them eats, and take them for a spin.

One Sunday, Harin and I were returning from an API meeting in Bhandup. The meeting had overshot its time and it was already past one o'clock. We needed to get home as fast as possible. Just then somebody waved us down at a bus-stop. The couple who had stopped us was clearly in serious trouble. The husband was just about managing to keep the woman upright with his support. It was a difficult situation. The woman, in an advanced state of labour, was on the point of passing out. They requested us to take them to the taxi stand. They had to go to a hospital in Bandra. Harin took them in and sped off. As soon as I saw a taxi on the road, I called Harin's attention to it. But he said nothing. The car sped on. At Ghatkopar, he turned right on to the road to Bandra. He took the couple straight to the hospital in Bandra. He saw them upstairs and said to me as he got back into the car, 'Mummy, suppose it had been Vijaya in place of that woman, would you have sent her by cab?' My eyes filled with tears. They still do at the memory.

16

The Theatre Again

The moment I got back from Europe, I was inundated with calls from the studios. Shooting commenced with all my producers claiming full compensation for my three-month holiday. In the midst of the hectic shooting, I found myself dragged into another art form altogether. Theatre. The background was the radio programme *Balidan* (Sacrifice), on Mahatma Gandhi's asassination, that I had participated in and that had been widely discussed. People had liked the programme very much. I too believe it was an innovative play. I was very happy to have had the chance to pay a heartfelt tribute to a great soul. After it was aired, some members of the Indian People's Theatre Association (IPTA) came to see me with a request to accept the presidentship of their organization. Many people from our friends' circle were members, Ramesh Thapar, Mulk Raj Anand, Anil D'Silva amongst them. This group used to do plays in English for IPTA. The Marathi wing was headed by Lalji Pendse and others. IPTA used to present different forms of entertainment including music, dance and theatre.

Members of the IPTA came from diverse linguistic groups. But I had not the faintest notion that the aim of all its programmes was propagation of the political 'red flag' movement. I was under the impression that it was just one of the many theatre groups that had sprung up all around. I explained to them that my only connection with theatre was as a specatator; that I could not work in theatre since my profession was films. Nor did I have the time. It would be wrong to accept the presidentship of a theatre organization. But they were adamant. 'Our organization would benefit immensely from having people like you in it. We will not expect you to act in our productions and if you don't have the time we'll be more than happy if you attended meetings once in a while.' They gave me these and many other assurances. I agreed at that point just to be polite, secretly resolving to tell them later that I would not be able to do it for lack of time.

A few days later I received a post card about their first meeting, with a request that I attend at least this one meeting. I received several telephone calls as well.

I went for the meeting that evening. After the initial speeches of thanks etc were over, the meeting began. The first point on the agenda pertained to a decision, already taken, to produce the play *Andolan* (Agitation). Written by Captain M.K. Shinde, it was to be directed by Keshavrao Date, in aid of the Gandhi Fund. Members were called upon to approve the list of selected artists, in which my name figured. I was furious. I objected to the list and made it quite clear that I would not act in the play. This caused quite a stir. There was much discussion. I informed everybody of the conditions under which I had agreed to accept the presidentship of IPTA and expressed grave displeasure at my name being included in the cast list without my consent being sought. I picked up a piece of paper there and then, to write my letter of resignation from the presidentship. Seeing that I was not to be persuaded, the committee decided to postpone the discussion for the time being and to proceed with the rest of the agenda. I did not participate in anything that followed. As soon as the meeting was over, I got up to leave. The committee tried to bring me around but I told them quite plainly that what had happened was highly irregular and I had no wish to continue my association with IPTA in any capacity.

The following day Keshavrao Date, Captain Shinde, and Lalji Pendse came over to see me. I told them firmly that I was not prepared to discuss the play. Mr Date said, 'I have no idea what happened between you and the others before our meeting. But this play is for the Gandhi Fund. People have been raving about your radio programme on Gandhiji's assassination and we assumed that you would agree to be part of a play meant to raise money for the Gandhi Fund. The entire project was based on this assumption. Please don't turn down our request, we beg of you. You have my personal word that the curtain will not go up on the play till you are fully satisfied that it is ready. We have made a public announcement of your participation. So please do just this one show.' After arguing long and hard, I agreed to do just that one show.

People liked the play. There was no way I could judge it myself. I had no stage experience to guide me in voice projection and audience response. But since four shows were sold out and invitations poured in from Pune and Nasik for more, I might be justified in assuming that the play was good. The press was also full of praise. Ultimately, there were five shows instead of one. I left for Europe immediately after that. As a result of this foray, I was labelled a communist. I am told that the CID tailed me for a long time after that.

I had to face a major problem when I returned from Europe. I had upset several theatre groups by my refusal, earlier, to act in their plays. Amongst them was Dr Bhalerao of the Mumbai Marathi Sahitya Sangh. He was very hurt and upset that the first play I had done was for IPTA and not for the Sangh, despite the close friendship that had existed between his family and the Lauds for so many years. Now he claimed his rights and insisted that I act in Sangh productions. He also pointed out that their approach to theatre was not commercial, but aimed at reviving the art. Dr Bhalerao shrugged off all my difficulties. Finally we settled on my doing two plays— *Bhaubandki* and *Keechakvadh*.

Mr Keshavrao Date took great pains over both plays. But the daily routine of shooting all day, rehearsals all night till 1 o'clock in the morning, and trying to get a grip on the two roles killed me. The unfamiliar language of the plays, long speeches that knocked the breath out of you, big roles filled with innumerable shades of emotion—it was an ordeal by fire for me. Dr Bhalerao and Mr Date allowed me, very generously, to choose my costumes and jewellery, and work out my own expressions and gestures. I was able to act with some sense of freedom because of that. I would not have been able to fit my performance into the highly theatrical mode of acting prevalent in those days.

It is difficult to describe that first show of *Bhaubandki*, held in the open air at Marine Drive. Everything was on a large scale—the enormous space of the open-air theatre, the mammoth audience crammed into it, the crowd of actors in the green room, the gold-embroidered costumes, expensive saris and stoles, stylish *pagdis*, ornaments, and jewellery. Everything was in Peshwa style. My legs trembled like jelly before I went onstage. But once there, I was oblivious to everything. The periodic exclamations of appreciation from the audience and their thunderous applause seemed to go to the actors' heads. Scene after scene took off and soared. Everybody gave excellent performances. Even minor actors were applauded. That day the patron goddess of drama showered all her grace on *Bhaubandki* and the Sangh.

Dr Bhalerao's wife stood by in the wings for the entire length of the play like a bridesmaid waiting on me. She stood there all those hours with an entire paraphernalia of things at hand that milady might want at any given moment—tea, water, fan, handkerchief, mirror, and whatever else—a guard of honour, so to say, for Anandibai. All my costumes, gold-embroidered saris, stoles and jewellery were my own. Mrs Bhalerao stood like a sentry over them, guarding them with eagle eye. Even otherwise, she was ever willing to do any work connected with the Sangh, whatever it was and whomsoever for. She would do the actresses' hair for them, help them drape their nine-yard saris, pick up costumes dropped on the green room floor and fold them up. We actors enjoyed the headiness of success, praise for our performance, people's admiration. But what did that dear mother receive except the satisfaction of serving the Sangh for her husband's sake? That was her share of the rewards. Nobody ever thanked her, or praised her, or expressed their gratitude to her. Only made her toil. She happily gave her own silverware, rich gold-embroidered silk saris and stoles—torn to shreds over time—for stage decor. Later many of her things were even stolen. But the smile on her face never faded. It vanished only once, in the first show of *Keechakvadh*, when the nose-ring which she had given Queen Sudeshna to wear, was misplaced. The poor woman was utterly distraught that one of the cherished symbols of conjugal bliss was lost. When it was finally found, she rushed to me in my make-up room with the nose-ring in her hand, and sobbed her heart out. Only she knew how agonizing the mental strain of those four hours had been.

I acted in many Sangh productions after *Bhaubandki*. It was a whole series—*Kaunteya, Patangachi Dori, Khadashtak, Sanshaykallol, Rajmukut, Shobhecha Pankha*—all these roles were different from each other and I loved them all. I had overcome my stage-fright enough for me to begin to enjoy acting. But *Vaijayanti* was a different experience altogether. I not only played Vaijayanti but directed the play as well. The task came to me because Keshavrao Datey, who had started rehearsing it, found things were not working out. He was not keeping well and the play was a great strain on him. Finally he said to Dr Bhalerao, 'Please get someone else to direct this play.' That was it. Dr Bhalerao roped me in. 'You must direct the play', he insisted. I was flabbergasted. I told him in every way I could, 'I just can't do it. I've never directed a play. I have no experience.' But neither reasoning nor pleading helped. 'Bai, you have to do it, otherwise we'll have to withdraw the play from the festival. The Sangh doesn't have time to start another play.' So saying he dumped the *Vaijayanti* script in my hand and walked off to attend to other work. The playwright, V.V. Shirwadkar, also added his oipinion in support of Dr Bhalerao's decision.

I could not sleep that night. I became agitated just thinking about the foolhardiness of what I had taken on. Finally by daybreak, I had read the play three times over. I made time, during shooting at the studio, to break down each scene into its parts, as I would do for a film. That was the only way I knew to handle a script. I made notes on each of these sub-scenes. In the evening I placed the whole caboodle before Dr Bhalerao. I consulted Mama Pendse. And taking God's name, I started rehearsals for the first act the following day.

The gaping holes in the production created by my ignorance of direction were covered by the performances of the seasoned actors. The flaws in the actors' movements were glossed over by the light design, the background score, and the sound effects, including terrifying screams from the battlefield off-stage. D.G. Godse's set was a huge help. The patron goddess of theatre favoured the Sangh once again. The play went off extremely well. Mama Pendse, Master Dattaram, and others gave superb performances. Dattaram's first scene and his and Pendse's last scene were incomparable. The playwright had written the scenes between Vaijayanti and Ratnakar almost like a silent film. Monosyllabic dialogue and a lot of movement gave the actors' performances a different quality. All the scenes became even more effective because of the lighting and music. *Vaijayanti* looked and sounded very different from the other plays in the festival. The great thing was that the audience accepted it. When the final curtain came down, that vast open space reverberated with thunderous applause.

Every time my acting in a Sangh play came up for discussion, it had to turn into an argument. This tradition continued with the all-India theatre festival in Delhi.

The moment I heard they were planning to put up *Bhaubandki*, I rushed to the Sangh theatre to meet Dr Bhalerao. I told him and other members of the Sangh, 'It will be impossible for me to participate in such a big festival. Theatre is not my profession. I have acted only in the Sangh's productions. I have no desire now to jeopardize my reputation as a film actress.' They tried hard to persuade me, but I remained adamant. We argued for a long time. Finally things came to a head and I burst out at Dr Bhalerao, 'You people do not have even an iota of concern for me. If the play goes off well, that's fine. If it doesn't, all the Marathi theatre people will heap curses on me saying, "Why did this film actress want to go dancing on the stage"! And if we don't win the competition, I'll have to hear taunts about "This forty-plus actress playing the sixteen-year old Anandibai".'

At the end of this long harangue, Dr Bhalerao looked at me for a second and said in a voice many registers lower than mine, 'Do you really believe we are not concerned about you? I can assure you that we think ten times more about you than you could be thinking about yourself. We are fully aware of our responsibility towards you. The Sangh has put an enormous burden on you and you have carried it without complaint. Now I appeal to you, please do this last thing for us. There is immense pressure on us from Delhi. Please do not refuse this request. I will never again say, "do this" to you.'

I could say nothing after this. I simply bent my head and agreed. To add to it, there had been constant calls from Delhi from Mr P.M. Laud and Mr Rajadhyaksha of the Indian Civil Service. 'Durgabai you must act in *Bhaubandki*. We feel we have the right to insist because it's for Marathi theatre.' With what words could I counter such a plea?

Preparations began in high spirits for the Peshwas to march upon Delhi. New costumes, upholstery, drapes and curtains were made, ornaments repaired. Rehearsals began in dead earnest. Everybody seemed to have taken an oath not to allow a single flaw to mar any part of the production. Everybody fell to work as if possessed by a new spirit. It must be said—the Sangh's *Bhaubandki* was of royal birth. On the day of the show, the premises of Sapru Hall were so packed with luxury cars that they overflowed on to both sides of the road outside. The hall was full to bursting with people. Amongst them were Pandit Jawahar Lal Nehru, Babu Rajendra Prasad, Dr S. Radhakrishnan, officers from the highest echelons of government service, the rich and the famous, and all the Marathi speaking people of Delhi. There was no place even for an ant to enter. Mr Laud and Mr Rajadhyaksha played enthusiastic hosts, personally welcoming and looking after all the VIPs.

The curtain went up punctually, and the audience gasped with delight at the sight of the Peshwa style decor of the Shanwarwada set. When Anandibai entered immediately after with her retinue, the audience greeted all the actors with applause. In that applause the Sangh received acknowledgement for everything—the set design, costumes, decor, and ornaments. The actors were pouring all the talent at their command into their performances. The audience broke into spontaneous exclamations at every voice modulation and every line of dialogue that was well enunciated and nicely delivered. Even those who did not understand Marathi sat rooted to their seats till the end of the play.

In the green room, the cast was overjoyed because the play had been a success in every respect. The audience was streaming out in a happy state of mind, singing praises of the play. The Marathi community in Delhi was excitedly discussing it, saying things like, 'We felt as if we were seeing people from the real Peshwa times.' Some were praising Ramshastri and others were cursing Anandibai. The whole atmosphere was brimming over with happiness. But in all this joy, Dr Bhalerao was lying supine after suffering a heart attack. We had no idea of this. That was the beginning of his ill health. After that he was always ill. He rarely came to the Sangh. But when he heard the news over the radio that the Sangh and *Bhaubandki* had won the first prize in the festival, he insisted on coming to the theatre personally to give the cast this piece of news. We could not bear to look at him, he appeared so exhausted. But his happiness, his joy knew no bounds. As it turned out, the doctor had spoken the truth! Never again was he in a condition to say, 'Bai, do this' to me. He was obsessed by just one thing till the end—the Sahitya Sangh.

Dr Bhalerao gave himself up entirely to the drama wing of the Sahitya Sangh. He poured home, family, work, practice, health, everything into the foundation of the Sangh auditorium, now named Dr Bhalerao Sabhagraha, to see it built. I owe some of the most successful, adventurous, and joy-filled years of my life in the performing arts to the doctor. The ten years I spent in his company as an actor of the Sangh remain with me as an enduring and deeply cherished memory.

My life in theatre was marked by an event of great honour. I was nominated president of the forty-third Annual Marathi Theatre Conference held in Delhi in 1961. The Conference celebrated Marathi theatre with great pomp and fanfare. Babu Rajendra Prasad inaugurated it. The presidentship of the Marathi Natya Parishad has a glorious tradition. I was acutely conscious of all the eminent men who had preceded me as its presidents—political leaders, writers, journalists, actors, musicologists, and jurists. I was not worthy of the honour. I have not studied theatre, drama, or anything pertaining to it. It was because of the Sangh's support that I achieved all the success I did on the stage. That was the sum total of my achievement. But some people have greatness thrust upon them. It was something like that with me.

17

The Boys Marry

BAKUL SETS UP HOME

Bakul's job with Air India frequently took him abroad, particularly to Europe. He went most often to Paris, which was an imporant centre of the company.

It was here that he met a Polish-Canadian girl, Krystina Skorzewska, who worked at the Paris office of the International Air Transport Association. Their friendship soon blossomed into love.

One day Bakul broached the subject of his marriage with me. He asked me if I would accept a western girl as my daughter-in-law. I laughed and said, 'The question is what kind of wife you want. Whatever makes you happy will make me happy.' One thing was clear that there was no question of the boys' marriages being 'arranged', given the unconventional lives they had led for the last ten years. Their ideas too were very independent. It was remarkable that Bakul was asking me at all while considering marriage. I had moved far away from traditional customs in my own life. There was no question then of controlling their choice of partners. Many proposals had been coming for them in the traditional way. It used to annoy both of them intensely. They would dismiss the whole idea with, 'Are girls inanimate objects that we should inspect them?'

As it happened, Bakul had found a girl who was just right for him. Tina, as he called her, came from an upper class family. She was about twenty years old. Her photograph showed a person of pedigree, not beautiful, but attractive. She was fair-skinned of course, her tall slim figure was strong-boned but delicate, and her simple elegant dress was testimony to a background of culture and education. 'She looks nice,' I said. Bakul was overjoyed. He flung his arms around my neck and exclaimed, 'Mummy, I'm going to marry this girl!'

I thought for a while and said, 'Bakul, will she like it here? Will our close-knit family ties suit her western ideas? You, Harin, and I share a small world. Even when we are physically far away from each other, we are bound by love. There are other things too—our lifestyles, the filth, poverty, weather, and food here. Will she put up with this happily? Think over all these things first. Don't create unnecessary tensions for yourself. Live in a place where both of you will be happy, whether it is here or in the West. It's your decision. There is no reason for you to think of us. Only keep our ties of love strong.' The question before me was of differences in ways of feeling. It had nothing to do with culture or religion.

Count Skorzewska, Tina's father—we call our daugter-in-law 'Tina'—had been a landlord in Poland. He had to leave his country after the Second World War when the Germans stripped him of all his property. He escaped to England with his wife and two children—Tina and her brother—and as many moveable assets as they could carry. Thereafter, they had to face many hardships before they found their way to Canada, where they settled. The Count died a few years later. Tina's mother single-handedly brought up her children. She educated them. When the children grew up, they made their own lives. Tina went to Europe and started working in Paris. Her bother, Olaf, took an engineering degree and settled in Canada. This was Skorzewska family history.

The next time Bakul went to Paris, I followed the Khote family tradition and sent a sari, blouse, and gem-studded necklace for Tina as an auspicious sign. Before he left we had long discussions. Finally we decided that Tina should spend three months with me, look around, make sure she would like it here and only then take a final decision about marriage. We also decided that Bakul should move out to a friend's place while Tina was with us, to allow her to move around with greater freedom.

Tina arrived soon after. Bakul was going away to Coonoor around that time as the Air India representative at the annual planters' exhibition. Tina and I went with him. We decided to drive down to make the journey there and back more comfortable and also to allow us to take a detour and see Bangalore, Mysore, and Shravanbelgola. The monsoon was on its way out. This trip of ours turned out to be very happy. When we returned to Bombay, we celebrated their engagement. The date fixed for the wedding was 24 November 1953. Tina was far away in an alien place and should have a loved person with her. That is why I invited her mother to visit us for three months. A very close friend of Tina's father's had also decided to come down later to give away the daughter.

The wedding preparations were hectic because there were only two of us—Bakul and I—who were organizing everything. Tina had begun to wear saris now. She had become quite adept at the art of draping them. She looked lovely in them too. She and I scoured the whole of Bombay to select clothes and jewellery that she liked and that would suit her. The Khotes provided all the bride's clothes, including those that her family would normally have given in a conventional marriage. When Tina saw all the things we had bought for her, she said, 'Banu (she calls me Banu), you do so much for me. What can I do for you?' I replied, 'I don't want anything for myself Tina. But if Harin needs anything, please give it to him. I'm sure he'll never be a burden on you and Bakul. After all, everything I have belongs to the two of them, Bakul and Harin. Use it all. But give Harin's share to him with love. Treat his wife as your younger sister. The older brother's wife is in the place of mother for us. Please keep that in mind.' I would recall the conversation repeatedly in later years. In the event it turned out to be no more than something said in the rush of emotion.

Since Tina's family was Roman Catholic, the wedding took place in a church as they had wished, on the morning of 24 November. The wedding lunch was also in western style. A reception had been arranged in the evening at the Baroda Raja's palace on Nepean Sea Road. Bakul had a large circle of friends because of Air India. There was also our huge family, my countless film industry friends, and Sahitya Sangh associates. As in all Laud-Khote celebrations, there was no place in the hall for even an ant to crawl in. All these people had gathered with love in their hearts to witness the first happy rite in my family. The whole sprawling place was decorated with lights. Unfortunately the generator failed at the last minute. We were terribly disappointed. My Sahitya Sangh friends ran around collecting as many Kitson lamps as they could get and saw us through. They saved my face. Unfortunately, my Harya could not be present at his older brother's wedding. It had been impossible for him to leave his work and come from Germany.

Three months after the wedding Tina's mother travelled all over India and then returned to Canada. Bakul and Tina continued to stay at Goolestan. They would normally have looked for an independent place. But the Goolestan flat is very large. They did not see any point in moving somewhere else when this huge space was available. Also it was not so easy then to find a place that you liked and that was convenient.

The first year of married life was all joy and excitement for the young couple. But once the first flush of happiness had subsided, the differences between East and West became apparent to everybody. Because our basic approach to life and ways of thinking were so different, adjustments were difficult to make, however hard one tried. The whole atmosphere began to change. The old family closeness gave way to distances. Tina used all the facilities of the home very cleverly to carve out her own niche. The idea of 'mine' and 'yours' began to assume importance in the home. Bakul's life was taking a new turn and we were going our different ways. The differences between eastern and western ways of thinking grew sharper. Finally I decided—they are happy together aren't they? Then it's best to put a lid on one's feelings. We were living together, but communication between us became more and more formal and functional. My heart harked back to Kandewadi and the warmth and love we had shared there. I had foolishly hoped, with a yearning for the old days, that my home would be happy again, and the family would consider everything—house, objects, people, money—as belonging to everybody. However, one thing is certain—Tina and Bakul are a very happy couple.

There is no doubt that Tina's presence brought a new vitality into Bakul's life. She made sure he met many of her people here and abroad. She supported him sympathetically when he was faced with problems at work. But it is equally true that the prestige of the Khote home gave Tina too a certain status. Be that as it may. I am content that they are a happy couple.

Bakul's married life began and soon three pretty fairies appeared in Goolestan one after the other. With Bakul's beautiful, intelligent daughters, my home became a true Goolestan—a bed of flowers! Their love and affection filled all the pits and hollows of my life. The thorns in Goolestan simply vanished under the soft, fragrant petals of these blossoms.

HARIN'S LIFE

I first saw Vijaya Jaywant at the rehearsal of the Sahitya Sangh production of *Othello*. Dr Bhalerao introduced her to me as a brilliant, promising artist. Around this time, a theatre orgnization headed by Kamaladevi Chattopadhyay had announced scholarships for training and I was on their selection committee. Vijaya was thinking of applying for a scholarship for Marathi theatre. She came to meet me one day to request me to accept her application and assure the committee that I would personally ensure that she acted in two plays as required for eligibility to the scholarships. Actually she was already acting in Ebrahim Alkazi's English plays. But her application was for Marathi theatre and so her experience had to be in Marathi plays. I agreed to her request and began rehearsals in the Sangh. Since I was asked to choose the plays, I chose *Bhaubandki* and *Khadashtak*. In the middle of all that I came down with flu and could not attend rehearsals for a few days. Vijaya came to Goolestan to ask after my health. We decided to read the plays at my house till I felt better. And so she began to come home everyday.

Harin happened to come down from Jamshedpur on leave around that time. He would peep in during our rehearsals to find out if I needed anything. I introduced Vijaya to him as 'Miss Jaywant'. Gradually he began dropping into my room everyday on the pretext of listening to the reading. One evening he asked me inquisitively, 'Mummy who is this girl, Vijaya?' I laughed and said, 'Why? You're asking too many questions. Interested?' Harin said nothing, only laughed. He had made up his mind firmly that he would marry only a Maharashtrian girl. Despite the eight years he had spent out of India, he loved the Maharashtrian way of life best.

The flu laid me really low. The doctor absolutely forbade me from leaving my bed. Naturally, our rehearsals suffered. But Harin's and Vijaya's meetings grew more frequent. Soon Miss Jaywant became Vijaya and next it was, 'Mummy we're going over to Bombelli's for an ice-cream.' And later, 'Mummy I'm taking the car to drop Vijaya home.' The gradual flowering of their friendship did not escape my notice. One day I said to Harin, 'If you're serious about Vijaya, you must ask her family's permission to take her out. That's our custom.'

Harin agreed to do that. He and Vijaya talked things over, and then Vijaya took Harin to meet the Jaywant family. The plans for the wedding were finalized before Harin left for Jamshedpur. The date was fixed for 18 February 1959. In accordance with Harin's wishes, the wedding took place in Goolestan. All the rites and rituals were conducted according to Maharashtrian traditions. A traditional engagement, the pre-wedding dinner, the wedding itself complete with white sheet to separate bride and groom and slokas to bless them, the feeding ceremony, and finally the famous non-vegetarian wedding dinner of Vijaya's CKP community. Harin loved every bit of it. The Jaywants too graciously kept up their end of tradition by giving Vijaya clothes, jewellery, and household goods. They honoured the bridegroom's side with the requisite gifts. On the whole, the event went off very satisfactorily.

After a short honeymoon, Harin and Vijaya returned to Jamshedpur. There, Harin's friends and colleagues at Telco also showered Vijaya with love and affection. They came back two years later at the time of Ravi's birth. Harin took up a well-paid job with Automobile Products of India (API). The company had given him a lovely flat in Bhandup. But Harin had lived away from me for so long already that all three of us felt that he should live somewhere closer. Seeing the general tenor of life in Goolestan, Harin decided to set up a separate home.

After a long search, they found the perfect flat in Nishad, an apartment block on Nepean Sea Road. It was a compact place with plenty of space around, a terrace on top and the Western India Automobile Association premises at the back. The Hanging Garden was practically next door for the children to go for walks and play in. So the boys had enough space. We loved the place so much that we did not haggle for a moment over the rent. We simply put a cheque as deposit in the landlord's hand and moved our stuff in the next day in the midst of a heavy downpour. Harin and Vijaya created a beautiful home for themselves. They had all the furniture made to suit the place. Every corner of the house was decorated tastefully and functionally. We had only two years in Nishad, but they were happy, joyous years.

Harin bought a small cottage on top of a hill in Khandala as a getaway. The place was located in beautiful surroundings, with woods and hills all around and a burbling brook nearby. The family went there every weekend. When I had the time, I would also go for a weekend. Devendra came soon after the elder, Ravi. Their pranks, boisterous games, singing, and dancing filled Harin with so much happiness that even the sky was not high enough to contain it. Khandala was one big romp for them with the local cowherds' and gardeners' children joining in. When the monsoon came, we would wrap the boys in warm shawls and go off for picnics to Igatpuri, Bhandardara, and Nashik. The beauty of these places in the rains was quite different from the beauty of Khandala. The two boys would jump about with happiness to see the drizzling rain, the all-pervading mist pierced by an occasional sunbeam, and the thick carpet of yellow flowers that covered the emerald green grass.

I used to visit Nishad at least three or four times in the week after my shooting got over. Harin and Vijaya would drop me home after dinner. On the way we would stop off at the *paanwala* opposite the Bharatiya Vidya Bhavan, fill our mouths with Banarasi *paans* spiked with scented tobacco, and drive down Marine Drive savouring them and laughing and chattering all the way to Goolestan. On days when I could not make it because of work, I was sure to get calls asking me to account for my absence.

After they returned to Bombay from Jamshedpur, Vijaya started acting in plays and other cultural programmes with renewed zest. While working in the Sangh and other theatre group productions she set up an organization called Rangayan with some enthusiastic and talented young theatre artists. The credit for making modern plays successful on the Marathi stage goes to Vijaya and Rangayan. Rangayan did not merely produce plays; it also introduced its members to allied arts, creating a taste for a vareity of cultural expressions amongst Maharashtrians and Rangayan's members. Rangayan presented music concerts, play readings, play discussions and critical appraisals of old plays on a regular basis, giving its members full returns on their subscription. Vijaya earned valuable experience in acting and direction because of the wide variety of plays Rangayan produced. She was soon firmly established in Marathi theatre. But juggling her life in the home and in the theatre became a hectic job for her. She would also help out occasionally at Durga Khote Productions.

How swiftly happy times pass! Those two years in Nishad flew away like a dream. Every small thing was full of innocent joy, sweetness, and enthusiasm. I have managed to endure many of life's cruellest strokes by drowning myself in those memories. Even the unceasing flow of tears from my eyes has not washed them away.

18

Fact Films

.

Fact Films, a production house for documentary films, was set up in 1952. Rashid came to Bombay years after he had returned from his European tour. He arrived with contracts from TCM (Technical Co-operative Mission), an American government agency in Delhi, which wanted documentary films made. In the intervening years Rashid had been shuttling between Delhi, Muradabad, Kanpur, and Lucknow. In that period he had entered into all kinds of business ventures, each of which ended in failure. And now his sights were set on the production of short films, in which, needless to say, he assumed I would cooperate. But I was determined to keep off. Now that Bakul was in Bombay, there was no danger of Rashid's cronies swarming all over Goolestan. I had enough work on my hands in theatre and cinema and had no time for his business.

After the first two years of marriage, we never did get along. And now that we were practically separated, I decided to rid myself of the whole business once and for all. But Rashid would not accept my decision. His visits to Europe and his expenses kept increasing. Everybody saw how things stood between us. I had told the boys about my decision. Rashid sent several go-betweens to explain the problems away and plead on his behalf but nothing worked with me. Finally, he agreed to go along with me if I first helped him set up Fact Films with the contracts he had brought from Delhi. This is where we left it for the time being.

TCM's work was to aid technical education in India through films. The contracts Rashid had brought from Delhi were very good both in terms of work and business, but only if they were handled properly. Deadlines were a vital clause. That is what Rashid was most nervous about. That is why he had tried everything in his power to involve me in the business. In the course of negotiations, I made sure my rights were legally covered. Our contract stipulated that Rashid would not interfere with my work but allow me a free hand to run the business. The financial responsibility would be entirely his. If he did not pay people in time, work would stop. These were the major conditions I got him to agree to. TCM had given us a large sum as earnest money. With this, we set up a neat office in Stadium Building. My own work in films and other commitments made it impossible for me to shoot all the films we produced. So I hired trustworthy technicians whom I had known from the Prabhat Studio days to do the actual work, but under my supervision. Soon we had completed two TCM films within the given time. TCM was very happy with them. Fact Films was now well established in Delhi. And in Bombay, big advertising agencies began coming to us to produce films for them. As the volume of work increased so did our enthusiasm.

I was now completely absorbed in making short films. I was learning aspects of filmmaking that I had not been exposed to before. We walked around small villages meeting and talking to ordinary people on whose lives our films were based. We made films on fishermen, weavers, carpenters, blacksmiths, and cobblers. We travelled over hills and valleys, to stone quarries and sandy deserts. I scripted films on farming, crops, fruit, and flowers. We also made films on urban problems, education, health and fitness. In short, we were experiencing at first hand what we had always known in theory, that the documentary film touches every aspect of human life. I saw how different this kind of filmmaking was from the studio-based film production that I had known. In the course of this work we enjoyed the rare opportunity of travelling from one end of the country to the other.

Some of our films won high praise. The *Evening News* wrote a laudatory review of *Parityakta—the Deserted Woman*, a film I had directed about women abandoned by their husbands. The other film that won a lot of praise was *Deepmala* which we made for the Life Insurance Company of India. The story used their symbol, the burning flame, as its leitmotif. We used *slokas*, prayers, and hymns about light from different religions and traditional rituals from different parts of India. Pandit Ravi Shankar wrote to congratulate us on the concept, music, and cinematography of the film which he had loved.

We travelled 2000 miles by truck into the deepest jungles of Orissa to shoot the ancient method used there for mining and processing iron ore. The iron column that stands in front of Delhi's Qutb Minar and the victory column in the Konarak temple in Orissa were made of this iron and still stand unrusted after centuries. We included all of this in the film. Making short films has been a fascinating and educative aspect of my work in the film industry.

When it became apparent that the films for advertising agencies were easier to make and more lucrative than documentaries, Fact Films began to incline more towards them. I could not always agree with the views of the agencies and resented their constant interference. Advertising companies insisted on having the last word on everything, from choice of technicians and models to expenditure. I could not tolerate this. Business began to suffer. Meanwhile, the film department of TCM closed down. When I saw how drastically the situation had changed, I said goodbye to Fact Films and to Rashid at one and the same time.

Many important events had occurred in my life apart from Fact Films during the ten years from 1950 on. Bakul and Harin had got married and were happy in their family lives. Little ones played in the house after many years. I travelled practically round the world, to Russia, China, and Germany, as a member of three government delegations. In 1958, I won the Sangeet Natak Akademi award for cinema. *Mughal-e-Azam* was finally released with great fanfare after ten long years under production. The film runs even today. I myself often marvel at those packed years.

19

Durga Khote Productions

After leaving Fact Films, I set up Durga Khote Productions (DKP). In fact I was so busy with my own work in films that I did not want to take on any kind of business responsibility. But some advertising agencies insisted that I should not discontinue my production work. They would support the venture all the way if I established a production house in my name with all my contacts in the film industry. There were very few short film production companies in those days, very few who even understood the nature of the work, while work in the field was increasing rapidly. People were trying to persuade me to complete the films left half finished by Fact Films through my company. Circumstances were strongly in favour of my starting a new business. Bakul and Tina and the staff of Fact Films were also of the opinion that I should start a company in my name.

After long thought Durga Khote Productions was born in Goolestan, with Tina, Vijaya, and I as partners. The financial investment was entirely mine. In place of the money that Fact Films owed me, I was given two invaluable pieces of equipment for filmmaking—a camera and a huge station wagon. The company got these assets without spending a paisa. The station wagon was a twelve-seater Volkswagen that gave thirty-five miles to the gallon. The camera too was a light, sophisticated German model of excellent design. Only one other camera of the kind existed in Bombay but nobody except I had the zoom lens to go with it. Of course only knowledgeable people knew the value of these things. Our cameramen used to guard them with their lives. These assets saved the company thousands of rupees in recurrent expenditure. Not only were they exhorbitant to buy but equally expensive to hire; in my opinion, having them was the best compensation I could have received for all the hard work I had put into Fact Films. These things happened around the time Harin and Vijaya returned to Bombay.

As luck would have it, the company got off to such a good start that soon we had to get ourselves a new place for a bigger office. We had to get a large staff together to handle the work. With the volume of work coming its way, Durga Khote Productions did not have a moment's breathing space.

Both my daughters-in-law were, without question, extremely clever. I had cherished great hopes that the three of us would work on the three main aspects of the business as we had unanimously agreed to do. Tina would liaise with the agencies, Vijaya would assist me in production, and I would administer the company while also doing production work. It was natural that the most complicated responsibility should devolve on me because of my close acquaintance with studios and filmmaking. These were the plans we made; but that was not how they worked out. Tina would spend almost six months of the year out of Bombay for one reason or another. Vijaya's work in theatre meant that she too was not able to give much time to the company. We had long arguments over this. At one point she retorted in anger, 'DKP cannot be my life.' She implied that she did not wish to dedicate herself to DKP. What she said woke me up. I asked myself why I was bothering with the work. I knew how involved Vijaya was with theatre, but up until then it had been regarded as her hobby, whereas DKP was business. Once she had taken on a certain responsibility and accepted the benefits that flowed from it, it was wrong to speak of it in the way she had done. I was very upset. But I did not breathe a word about it to Bakul or Harin to avoid friction in the family. With business and family relations intertwined in DKP, I was in a difficult bind with both my daughters-in-law. I had to bear the entire burden of production because it was through my contacts that work came and got executed. Fortunately all the work was efficiently and successfully completed because I had extremely bright, responsible, and honest people working with me. The Durga Khote Productions business soared. Our profits for the year 1963 were extremely satisfying. But I had lost the mental satisfaction and joy of work.

I felt sorry that Vijaya had not taken this opportunity to find a footing in DKP and to learn the ropes. A number of reputed companies were giving us work and documentary filmmaking was a new thing then. We had been commissioned by the Films Division to make a film on the traditional method of mining and processing iron ore practised by Adivasis in Orissa. The columns near the Qutb Minar in Delhi and at Konarak in Orissa, built from this iron, show no effects of centuries of exposure to rain, wind, and sun. The whole world has been intrigued by the phenomenon. And I had been assigned the job of recording for posterity, this method of making iron.

On 15 November 1963 I set off from Bombay with a crew of six technicians. We had been warned that Orissa would be very cold. We thought we were fully prepared for it. But when we actually faced the cold, we froze. We arrived in Raigadh, Orissa after travelling all night on a slow passenger train from Raichur. From there the Sarvodaya people made arrangements for us to go to Jirapada, Guriwada, and Kharapada. The iron mines were spread out in the hills around these villages. We made this journey of around 350 miles by truck. There was no other mode of transport in that region. In my entire experience of making films, our outdoor shoot in Orissa was the most awe-inspiring. The road wound around hills and was covered with tall trees and dense creepers. The forest was so dense that no sunlight penetrated it even during the day. At high noon, the cold was sharp enough to hit one's bones.

The only inhabitants here were the half-naked Katkaris. Occasionally one would notice a tiny hut here and there. Wild animals were known to roam the jungle. We did not see any other truck on the road throughout that long day's journey. At sundown we reached the Sarvodaya rest house, also located in the jungle. Since there was neither bed nor bed-linen in the place, we spread our bedding on the floor for the night. After the strenuous journey, we did not need more than a moment to fall asleep. But the next morning we were startled to see the clear pug marks of a tiger right outside the doorstep! From the next day, the Sarvodaya people organized gangs of Katkaris to keep wild animals at bay. They also arranged to keep the lights burning all night.

The shoot went off extremely well. The local people were desperately poor but very warm and friendly. We mixed with them, danced and sang with them, and got them to work for a month and a half on the film. The film earned much praise and fame.

20

1964

I finished the Orissa shoot in December 1963 and was returning home after being away for a month and a half. Bakul, Tina, and the girls were to go out of Bombay for Christmas. So, instead of going to Goolestan, I got off the train at Kalyan and caught another train to Khandala. Everybody was thrilled to see me come like this, unannounced. Harin and the boys gave me a noisy welcome. I cannot describe how moved I was by their loving welcome. Harin's first question as soon as I had had a bath and tea was, 'Mummy, will you make fish curry? We'll go get some fish and prawns from Lonavala.' And we did just that. Harin loaded all of us into the car and drove us down to Lonavala. On the way back we stopped off at Maganlal Chikkiwala and picked up a whole basketful of eats—peanut crunch, hot *jalebis*, fresh *gulab jamuns*, and piping hot onion fritters which Vijaya and I loved.

Harin used to love my cooking, my fish preparations in particular. Lunch was very late that day but tremendous fun. At night, after the boys had gone to bed, we sat out in the garden chewing *paan* and chatting away. I told them stories about my Orissa shoot. We talked about all the good and bad things that had happened during the past year. We talked of plans for the coming year, about the children's pranks, Harin's career, things they wanted to buy for Nishad . . . we talked of everything under the sun. It was only when all the paans were eaten and Harin's cigarette case was empty that we finally called it a day. We hardly knew how the next four days flew by. The memories of that time are buried deep in my heart. That was the last time I went to Khandala.

January 1964 was a very busy month. Apart from my regular work—shoots and DKP—Vijaya's eldest niece was getting married and her house was in a whirl. The Marathi Natya Parishad was holding a festival of plays to mark Bal Gandharva's seventy-fifth birth anniversary in which Vijaya and I were naturally involved to some extent. Yet, in all that frenetic activity, Harin did not forget my birthday. Early on the morning of *Sankrant*, 14 January, a beautiful bouquet arrived at Goolestan from Nishad with a loving note from Harin and Vijaya on which the boys too had scribbled their names. That night Harin and Vijaya took me out to a Chinese restaurant for dinner. They had already ordered my favourite dishes in advance. Dinner ended with a delicious Banarasi paan. As I got out of the car at Goolestan, Harin said, 'Hey Mom, we're booking you right now for the 1965 Sankrant. So keep yourself free.' We laughed a lot over that. But the 1965 Sankrant??

I called Harin on 7 February to remind him that we had planned to see a plot of land in Panvel on the 8th. He and Vijaya were going to see a play on the night of the 8th with Pu. La. Deshpande and Sunita. Even then Harin assured me repeatedly that he would take me to Panvel. 'I'll come and pick you up first thing in the morning,' he said laughing. I heard him whistling as he called off. I had been very busy shooting the whole of that week and was feeling so tired that I gave dinner a miss and went straight to bed. I do not know when I dropped off to sleep, but sometime in the night I became aware of a bell ringing in the distance. I got up with a start and put on the light. My phone was ringing and it was two o'clock in the morning. Harin's servant was at the other end telling me in a frightened voice, 'Sahib is very ill. Please come as soon as you can.' I quickly woke Bakul and we got ready to leave. Just then the phone rang again. It was Harin's neighbours asking me to hurry. Bakul and I rushed to the car and drove to Nishad. Questions hammered away inside my head—what could have happened? Could it be food poisoning?

All the lights were burning in Nishad. The neighbours had gathered in front of Harin's flat. The doctor was there. When we went in, we saw Harin lying on the floor groaning. Nobody would tell me what was wrong, but the doctor took Bakul aside and told him it was a massive heart attack. He advised us to immediately call an ambulance and take him to a hospital. A doctor we knew well lived close by. Bakul called him and then called for the ambulance.

We took Harin to Breach Candy Hospital. Though I was very much in my senses I could still not comprehend what was happening. I pulled Vijaya close to me and stood rooted to the spot. The two of us rode in the ambulance with Harin while Bakul went ahead by car to the hospital. Harin had been so happy when he talked to me that evening. What could have happened all of a sudden?

Harin was put in a special room. The cardiologist was called. Nurses and others ran back and forth while Vijaya and I stood outside the door. At one point the door opened and I took a step forward thinking Harin had finally regained consciousness. But when I entered the room I saw Bakul, head bent low, holding Harin's hands tight in his own and sobbing. My heart just broke. That was it. Everything was over. My Harya had gone away whistling, at the age of thirty-six, leaving us bereft. The doctor held my hands tight and said, 'I did my best. Such a young man.'

I brought Vijaya home to Goolestan. What was to be done now? The exact question that I had faced twenty-five years ago was back before me. Harin's father had died leaving two children behind. And now the son was gone, also leaving two children behind. Both had died at the same age and of the same condition. What was I to do now with my cursed life? I no longer had the strength to face it.

The days passed one after another. I had no desire to do anything. I wanted to give up work, DKP, everything, and run away somewhere. But what was I to do with Vijaya, Ravi, Devendra? The office staff came over. 'Bai, we are like your children. Where will we go if you close DKP,' they asked. Finally Bakul took the decision Papa had taken thirty-seven years ago. He called the DKP staff over and told them, 'Bai and Vijayabai will come to the office from tomorrow. Put them to work. Tinabai will take the unit to Kanpur for the shoot.'

My dazed mind could think of only two things—Vijaya and her children. Bakul told me firmly, 'Vijaya must work. That's the only way. We will look after the boys. She must do what you did.'

I went to work like a blinkered animal tied to the oil-mill. I picked up the whole burden of DKP in addition to my own work and stepped out. But I was not aware of the pitfalls that lay on the path ahead. We began hunting for a separate flat for Vijaya and her children. After a long search we decided to buy one in Ashoka

Apartments. It was a time when everything was going up in flames—
at home, outside, in the office, in the theatre world. The flames
continued to scorch me for the next two years. I did all I could to
bring the situation under control, but failed. I tried with all my heart
and soul to protect Vijaya and the boys. I struggled hard to make
sure that these three souls did not suffer the agonies that I had
suffered; that they would always have the shelter of my love. I wanted
them to live in the same style they had grown accustomed to when
Harin was alive. I spared neither effort nor money to ensure that
they did not fall short of anything. They had a car, a flat in Bombay,
and the house in Khandala. The flat in Nishad belonged to the
company. After a long search we found a suitable flat in Ashoka
Apartments on Nepean Sea Road. We bought it in Vijaya's and
my names.

But soon I began to hear strange stories. Vijaya appeared to find
my closeness inconvenient. Expenses on the car, petrol, visits to
Khandala were increasing. A smouldering tension was building up.
The boys were affected by it. Their health began to suffer. Their
faces looked pinched. Everywhere I went, people were talking about
just one thing—Vijaya and her theatre tours.

I tried to explain a few things to Vijaya. But it made no difference.
The problems festered. Finally I told her frankly that if she wanted
to continue in the direction she had chosen, she should leave Harin's
boys in my care and then do what she pleased without expecting
anything further from me. After that she stopped coming to DKP.
We too stopped going to her place. The boys were also separated
from us. That hurt me very deeply. I was consumed with anxiety for
my grandsons.

Then one day we heard an unexpected bit of news. Tina brought
home the news that Vijaya was going to marry Farrokh Mehta. I was
aghast. Who was this unknown person? What would happen to the
boys now? I could not get the question out of my mind. I could not
understand where this Farrokh Mehta had sprung up from in the
midst of the upheaval in our lives. I went over to see some friends of
Vijaya's with whom I was acquainted, to find out. I suggested that at
least the Ashoka Apartments flat should be put in a trust for the
boys. But nobody was willing to listen to me or do anything about it.
They all shrugged off responsibility. Not just that, my suggestion led

to more battles. I could do nothing after that except feel helpless and keep mum.

Ultimately DKP split up. Vijaya married Farrokh Mehta in December 1965. Vijaya Khote became Vijaya Mehta. Tina and I were now the only partners in DKP. It was not even eighteen months since Harin had died, and our lives had turned topsy-turvy.

21
Tours Abroad

It was July 1951. The post had come in and I was utterly surprised to find a letter addressed to me from the External Affairs Ministry of the Government of India. Assuming it must be a notice about some meeting or the other regarding the film industry, I pushed it aside. I realized then that the envelope was pretty thick. So I opened it, and couldn't believe my eyes. Attached to a long letter from the Ministry was another from the Russian Embassy inviting me to Russia as a member of an Indian film delegation. Amongst the ten invitees were some people from Bengal, two from the South, and two from Maharashtra. My first reaction was 'Russia? Gosh, no thanks. Who knows, I might never come back.' One had heard such stories about Russia. But Bakul was sitting nearby and he scolded me, 'Don't be silly. It's a wonderful chance. Write back this moment, saying you're going.'

The next minute he had pulled out a notepaper pad and drafted the letter for me. That was only the beginning. After that he became a regular nag. 'Show me what you're taking with you. Where's your coat? And gloves? You must wear shoes. You're not used to them now....' It was with such loving attention that Bakul helped me pack. He got my visas done through Air-India, one for Russia and one for Britain so I could meet Harin. Our itinerary itself was charted by the Russian Embassy through an unusual route.

The delegation assembled in Delhi. From there we went to Peshawar by train. Our Russian visit started the following day. After an early bath and breakfast, we set off in three huge station wagons, preceded and followed by two touring cars. The one behind carried Embassy officials and the one in front carried our luggage and an armed Russian escort. Our convoy set off in great style. All the vehicles belonged to the Embassy. Throughout our journey from Peshawar to Kabul, where the road was flanked on either side by mountains that touched the sky and valleys that plunged deep, we did not see a single living thing, neither bird, leaf, nor twig. Our minds grew numb as we travelled through that desolate wasteland where the shadow of one cliff fell on the face of another and made the road in between freezing cold. The landscape seemed never-ending and harsh.

In this mountainous terrain we noticed no more than four or five small hamlets. At the entry to each, tall, rugged Afghan soldiers armed with guns stood guard. They would order our convoy to halt in rough, rasping voices. Once we had clambered out of our vehicles, they treated us with utmost courtesy, leading us to the nearby sentry post where we could relax. All our stuff, including handbags and passports, would then be offloaded and brought to the post. A particularly strict watch was kept on our cameras. When they had inventoried all our stuff and handed the list to us, they became the warmest of hosts. They plied us with succulent meat dishes and grapes. The vegetarians were offered vegetables, peaches, apples, and dry fruit. Everything around these hamlets was green and verdant. From the sentry post, one had a clear view of the land for miles around. But not for a second through all this time did the guards relax their vigilance over us.

We finally arrived in Kabul the following morning. The Indian Embassy there took us around the city. We visited factories where wonderful cotton rugs were made and also breathtakingly beautiful and extremely expensive carpets. A Russian plane was waiting at Kabul to fly us to Tashkent. It was a crude-looking aircraft unequipped even with seat belts. It must have been built out of scrap left over from the war. We took off at noon and reached Tashkent without a halt at five in the evening. On the morning after that we left for Moscow.

Before I left India I had been collecting information about Russia from friends and acquaintances who had been there. The one common thing I heard from them all was that we would be welcomed with a lot of respect and curiosity. Even then we had not been prepared for the sea of people waiting patiently at Moscow airport to welcome us. I had expected a few handshakes, bouquets, and an exchange of brief formal speeches. I decided the crowd out there was waiting to receive some celebrity expected later. But it was actually for us. In that crowd stood established film artistes, workers and representatives of studios, directors, cameramen, producers, and the Minister of Film Production with his entire retinue. The flowers that welcomed us would have filled a whole garden. This kind of welcome was repeated at every railway station and airport and even in the smallest village that we visited.

Receptions, dinners, and special cultural programmes had been organized for us everywhere we went. It was as if everyone was competing to outdo the other. Everything was on the government level. I wondered whether the Russians were under the mistaken impression that our delegation enjoyed a similar status in the eyes of our own government! But it was not so. Inquiries revealed that the Russian government had complete information on us. They knew precisely what our status was in our private, social, and professional lives. It was just that in Russia artists are held in the highest esteem. The members of departments of arts in every ministry are selected from the relevant fields of art. Art and artists are looked upon as national treasures. That is why they are honoured. The government is responsible for ensuring that this national wealth does not go waste, but is preserved.

In our country, if an artist cannot contribute to the business side of art, he no longer exists as an artist, however great he may be. Only the artist who has accumulated wealth can make use of his talent in the business of art. But in Russia, the older an artist is in years and knowledge, the more he is respected nationally. Great value is attached to the years of dedication he has put into his art practice. His experience is considered useful for research and his guidance for nurturing a new generation of artists. Artists are given great importance in government departments, and are appointed to key posts. We saw this clearly in the ballet school where the faculty and students together covered a span of over seventy years from the oldest professor of eighty to the youngest student, five years old.

In Moscow, we were housed in a luxury hotel. Two interpreters were appointed to be with us constantly and look after our needs. So the problem of language did not hamper us. The day's programmes were always fixed beforehand. We would be handed the schedule for the day with our first cup of tea. Our cars were always ready in all respects, round the clock.

Since we were from the film industry, the first events lined up for us were meetings with our counterparts amongst artists and technicians, visits to studios, and film screenings. That took care of the first five or six days of our visit. Russian films were very much like Indian films, with long, tortuous plots, a heavy dose of propaganda, and were visually loud and crude. We did not feel Russia was ahead of us at least in this field. But their children's films were extremely entertaining and educative. We saw many in the film department, but I soon lost interest in seeing the same kind of films day in and day out. What I was waiting eagerly to see was the Bolshoi Ballet. I had seen Anna Pavlova dance in the *Dying Swan* in Bombay and that memory was still as vivid as ever after all these years. I was also fascinated by Bolshoi theatre. I could not resist asking our interpreter about Pavlova. His face grew suddenly serious when he heard me mention her name. Let us not talk about her, he said. I was baffled. I gathered later that artists who had performed during the Czarist years were persona non grata in Russia. But the following day we saw the ballet *Red Rose* at the Bolshoi.

With what words can I describe the Bolshoi theatre. It was a palace. The lights in the enormous chandeliers that hung from the high ceiling were reflected in the mirrors that lined the walls, sparkling like a thousand stars. The paintings on the dazzling white walls showed scenes and poses from ballets. They were so lifelike that you could mistake them for live dancers. The seats were upholstered in velvet, and the vast stage and velvet curtain with golden tassels all bore witness to the splendour of Czarist Russia. The ballet was beautiful but its grace and beauty were marred by political propaganda. The theme was the Russia-China friendship of those times.

We saw an even more beautiful ballet in Leningrad that included a scene showing a flood. The flood was so effectively contrived that the audience experienced a strong illusion of the water actually rushing towards them. I had not seen such a sophisticated stage set or lighting design even in Europe. We got to see some marvellous operas in Leningrad. The singers, both male and female, had such rich, sweet, and resonant voices that they seemed to shake the whole theatre to its foundations. But the actors struck me as rather unattractive. After we had seen all the world-famous sights in Moscow and Leningrad—the Red Square, Lenin's tomb, the Kremlin, and numerous museums—we turned southwards to the Balkan State across the Black Sea. The journey was by air but I found it terrifying. I longed for that black sea, spread over miles, to end. A terrifying sea of pitch black water with neither ripple nor fish to show signs of life! It was like an unending deep black tunnel. The sky above. The water below. Both utterly still.

The natural beauty, climate, and food habits of the southern part of Russia were exactly like ours. We threw away our Moscow gear—woolies, coats, and gloves. We were actually feeling hot. How long it had been since we had seen banana trees, coconut and date palms. We began to have fruits like figs, dates, and bananas. As for the food, it was exactly like the kind one got in Delhi and Lucknow, with rotis and naans and kababs. The local dances were like our own Manipuri style and the music was like qawwalis and ghazals. The people were good-looking but dark-skinned like us. We felt we were near home. The small seaside town of Sochi was like Bombay's Vesave or Juhu. I returned to Moscow from here because I wanted to spend some time with Harin before meeting my shooting dates in Bombay.

It would be presumptuous indeed to say that I had seen Russia in this brief period of five weeks. It was impossible to see, understand, and know a nation that its citizens had worked hard for thirty years to build in so short a time. But we did see a lot. We saw places where none of our people had ever been. We saw fascinating sights that it would be impossible to forget. The Russians live artistically. Every city and small town had its own theatres. But, more importantly, all of them were packed with people everyday, whether it was an opera, ballet, play, or film. Art was an inseparable part of their daily lives.

The general interest in the arts comes from the numerous institutions there that teach art. The Russian schools of music, dance, theatre, and film are like universities where you start as little children. Other subjects are also taught there along with the arts. Thus the artist is never just an artist. He is an educated citizen too. The way nurseries and playschools were run in Russia gave us an idea of how the nation looked upon the future generation. All the children we saw looked healthy, happy, smart, and had alert, inquiring minds. As far as art was concerned, one felt almost envious of the way it was nurtured.

Russian women were generally tall, large, and rather plain looking. But they worked shoulder to shoulder with men in every sphere of life. We met any number of women who were pilots, engineers, hydraulic engineers, scientists, doctors, and bus and railway-engine drivers. Several of them had won government awards for their work. We noticed a strong commitment to the cause of national welfare amongst them. The spark that had been lit in them during the years of labour, hardship, and self-sacrifice when they were building their nation, was still alive. Women had been made responsible by law for several aspects of child-rearing such as education and health. They controlled sectors like health and education, aimed at the development of the future generation. Women also headed children's institutions and had direct access to the highest ranks in government. These were aspects of Russia that I found extremely admirable and inspiring.

CHINA

My casual encounter with IPTA through their play *Andolan* must have been the reason why I was marked as a communist. After Russia, I was invited to China in 1954. An eight-member delegation of the Democratic Women's Federation was to be sent to Peking. It was largely political in constitution. Some of the members were Members of Parliament while some were relatives of Indian Administrative Service officers. Ms Ammu Swaminathan, Member of Parliament, was the leader of our delegation. The other members were the Queen Mother of Tehri Garhwal, a member of the Rajya Sabha, Renuka Chakravarti and Anutai Gyanchand of the Labour Party, Mrs Rajan Nehru, wife of the Secretary of the Ministry of External Affairs, and the famous Urdu writer, Ismat Chugtai, a known communist. I was the only person from cinema. I felt a little out of place initially in this political group. Anutai was the only person who belonged to our circle. But everybody treated me as one of them.

As usual we made a respectful bow to Delhi first before proceeding to Calcutta and from there to Hong Kong. Every journey is marked by its own unique experience. The pilot of our Air India flight invited me into the cockpit to observe our approach to Hong Kong. I was stunned to see how skilfully he piloted the craft through the narrow rift between two cliffs that rose on either side of the sea. This narrow creek guards the entrance to Hong Kong. As you cross the creek, the beautiful sight of Hong Kong, spread out on two levels along the seaboard, rises to meet the eye. Soon after that we landed at Hong Kong airport. I thanked the crew and returned to join the delegation and collect my baggage.

Arrangements had been made for us to stay at the Miramar Hotel. That massive five-storey building looked as if it had been lifted straight out of Europe and transplanted here in the East. The style was wholly European. Only the staff was Chinese. As soon as we had eaten our lunch, we stepped out to see the city. Because Hong Kong is a 'free' port, the shops were stuffed with merchandise from all over the world. Tourists were everywhere, in the thousands, busy shopping. Goods like cameras, textiles, off-the-peg clothes, household products, watches, shoes, perfumes, soaps literally overflowed from the shops. It was a trader's paradise. The shoppers came from every continent, women outnumbering men. Though the population was mainly Chinese, there was a fascinating mix of East and West everywhere. Hong Kong suffered from one major problem—shortage of water. Even bath water was rationed. But preparations were already underway to build a series of canals.

From Hong Kong we went to Canton. This was like suddenly entering another hemisphere altogether. The people were quite different from any others I had seen, in build and looks. They were short and stout, with yellowish skins, broad, flat faces, and narrow almond-shaped eyes that slanted upwards towards the temples. They wore unisex clothes—blue-black trousers topped by long sleeved shirts with Mandarin collars made from the same uniform material. The women wore cloth shoes on their small feet and most of them carried infants strapped to their backs.

At first sight the place did not strike us as prosperous. Canton had an old-style atmosphere, a lot like Calcutta's Barabazaar. The streets spilled over with crowds, rickshaw bells clanged continuously, small eateries lined both sides of the road, and colourful paper lanterns hung everywhere. Our cars somehow managed to carve a way through this chaos to where we were going to stay. The hotel was large but its doors were like those of a pilgrim dormitory, made of heavy wood and carved. The rooms themselves were clean and well furnished. Photographs of Mao and Ching Len hung on all the walls. No interpreter seemed to have been appointed for us yet. Before we began to wonder what next, we were served fragrant black tea in delicate cups and informed by an elderly woman that lunch was served. She was probably the chief Amah (chief of staff). She had a smattering of English.

We trooped into a huge hall for dinner. The food brought back memories of Calcutta's China Town. The large table was made of marble. The chairs were made of carved black wood but their seats and backs were of marble. Though we knew how the Chinese ate, it was still an amusing sight to see over fifty people in one hall eating rapidly with their chopsticks. It was quite a feat to pick and carry pieces of meat and vegetables to the mouth with those slender sticks without dropping or wasting a single grain.

We left very early next morning for Peking. Not too many flights operated from Canton in those days. Flights to Peking were organized only for very special occasions. From Peking there were regular flights to Nanking, Shanghai, Penang, and even Rangoon and Bangkok. It was a great relief to see officials from the Indian Embassy at Peking airport. After we left Hong Kong, our halting conversations in broken English had not resulted in much mutual understanding. Beginning a sentence in broken English and completing it with mime and smiles was the only means of communication we had. At the airport, our co-passengers stared at us all the time with frank curiosity. Their expressions suggested that they had practically no links with the outside world.

Travelling around Peking, we could see clear evidence of how complete Russia's influence over China was. The Russian and Chinese flags flew together in many places and photographs of Stalin were displayed everywhere. Military discipline governed life. People wore uniform-like clothes and spoke no more than required. Flocks of white pigeons were kept for propaganda. Even the slight openness we had noticed amongst the ordinary people in Russia was missing in Peking.

As expected, we were put up in a large, brand new hotel. Each of us was now given two women interpreters. Though they spoke English well, they would answer our questions or give us the day's itinerary only after they had consulted each other in their own language. Since China was celebrating its republic day anniversary during our visit, we had occasion to attend many public meetings and functions. The meetings followed the Russian format. They began with the hoisting of the Russian and Chinese flags. Military parades, peasant processions, and children's programmes followed. Mao and Ching Len were both present at these meetings. We had the opportunity to meet them though our exchange was strictly formal and conducted through interpreters. We got the impression from their faces and those of other top leaders that they knew other languages. Their sharp, stern eyes were fixed on every object, every gesture that a speaker made, and every shade that passed over her or his face. Their own faces, however, remained inscrutable, their eyes almost closed. One thing we noted was that all the interpreters were in their early twenties and talked to us in the presence of their leaders with bold self-confidence. The new generation was completely at ease with their leaders and there was an equal give and take between them and the elders. In India we deify our elders. This represses our youth and stunts their growth.

In Peking, we attended a few meetings with local women's groups. They would make speeches in Chinese, which would then be translated into English. But they all said the same things. They spoke glowingly of China's policies, of the Russia-China friendship, of agricultural education, and of the progress made in small-scale industries. Not only were the contents of the speeches the same, even the words they used were similar. The subjects closest to their hearts were floods and famine, both terrible calamities.

Many new buildings had sprung up around our hotel. They housed several museums, huge 'peace' halls, trade exhibition centres, and other such organizations for propaganda. The Soviet Union was given pride of place here. There was only one film studio that was working, equipped with basic requirements. Since I was a film artist, the studio invited me to attend a shoot. The story was centred round the hot topic of the day—Tibet.

Old Peking is just as picturesque and full of historical interest as described in Pearl Buck's novels. The roads surrounding the fort are lined on both sides by beautiful gardens. The houses are like pagodas. Their design too is unique. There is a central hall, surrounded by a number of rooms. The main part of the house is connected to the outlying rooms by beautifully wrought low, colourful bamboo banisters. The dainty paths leading to the rooms are lined with flowering bushes. It is here that we see the splendour and aesthetic sense that China once possessed.

After Peking we visited small villages by train to see China's rural industrial centres. Many things were on sale here—beautiful hand woven fabrics, intricately crafted objects, and brocades woven with flower, creeper, and peacock motifs. None of us could resist the temptation of buying them. We bought practically all the stuff in the centres. Mechanical manufacture appeared to have begun recently, but the people were full of enthusiasm. Here again the young were in the vanguard.

The next large city after Peking is Shanghai. Till the second World War, Shanghai was a famous trade centre. The tall buildings here were equal to any in the cities of the West. But they seemed to be in a state of disrepair now. Despite this, the city still ranks among the famous markets of the world.

The best sights to see in China are the historically famous Great Wall, Buddha temples, and the temples and monasteries of the lamas—the finest achievement of human labour and abodes of peace. Legends about the building of the Wall of China are legion. One of them, a tender story, is still recounted by the people. This is how it goes. When the Wall was being built, there was a shortage of ropes to lift stones. Work was interrupted. To prevent long delays, the women filled the lacuna by cutting off their hair and plaiting it into strong thick ropes. The story sounds perfectly credible when you see the thick, long, black braids of Chinese women even today.

The Buddha temples as well as the monasteries of the lamas have been carved out of gigantic rocks. There is some similarity between this sculpture and our Ajanta-Ellora caves. The temples are decorated with delicately carved figures, short and a little squat. They bear some physical resemblance to Tibetans. The atmosphere is solemn and tranquil in both places. Though not too many lamas live in the monasteries, they recite the scriptures and chant through the day and night.

22

The UNESCO's World Women's Conference

Bakul's daughters Anjali and Rekha are settled in Canada and France. They come to India every two years during their college vacations, but since their vacations don't coincide, the girls are rarely home together. Both have graduated now. Anjali works in the film cell of the sociology department of the Vincennes University where she studied, and Rekha has a degree in hotel management and has an important designation.

I made a trip to Europe quite unexpectedly in 1975. UNESCO had invited me to attend its International Women's Day meeting as a representative of Indian cinema. I stopped off in Paris on my way to Italy and spent eight days with Anjali. She was overjoyed. She had assumed I would stay in a hotel and had even booked a room for me in one. But I told her quite categorically, 'I have made this stopover only to see you and be with you. I'm not going to stay in some fancy hotel.' Anjali gave me a big hug then and said, 'Granny, won't you feel cramped?' I gave her a litle tap on the cheek and said, 'Cramped with you? What a little idiot you are.' When she heard me say this in Marathi she burst into peals of laughter. She said, 'This is just like being back in Goolestan.' We spoke Marathi with each other throughout those eight days. Anjali's Marathi is not too bad. She fumbles sometimes. But she speaks very sweetly with a liberal sprinkling of French words.

Paris had changed a lot. Also, thirty years after my first visit there, I was seeing the city through the eyes of the young. Anjali and her young friends took me to places I had not seen in my previous very hurried visit. Art galleries, museums, exhibitions, conservatories, small theatre companies—Anjali's friends brimmed over with excitement when they spoke of these. We had a language problem, of course, but Anjali helped us over that hurdle. And the bookish French I had learnt at college had not rusted entirely.

Anjali's friends were quite impressed that I was going to attend the UNESCO meeting. The Hindi film *Bidai* in which I had acted, was running in Paris. I had even won a Filmfare award for my performance. Anjali's friends had got hold of the film posters carrying my photograph. They gave me a genuine French dinner in a small riverside cafe. It was simple food but they showed me so much affection that I did not need anything more. Another day I cooked Indian food for them at Anjali's place. They loved it. The puris disappeared as soon as they came out of the fryer. As for the bowls in which the mango pulp had been served, we did not even need to wash them. Anjali and I were in splits. Christian was the one who particularly loved the food. I saw signs of the Khote family soon acquiring a French son-in-law. After Anjali and he were married he told me, 'I knew I had to marry Anjali the day I had that dinner you cooked!'

The conference in Italy was attended by film artists from thirty countries. We travelled from Zurich to Aosta Valley by luxury bus. It was a beautiful place and the 200 mile journey to it was a happy experience, surrounded as we were by hills, green fields, and clear springs, with snow-capped mountains behind us and a fine smooth road beneath. The journey lasted five hours but we hardly noticed the time. I have travelled by road on many occasions, but each time the experience has been different. Nature has many faces and each of them is unique.

Our buses came to a halt in front of a magnificent building, the Grand Hotel Billia St Vincent—Aosta, Italy. As we gathered our things together, we craned our necks from the bus windows for a view of our surroundings. After we registered our names at the reception, the bellboy escorted us in grand style to our rooms. My room was on the third floor. I had to cross two large halls to reach the lift. As we went up I noticed that the white marble staircase was as sweeping and splendid as the one in Taj Mahal Hotel. Thick red carpets covered every inch of the floor. The view from my window was so beautiful that all I wanted to do was stand and stare. There was a lovely garden, swimming pool, and tennis court outside with lounging chairs under the trees. It was as if the whole place had been awaiting our arrival. After all, we were the guests of the Regional Government of Aosta.

I could see far into the distant countryside from my window. Even the serpentine road that wound through the mountains was sharply visible, like an etched line. The hotel grounds were spacious and filled with the beauty of nature. Gardens of different shapes, enormous trees covered with thick creepers, lotuses nodding their heads in an artificial pond, bushes heavy with clusters of wild multi-coloured flowers, and spread underneath it all, a thick carpet of green grass. The place was a perfect blend of nature and art.

The telephone rang as I stood absorbed in my enjoyment of the scene outside. Dinner would be served at seven o'clock, I was told, and was requested to be there on time. I changed and took the stair-case down to get a grip on the geography of the hotel. The UNESCO director Mr Joel Blocker, and the secretary Ms Ezra Marshall were at the reception to introduce the delegates to each other. With conference badges pinned to our shoulders, we then made for the spacious dining hall. After dinner we trooped upstairs to a small auditorium where two of the films that delegates had brought for the conference were screened. They were not particularly well made.

The conference was held in the conference room of the hotel. The arrangements UNESCO had made for the conference gave us an idea of the sheer scale of their work. We had microphones, speakers, interpreters, secretaries, and a telephone exchange. The conference started the following day. The director of UNESCO's women's department, Marie-Pierre Herzog, made a welcome speech and proposed that the delegate from India, Mrs Durga Khote, should make the first presentation. The committee approved the proposal and a resolution was passed that I should start proceedings.

In my speech I gave a brief sketch of the film industry in India. I made special mention of women characters in Indian films. Other speeches that followed mine covered many aspects of filmmaking, including the conditions and problems that afflicted it. The problems were the same everywhere, the chief one being finance. A common complaint made by all delegates was that women had to face more difficulties in the business than their male counterparts. They contended that it was easier for men to find funding and have their work distributed and exhibited compared to women, who were neither helped nor encouraged by the social environment. UNESCO's women's department was requested to intervene to help women filmmakers.

I was surprised to hear women from western countries complaining. The reaction of the Egyptian delegate, Mrs Attyan Abnauri, was similar to mine. Both of us, coming from the developing world, were astonished to hear that women suffered such handicaps in the developed world. I made my opinion very clear in my response. In my experience, the film business was fraught with the same difficulties for everybody. Both men and women had to fight against prevailing conditions. If you had a good story and your crew was technically sound, it made no difference whether you were a man or a woman. Everybody could do well if care was taken to raise capital according to the rules of good business. I said Indian women were doing pretty well, by and large, in the film business. The real problem for women had existed two decades earlier when they had not been allowed to practise music, dance, theatre, or cinema. But those days were gone. Now women in these arts were admired. Perhaps it was the money that women were earning in the business that had prompted this change in attitude.

We saw several films written, directed, and produced by women in the course of the three-day conference. I was not terribly impressed by any of them. The Egyptian film was realistic and had a powerful story. Some of the films were downright obscene. I objected to them. Some other delegates felt the same way as I did. On the whole, I did not think the conference was terribly productive. The idea of setting up a central distribution facility with a library of shots for sale was very good, but would be impossible to implement because of the exorbitant costs involved.

I had hoped that new ideas regarding collaboration in making, distributing, and exhibiting films would emerge and be discussed during the conference. But nobody touched on those issues. Some of the delegates, whom I met later in India, had also expected the same.

23

The Body's Debt

Ever since I returned from Europe, my health had begun to give way. I tried every kind of treatment—allopathy, homeopathy, ayurveda. I, who had never had a day's illness, now slept with a chemist's shop next to my bed. My body was like one of those obstinate ponies that nothing can budge. My worst complaint were my legs. I had hurt them long ago; an accident during shooting had returned to haunt me now with double effect. It was so bad that I could not take a single step forward. I fasted, prayed, made pledges for a boon, asked for blessings from distinguished elders. But my legs had neither fear nor respect for any of these!

In my case, the opinions given by doctors and *vaidyas* were poles apart. Some said I needed to take complete bed rest; others that I must keep walking. Some that I should give up work altogether; others that I must not stop working whatever happened, because that would affect me psychologically. One would prescribe fomentation, cold water bandages, and massage; another would advise dipping my feet in hot salt water. Some were of the opinion that I should sleep with my feet placed on a high bolster while others were certain I should let my feet hang at all times, otherwise there would be no blood supply to them. However, nobody could diagnose the root cause of the complaint. Some thought it was arthritis; others decided it was the kidneys. But there was no external sign such as a swelling on the legs. X-rays, electric shock therapy, every investigative test that could be done from top to toe was done at Breach Candy Hospital. Nothing helped. Whatever the treatment, it had only a temporary effect; then the agonizing pain would come surging back. My predicament reminded me of Taliram's condition in the sick bed scene in *Ekach Pyala* and I laughed at myself. In all of this, one thing remained constant—the excruciating pain. I had also begun to feel anxious. I pushed myself to finish the films I had in hand and refused all other offers. I somehow managed to get through 1976.

Tina was away in Europe with Bakul and I was shouldering the entire burden of complicated and stressful work at DKP. I wrote to them to say I could not handle it anymore and asked Tina to return as early as possible and take over. But by the time she returned, it was December 1976. On 16 December, I left the office, came home and collapsed into bed. I did not get up from it for the next month and a half. I informed DKP that I wished to retire, and went away to Jhirad. The question now was what to do with myself.

I spent the next fortnight lying on the verandah of the house in Jhirad, looking at *the tulsi vrindavan* in the yard. The women of the neighbourhood collected and burnt the dried leaves in the garden. The next two months were very difficult. Nothing helped me feel better. My mind refused to function. I could not remember any time in the last forty-five years when I had sat like this, without work, unmoving. There had been occasions when I had even been at work all day and night. It was extremely difficult for me to lie around like this doing nothing. I was very angry, furious with my illness. But after thinking about it for a long time, I asked myself why I should complain about returning the debt of a body that I had pushed so hard all these years. What was the point in getting angry? Who was I angry with? I decided then that I would walk. If my legs hurt, well then, that was just too bad. But at least they would loosen up. I began to walk around in the yard for as long as I could manage. When the stab of pain came, I would sit down, rest for fifteen or twenty minutes, and start walking again.

In the next ten days or so, I found I could walk pretty well despite the pain. I felt relieved. My legs were losing their stiffness. Soon I was able to make it to the garden. I began doing a bit of gardening to keep myself occupied—collecting dried leaves, plucking dried twigs off flowering plants, gathering *parijat* flowers that fell in a carpet every morning, plucking *mogra* flowers and stringing them for the hair. I enjoyed doing these things and they helped me pass the time. I continued with this routine till the monsoon.

That year I experienced the amazing joy of watching heaps of vegetables, onions, and mangoes from my own garden piling up in the yard. Every other year the gardener would show me the produce and, if I had the time, I would glance briefly over it, before telling him to arrange for its disposal. That year my closeness to it added a rich value to my life. I used to imagine trees, flowers, and leaves whispering their joys and sorrows to the wind. It did not seem to matter to them whether anybody heard them or not. They were in harmony with the rest of nature.

I now decided to take over small kitchen jobs while the servants dealt with the heavier tasks. As I sat down, got up, bent, and stretched, I was automatically exercising my body. By the time I returned to Bombay at the beginning of the monsoon, I was feeling much better. Was this what people meant when they spoke of nature therapy? Once my health was under control, I started work again. I decided now to accept only those roles that I could do without strain, and return to Jhirad as soon as the shooting was over. This helped me keep in good health. The first role I accepted was in *Paheli*. The shooting was to start in September. It was a whole year since I had made up my face. The year had seemed like an age to me. The film told a simple homely story. The director and crew were all young and worked with tremendous zeal. The cinematography was particularly beautiful. We shot outdoors in Kolhapur. In my film career, Kolhapur had been like a mother's home to me. Returning to it now seemed like an auspicious sign. My legs hurt occasionally but that no longer bothered me very much. The shoot was completed in a spirit of bonhomie. The film was well made and became success- ful too.

I returned to Jhirad as soon as the shoot was over. Monsoon had broken and the rain was coming down in torrents. It was past ten. Normally not a soul stirs abroad around Alibag after seven in the evening. But I thought I heard sounds on the road. I thought it could be somebody stopping by to ask the way. When they blew the horn the gardener went out to open the gate. A huge Matador van turned in, its headlights full on. I was surprised and also a little nervous. Who could it be so late at night? The gardener called out saying it was some film people come to see me. I stepped out to inquire who they were. I did not know any of them. But they said they had come to meet me and had got so late because they had had to ask their way to my place. Finally a gentleman from Jhirad had accompanied them. They had not eaten, so I gave them some tea and snacks and asked them what brought them there. They had come to persuade me to act in their film. I made many excuses. I had just finished a shoot. I had cut down on my work on account of my poor health. The role was also not very big. But they continued to press me. I too could not turn down their request seeing that they had spent four hours trying to track me down.

There was another instance when a producer came all the way to Jhirad looking for me. He, too, arrived late at night and would not take no for an answer. I am deeply grateful to all these people and to the film industry. They have always understood my problems, agreed to all my conditions, and treated me with great respect and love.

24

Life: A Void

After Harin's death on 8 February 1964, hopelessness and despair made a permanent home in my life. A well-known personality, describing my psychological condition, once said that somebody appeared to have extinguished the light in my life. Everything seemed joyless to me. Problems had gradually begun to surface in DKP. Vijaya was completely absorbed in her theatre and other activities. Tina was busy creating obstacles and difficulties to gain an upper hand in the business. Nothing seemed to be working out. The situation was getting worse by the day. But I had no desire left now to face it. My life seemed to be devoid of all meaning. What had I done in life? What had I got in return? Bakul's daughters were out all the time with their gang of friends. They had no feeling left for home and family. Their life had become rootless, showy, and superficial, guided neither by eastern culture nor by western discipline. The girls began to see this when they went to Europe. They began to sense their inner emptiness. 'What is our background,' they would often ask. How would they understand at that innocent age? Fortunately, they found their own answers and everything turned out right, but much later.

I did not really know Farrokh Mehta. We had met a few times in the general course of business and that was about it. I had no idea where Vijaya and he used to meet. But things happened in a very short time, by the December of 1965. The speed at which they happened was astonishing. I had begun to feel very anxious about Ravi and Devendra because of the way things had turned out in the interim period of eighteen months. We had bought a flat in Vijaya's and my name in Ashoka Apartments for the boys. Bakul and I were of the opinion that the flat, along with whatever silver and gold

Vijaya owned, should be put in a trust for their exclusive use. But Vijaya and her people rejected the idea. After she and Farrokh married, they began living in Ashoka Apartments. We were told that we would be paid back for the flat in gradual instalments. I was shocked that Farrokh had done this. I had hoped and expected that they would think about the issue responsibly. However, I did not get into an argument. I simply descended the stairs of Ashoka Apartments and did not turn that way again for the next ten years. The boys used to come to Goolestan occasionally to meet me. Once in a while, when I could not resist the urge, I too would call them up to find out how they were. This connection did not last too long either. The same year Farrokh and Vijaya went to England, taking the boys with them. They were away for three years.

The events of the intervening years had disturbed the working atmosphere at DKP. My staff had left one by one for a variety of personal reasons. The casual way in which the new staff worked created problems. There was no satisfaction in work. The employees had become slack because of the prevailing atmosphere and differences of opinion. Each one took sides to promote his personal short-term benefits, and spoilt the atmosphere further. The quality of work suffered as a result, and clients were beginning to lose their confidence in us.

My self-confidence was thoroughly shaken now. I was fed up with the whole thing. I often felt like dropping everything and simply going away. But where could I go? At no time in my life had I been able to find a true friend, the warmth and affection of a close relationship with no strings attached. I had been friendly enough with everybody, but had not really looked for anything beyond my home, my children, and their families. I had never gone to clubs for recreation, nor had I pursued hobbies like games or cards. Today I felt acutely the need for a sympathetic individual who would listen to me and share my pain. But friendship has to be nurtured and cared for. It is a mutual give-and-take. I had kept away from that. I had stopped all socializing because I was convinced it would do nobody any good for people to see the rifts and frictions that had surfaced in our family life. Such relationships as I had outside the family were formal. Besides that, nothing else existed for me except work, whether in the studio or in the office.

Once, a woman architect came to DKP to discuss the renovation we were planning. I had known her for many years. Sharp and observant, she had made careful mental notes of every detail. After she had spoken to Tina, she said to me with genuine feeling, 'Ma'am, why did you have to get involved with this mess after you left Fact Films?' I laughed at the question and said to myself, 'Debts from some previous life.'

From 1966 onwards, my own work increased enormously. I worked for Prasad Productions, Hrishikesh Mukherjee, R.K. Studios, and Gemini and AVM from the South, besides several smaller producers. I was shooting all day for months. It was like a gift from God. I was so busy that I had no time to think. Work too was satisfying because the roles I was playing were varied. Many years of my life passed by in this fashion. I was looking for a peaceful place in the vicinity of Bombay where I could stay quietly when I had the time between shooting dates. I went as far afield as Tarapur; but finally it was in a small village called Jhirad in Alibaug district that Bakul discovered a small house surrounded by fields and a mango orchard. I went to Alibaug on Guru Purnima day at the height of the monsoon, paid for the place and took charge of it on the spot. I thought sadly of Harin. We were going to look for a place in Panvel in 1964. Now in 1968, I had a place, but Harin was not with me.

I returned to Goolestan the same night with a basketful of mogra flowers from the garden and a pitcher of water from the well of the house. Anjali, Rekha, and Priya danced with joy. They threw their arms around my neck. Widening her large light eyes in wonder Anjali said, 'You mean you just went in the morning and came back at night with a huge property? Granny you are incredible.' I was touched by her affection.

Mangoes from Jhirad are a great treat for us. Even today, I send them all the way to Europe for the girls. Not a single letter arrives without their asking after Jhirad, its trees, rice, onions, and even the dog. All the children loved the place. Even producers who came there to meet me were reluctant to leave. One producer told me admiringly that the approach road to the house reminded him of the opening shot in *Rebecca*. The house itself is small, very much like a farmhouse, and is tranquil, quiet. When I enter the garden, I seem to leave all my mental turmoil outside.

There's a tulsi vrindavan in the frontyard of the house. Our gardener lights an incense stick and prays there morning and evening. During Diwali, the whole yard is covered with *rangoli* patterns with oil lamps burning around them. The air is heavy with the scent of the night queen at night, and the *prajakta* in the morning. In spring, the mango blossom hangs in heavy clusters, spreading its fragrance everywhere. Jhirad brought peace, stability, and a sense of balance to my life which, till then, had been empty. I thought of all the people who must have had to endure sorrows worse than mine. Why then should I sit around coddling mine? That is how I thought, but I don't act that way even now.

My grandchildren had now grown up. After her school certificate examination, Anjali had won a scholarship to Atlantic College in the UK. I thought she was still too young to be sent so far away. In my opinion, it would have been better for her to go after graduation. But her parents had decided that it was better for the girls to take their higher education in the West. Anjali gave me a big hug. Before she walked to her plane she said to me with tears in her eyes, 'I'll write to you granny and don't worry. Look after yourself.' That was three years ago, and there was no sign of her returning. Preparations were now on to send Rekha away. That left Priya.

I now started getting small notes and postcards from Ravi and Devendra. Farrokh and Vijaya also wrote occasionally to give me news of the boys. I felt very reassured to see their photographs. They looked healthy, happy, and utterly sweet. To know that they were happy lifted a huge burden off my chest. I could see from their faces that Farrokh was looking after them as he would after his own sons, giving them all the love and care they needed. I used to thank him silently for this. The boys now had a sister. Judging from their letters, the new baby was like a toy for them. Two years later, the children were back. Everything in India was new to them. Even the language was a problem for some time. It was very amusing to hear their British accents.

The boys used to come over to Goolestan occasionally. Their first question was always, 'Where's Anjali?' They had both retained a vivid memory of her. I found it surprising that Ravi and Devendra talked about Harin quite easily as Harin Daddy. They knew all his cricket and hunting stories. There was a bearskin in my room with stuffed head, which Harin had given me. They would sit on it, stroke its head and talk about Harin. You could see Harin in their expressions, their gestures, and the way they talked.

Sitting in the office one day, the last ten years unspooled before me like a film. It was Sankranti day in 1974. The office staff had brought the traditional Sankrant sweet of sesame seeds and jaggery for me. They put it on my table, pressed their palms together in a *namaste* and then gave me pedhas to mark the fourteenth anniversary of DKP. I was sitting absolutely still with the sweets in my hand when I heard a voice ask, 'May I come in?' I looked up and saw it was Farrokh Mehta. He came in carrying a huge bouquet of flowers. I was a little flustered. I was seeing him after many years. We had corresponded quite a lot, but on the few occasions that we had met socially, we had not exchanged more than formal greetings across the room. I asked him to sit down but did not know what else to say. But Farrokh took the initiative. He said, 'Many happy returns of the day,' and handed me the flowers. My eyes suddenly smarted with tears. Farrokh held both my hands and said, 'I have come to invite you to dinner at Ashoka Apartments.' I began muttering something about going another day, but he interrupted me. 'I have invited you many times. But now you must name the day. I have promised the boys I will bring you.' I was speechless. Farrokh continued, 'It's ten years now Bai. Don't you trust me yet? The boys want you to come over home. Won't you listen to them?' I was very moved. Swallowing the lump in my throat I said, 'You decide which day, and I'll come.' He responded instantly with, 'No. I will come and pick you up.'

Though I had agreed to go, I was feeling extremely uneasy. I had not visited anybody at all in the last ten years. Yet I could not hurt the boys. The next Saturday, Farrokh came to pick me up as planned and drove me to Ashoka Apartments. My heart was thudding at the thought of stepping into that building again. But the boys came racing towards the car, took hold of my hands, one on each side, and dragged me upstairs. Anahita, their sister, stood at the top of the stairs enjoying the sight. When I called her to me, she smiled bashfully and ran to her mother.

During dinner old memories and new images mixed and merged, throwing my mind into turmoil. I doubt if I was talking very coherently. But what held me together was the children's laughter, their pranks and the tales they carried about each other, always beginning with, 'Granny you know what . . . .' I thought Ravi and Devendra at twelve and ten were spitting images of Bakul and Harin at that age.

25

A Different View

I must go back at this point to write a few words about Farrokh Mehta. I was very upset that, when he and Vijaya got married in December 1965, he gave up his own flat to live in our flat in Ashoka Apartments. Dear Lord, was it for this that I had strained and struggled for two years, I thought. It made me so furious that my mind simply stopped functioning and everything seemed beyond endurance. Ultimately I decided to lay Harin's children at God's feet and brought the shutter down on my heart. I would yearn to meet my grandsons, but that was not to be. And time moved on.

After some time I began getting news of the children from relations and friends. I heard they were doing well. That Farrokh was very caring. That he loved children. Much of my anxiety subsided when I heard that the boys got on well with him. After that the boys began to visit me in Goolestan. I saw that they were well, that they were fond of Farrokh and that he had brought stability to their lives. This could not have happened if he had not been tender and caring by nature.

Yet, see how strange the mind is. When I heard that Farrokh referred to Ravi and Devendra as 'my sons', it upset me a little again. Doubt and suspicion raged in my mind. If the two boys were going to be legally adopted, the last sign of Harin's existence would be erased. How then would the boys relate to us? However, another thought soon replaced that. Suppose Farrokh was not to treat the boys as his own? How would I feel about it then? Finally, I just stopped thinking about the problem. When the boys started going to playschool, their names were registered as Khote. And I heaved a sigh of relief.

It was soon after this that word had come from Ashoka Apartments that Vijaya and Farrokh were taking the boys to England for three years. I was very unhappy. To be separated from them for three whole years! How was I going to live through the time? When would it end? I sent a trusted servant across to Ashoka to tell Farrokh to send me the bill for whatever woolies and other clothes the boys would need for England. Back came Farrokh's courteous response— Please do not worry at all; my company is making provisions for all these things; please trust me to take good care of the boys; I will not let them want for anything.

Before they left for England, Farrokh sent me an affidavit for the full price of the Ashoka Apartments, pledging to return the entire amount to me with interest in instalments. He also paid in cash for the jewellery and silverware. I put all the money in a trust for Ravi and Devendra and handed over charge of the trust to Farrokh as soon as they returned. Because I saw Farrokh now as a rare human being.

Farrokh and Vijaya wrote to me regularly from England. They gave me news of the boys and it made me happy. Later I began to receive letters in which Ravi and Devendra had scribbled pictures and added crooked letters of the alphabet at the bottom. The boys now had a new toy—their younger sister, Anahita. The photographs Farrokh took of the way the three spent the day were very sweet and amusing to see. The boys looked plump and healthy. I longed for the time I would see them and hold them close.

During those three years, the boys travelled to many places with Farrokh. With their inquisitive minds, they learned a lot of valuable things. Their report cards from school showed they were doing well. In fact, they were doing better than one would have expected at their age. Finally came news of their imminent return. I could hardly wait to see them. My mind was racing faster than the flight they were to arrive on. But just then Farrokh wrote to say they were not coming by air but by sea. That meant a whole month more of waiting. I was almost in tears.

But then I realized Farrokh was doing this in the children's interest. The idea was to give the boys a chance to see many more places on the way. He was even planning to stop over in Africa to take them on a safari. I felt grateful to him and pitied my own miserable thoughts. The end of his letter touched me deeply. He had written, 'It is our wish that you should be the first person the boys should see and spend time with. Please come to Ballard Pier and take them with you to Goolestan for a few days. We will be waiting for you. Please do come.'

Once in Bombay, it was Farrokh who did the running around required to get the boys into school. I was very keen that they should go to Cathedral where all of us siblings had gone. And so had Bakul and Harin. Farrokh himself had gone to the same school. But getting into it had become very difficult. However, we marshalled every contact old and new, pulled several strings, and got them in.

Both boys did extremely well at school over the next ten years. The credit for that goes to Farrokh again. Every year's report cards were excellent. Besides studies, the boys were good at extra-curricular activities too, like sports and elocution. They had been provided with a broad and progressive foundation for life. Farrokh had spent a lot of thought, care, and effort in managing this. Both Ravi and Devendra were appointed head boys in their final years. It was rare to see one brother handing over charge as head boy to his own brother in a grand ceremony.

Ravi and Devendra are both at college now. They are also entering the world of art in different capacities. Ravi is doing very well in painting and music while Devendra excels in sports and does sound and lighting design for theatre. Farrokh has nurtured them carefully from boyhood to the threshold of manhood and done it with a model father's love and care. Today he treats the two young men as equals while continuing to guide them.

I must frankly admit it now. I would never have been able to do all this for the boys. I would have sheltered them with my love, but that is all.

Thank you Farrokh!

26

Some Moments of Joy

In July 1977, Anjali came to Bombay with Christian. They had decided to get married. They were married on 28 August in a private civil ceremony in Goolestan in the presence of very close relatives and friends. We decorated the whole house with marigold flowers and mango leaves. Two banana plants flanked the front door and a rangoli pattern made with balsam flowers covered the floor between them. A metal plate containing a flower rangoli replaced the vase of flowers that generally stood on the table. Christian loved the way the house was decorated. He kept putting Anjali or Priya against this or that bit of decoration and taking pictures. He must have exposed dozens of film rolls.

Anjali looked beautiful with traditional flower decorations in her hair. Her face was luminous with that special radiance you see in brides. Priya was the bridesmaid. Dressed in a sari, she was busy greeting and welcoming guests. Unfortunately Rekha missed the wedding. She could not come from Canada at such short notice. But she had a long, sisterly talk with Anjali over the phone. Tina and Bakul made a handsome couple. Ravi and Devendra as the bride's guardian brothers loved the ritual of tweaking Christian's ears to make him give them a token gift. The most surprising thing was that my legs suddenly found strength to allow me to serve at the wedding lunch.

Christian loved the food. It reminded him of the dinner in Paris, which, he said, had made him decide to marry Anjali! The atmosphere was so informal that guests went straight into the kitchen to help themselves to hot jalebis as they came out of the frying pan. It was a beautiful wedding. Four days later, the hustle and bustle was over and the couple had returned to Paris. As they left, Christian said to me, 'Banu, you must not worry. I'll take care of Anjali. I'll make her happy.' Of course I was already wondering when I would meet her again. As it happened the family had occasion to come together again the very next year.

By the time I finished the films I had in hand, it was 1978. It was Tina and Bakul's silver wedding anniversary that year. By the grace of God they had had a happy married life. Rekha, Anjali, and Christian had all reserved their annual leaves for the occasion. They were in Bombay on 24 November and came again later for Christmas. Rekha was the first to arrive. I was seeing her after two years. We hugged each other and stayed that way for a long time without saying a word. Finally Rekha said, half laughing, half crying, 'Granny, how I have waited for this.' I could not even see her face properly through the mist clouding my eyes. What a smart and beautiful woman my little girl had grown into! I still thought of her as a little girl. Tina had left her with me and gone to Europe when she was ten months old. When she fell ill with measles, I did not know what to do. I sat up all night holding her on my lap. And all the time she too kept babbling 'Gyanny, Gyanny' and clinging to me. I still thought of her as a little baby. But she had grown into an all-American woman with a strong American accent. She opened her capacious handbag now and pulled out two hand-embroidered handkerchiefs with my name on them, two bottles of perfume, a small torch, and a keychain. Stuffing all these gifts into my hand she warned me, 'You better use them. Or you'll lock them away in the cupboard.' While I was looking at my gifts, Rekha put her hands around my face and lifting it up asked, 'Tell me the truth. How are you feeling?' I was near to tears. I could hardly speak. But then I said, 'I'm fine Rekhibekhi, truly.' Rekhibekhi was my pet name for her. Just then Priya called out, 'Hey you two. Come out here and talk.' Rekha put her arm round my waist and we went out into the sitting room.

Anjali and Christian arrived two days later. They had managed to get tickets at the last minute. Their whole style was outlandish. They had brought just one suitcase of clothes between them. The rest of their baggage consisted of dozens of plastic carrier bags stuffed with cheese, chocolates, soup packets, salami, frozen puddings, and bottles of French wine and champagne. They were a veritable food store on the move. Anjali said, 'I've only brought pants and a swimming costume. I'm going to wear granny's saris.' Christian said, 'I'm only carrying the *lungis* I took from here last time except for one suit for occasions. I'm going to go everywhere in lungis.' They were like gypsies, but they looked so happy together.

Goolestan came truly alive then. Tina and Bakul's silver wedding anniversary was celebrated in grand style. Our Piyuma (Priya) was organizer-in-charge of the event. She had ordered everything from flowers to dinner to ice-cream. They had all planned to stay till January. Not for a moment did I suspect what the naughty dears were planning, because I had clean forgotten that I was going to enter my seventy-fifth year on Sankrant day in 1979. On that day all three girls were bustling around from the morning. They turned my wardrobe topsy-turvy till they found a sari they liked. They laid it out on the bed with its matching blouse and accessories and ordered me to wear them in the evening. I said, 'But I'm not going out anywhere tonight.' They hummed, hawed, and giggled, and I still did not catch on to what they were up to.

That evening I was stunned. They had arranged a huge dinner for me with all kinds of sweets. Greetings sent by people from the film industry were neatly stacked in a silver salver. Bouquets, including a basket of flowers from Mr Kiran Shantaram of Rajkamal Studios, filled the hall. Bakul, Tina, and the three girls were dressed up to the nines. Christian was in his 'suit for special occasions'. I was too moved to actually take it all in. They put candles on the cake and showered me with gifts. How can I describe my feelings at the time! I was simply overwhelmed by their love. Christian had brought French champagne especially for the occasion. So much love! So much affection!

Ravi and Devendra's telegram had arrived that morning and later there was a huge bouquet from Vijaya, Farrokh, the boys, and Anahita. They were spending the Christmas vacation in and around Delhi. They called that night—'Many happy returns of the day granny and lots of love.' It was a moment I would have wished to last all my life.

27

A Film on Fifty Years of Filming

When I look back on this span of fifty years, I am amazed at how long the march has been. The distance between *Ayodhyecha Raja* and *Karj* is like a trek from Ayodhya to Kodaikanal. The last scene of *Karj* was shot in Kodaikanal. I have branched off in other ways since then, but not yet found a clearly visible path. My very first role in this long string of films was *Taramati*. It became very popular with the Marathi audience. They were enthralled by its sweet songs, the scenes that brimmed over with maternal love, its beautiful location on the banks of the Krishna, and its magnificent sets. My role made a terrific impact, for which the credit must surely go to Prabhat; it was also the brightest flame that lit my career in film art.

The audience fell in love with my role as the fiery Kilotala in *Maya Macchindra* because she was brave. The cheetah which sat at my feet filled them with fear and awe. The pair of swords hanging at my waist added a stern power to my personality. This was the second grand step I took in filmdom.

My Saudamini in *Amarjyoti* still flickers on the silver screen. No words can suffice to describe this film. These three Prabhat heroines are not only my favourites but have also found a permanent place in public memory. They came with the Prabhat aura, they were directed by Shantarambapu, a great filmmaker, and they succeeded at the box office—what more could an actor want?

My Mathukaki in the late P.K. Atre's *Payachi Dasi* put fear into all daughters and daughters-in-law. What a terror the woman was! Her short sari, her bald head, her scornful sniffing, made this mother of all mothers-in-law the talk of the town. I had initially refused point blank to accept such a role, but Atre needled me. He said, 'If you're a true artist, you'll want to take up this challenge.' That was it. Lo and behold! Durgabai soon materialized as Mathukaki in two language versions—Marathi and Hindi. Shooting for the film was great fun. The scenes were so funny that Kusumtai Deshpande, who played my daughter, and I would break into constant fits of giggling. Even the studio hands used to be in splits. The best scenes were the ones that featured a souped-up jalopy, Mathukaki's torn umbrella, and the unending arguments between her and her husband. I performed these scenes with extra gusto. Another scene in which my performance went down well was where Mathukaki slips at the well and falls on her behind; also the scenes where her back pains come on. Vanmalabai's sweet homely songs and traditional couplets sung at the handmill imbued the film with a lot of charm.

I took the washerwoman who lived at the back of our house as my model for the Hindi version. I wore chunky brass and silver ornaments, pulled my hair up in a top knot, kept a wad of paan permanently in my mouth and copied to a 't' her style of continually spitting out its juice. Practically everything I said was accompanied by swearing or cursing. The character I created looked so outlandish that people could not stop laughing. The Hindi screenplay writer Anandkumar did not recognize me when he saw me the first day. He asked Mr Atre, 'Atresaab, who is this battle-axe?' I had a lot of fun playing the role.

Mr Debaki Bose, the director of the New Theatres' film *Sita*, made the heroine an incarnation of compassion. He had bestowed on this saintly woman who lived in Valmiki's ashram a fine mind as well. He showed her in many emotional states. She was a wife sorrowing over her unjust separation from her husband, shouldering the responsibility of bringing up the princelings, Luv and Kush. The queen of Ayodhya was full of grace and courtesy. Despite her exile in the jungle, she continued to live with dignity and courage. These emotional nuances were subtly written and Debaki Bose directed me to play them just as subtly. One of the best things about this performance were the minute inflections of voice that I was encouraged to use. The dialogue was sparse. Looks had to express more than words. The performance had to be low-key, the emotions under control. I had to learn many new aspects of acting for this film and I learned them success-fully. This was the first Indian film to be screened at the Venice Film Festival.

My role of Kaikeyi in Prakash's *Bharat Milap* was exactly the opposite of Sita. She was King Dashrath's favourite queen. She ruined the life of the palace in a fit of rage. She brought about a calamity by insisting that Rama should give up the throne and go into exile in the forest for fourteen years. The audience showered me with extravagant praise for my performance as Kaikeyi and the look I had created for the character.

The character of Mrinalini in *Prithvi Vallabh* created by Minerva's Mr Sorab Modi was somewhat reminiscent of the old Urdu theatre. The film, based on a novel by K.M. Munshi, was full of mouth-filling dialogue, exaggerated gestures, and unnatural movements. The last scene called for a dash of daring. Mrinalini and Prithvivallabh are sentenced to death by trampling under an elephant's feet. As I lay under that gigantic animal's feet, I knew it was goodbye to life if the animal got distracted even slightly or actually brought his feet down. We would have been buried deep in the earth if he had done that. My eyes were fixed on the elephant's raised foot. All ideas of acting had flown away. Fortunately the elephant turned out to be a gentleman!

There was a period after this when most of the films I did were based on social themes. They were full of mothers, aunts, grandmothers, and other stereotypes. They were mostly pedestrian roles devoid of life. But then a role came my way that gave me scope for a different kind of performance. This was Raj Kapoor's *Bobby*. I put some Konkani phrases in the mouth of Ayyakka, the Goan nanny I played. The character fitted perfectly into the Goan atmosphere created so beautifully for the film. The performance made a considerable impact on the audience.

Some of the roles I played in Prasad Production films were interesting. There was the old woman in *Dadimaa* who fights for the village boundary, and the middle class mother-in-law in *Jeene ki Raah* who takes her daughter-in-law's side against her son. The film *Bidaai*, which became very popular, effectively portrayed the complex problems that crop up between the old and the new generations. Mr Prasad had worked very hard on this film. We shot continuously for a whole month from nine in the morning to ten at night. It was a condition in my contract that I give him one month at a stretch for the shoot. They had constructed a huge house for the set. All the action took place in various rooms of this house. It could not be dismantled and put together again. When the film became a hit, Mr Prasad was extremely generous in giving me all the credit for its success. He unhesitatingly told everyone, 'This is Durgabai's picture. She made it. It is her credit'. The film was widely talked about. The Filmfare jury was unanimous in nominating me for that year's best actress award. I was told this had never happened before. 'There were no two opinions about it,' they said.

None of the usual tensions and friction occurred during the entire duration of the shoot. There were plenty of arguments, of course; but Mr Prasad had planned every shot in such great detail that he knew exactly what every movement and expression was meant to convey, and would himself demonstrate what he wanted. All the actors felt deeply inspired to see this venerable old man act with so much spirit. It made us work even harder at our roles. I had not been part of such a smooth, well-planned shoot in a long time.

Mughal-e-Azam was my zenith in this series of films. The scale on which the film was conceived and executed put it in a class by itself. The story was about a Mughal prince. Naturally everything—the budget, schedules, sets, make-up rooms, costumes, jewellery and call-sheets was on a gigantic scale. A unique feature of the film was that it had been financed entirely by one individual. *Mughal-e-Azam* forms an important chapter in the history of Indian film-making.

The shooting for *Mughal-e-Azam* was completed in four schedules. The original cast comprised Nargis, Chandramohan, Sapru, and Durgabai Khote. We were shooting in Bombay Talkies, but the film was abandoned when we were about a quarter of the way through. This footage was rejected after a lapse of two years. The exposed stock filled ten trucks. Who knows how much other stuff like costumes, jewellery, and wood had to be scrapped.

The new shoot began around 1950. Practically the entire cast had been changed. I was still Jodhabai. Now Prithviraj Kapoor replaced Chandramohan as Akbar. Some of the scenes between Prithvi and I were shot in a magnificent palace and in the ammunition room next to it. They turned out beautifully. Huge crowds would throng to see the shooting. But *Mughal-e-Azam* could not retain its splendour for long. There was again a lapse of a year because they could not decide whom to cast in the lead roles of Salim and Anarkali.

Many well-wishers tried to promote their own favourites. Finally Dilip Kumar and Madhubala were chosen. And so began preparations for the third part of the shoot.

It had been decided now to shoot the film in three versions—Hindi, English, and Tamil. A *darbar* of Urdu litterateurs was set up in the studio for the Hindi version. Huge packets of the Tamil version used to be flown in from Madras. Innumerable flights were taken to Delhi for the English version. Everything was happening in royal style. In the Hindi version, three forms of language had been skilfully used—Urdu in the court, Hindi, and occasionally the local Braj dialect in Jodhabai's palace. Braj is a sweet dialect and the creative meld of the three languages was extremely effective and gave the film a lilting lyricism. It also made the performances more expressive. The English sounded very stilted. As for the Tamil, it was very painful working with the dialogue director who had been appointed for it. Finally I got myself a Tamil teacher to put me through my lines so I could learn them by heart. If I had not done that, I could not have performed at all.

While the dialogue for the three versions was being written, other preparations had to be attended to simultaneously—costumes, jewellery, and other props and accessories were to be collected anew. Tailors from Delhi were summoned to stitch the costumes, goldsmiths from Hyderabad to make the ornaments, and craftsmen from Kolhapur to create the crowns. Blacksmiths from Rajasthan provided the swords, armour, shields, spears, and daggers, and the footwear was specially ordered from Agra. Embroiderers from Surat and Khambayat were recruited on monthly salaries to do the gold thread work on the royal costumes. The wigs were ordered from England and the actors had to make trips there to be measured. But ultimately we had to use the ones made by our own studio wigmaker. The Indian weather did not seem to suit British hair. It came out in bunches every time a comb was passed through a wig!

Finally the court set was ready. But when it was erected it extended beyond the studio premises into the garden. Even then it was too small. So the entire space by the roadside, right up to the boundary wall, was utilized. A few corners had to be cut before it was ready at last for the shoot. It would take three days to light every shot and three weeks to shoot it. We shot for six months at this pace. Many actresses of Hindi films, some established, some new, were invited for the scene of Salim's arrival. They were to fetch flowers, sprinkle attar, and scatter pearls. At the end of six months, the film came to a halt once again. It had exceeded the budget many times over and the producer had now tightened his purse strings.

The director too would not budge. It came to a point where he announced he would not shoot unless this or that was done. The friction escalated to such heights that there was talk of changing the director. Six months went by. Finally some elders from the industry prevailed on all parties to come to a compromise and finish the film. With much discussion back and forth, it was decided that, apart from one song-and-dance sequence that would be shot in Eastman colour, the rest of the film would be completed in black and white.

Mughal-e-Azam was released in 1958–9. Even today, screenings of the film run to packed houses.

28

My Friends in the Film World

 There is a lot of curiosity among the general public about film actors and their lives, particularly about their relationships. This is quite natural. After all they see them romancing each other, they see them sharing joys and sorrows. They see miraculous things happening to them. The audience inevitably begins to wonder whether the relationships that actors have on screen are carried over to their private lives; and if so to what extent. They then begin to make all kinds of conjectures.

It is difficult for people to understand that what they see on the screen is mechanical, a calculated use of technique. It would be a revelation for them to see what actors look like after a shot is finally approved. They are tired, irritable, and sweaty. Yet most of them go around with a permanent smile, a mask. Only actors know what it is to wear this mask and be conscious of their image all the time. Just the other day a love scene was being shot. The minute it ended the actor and actress glared at each other as if they wished the other person dead. The actor kept muttering, 'I hate her, I hate her. . . .' The actress was also furious. It was in this state of mind that both flopped into their respective chairs, waiting for the next love scene to be announced. This is often the off-screen story of on-screen romances.

The cinema world looks very attractive from the outside—it certainly is to some extent. But the lives of film artists are very unstable, uncertain, and irregular. There is a lot of competition and business rivalry. In the middle of all this you are trying to understand your role and working out how to handle it. With such preoccupations burdening your mind, where's the time for friendships and love?

A film actress meets so many people in the film world or in her social interactions that it becomes very difficult for her to keep count of all the people she has met, and where. Some of these associations deepen into friendships; others are temporary, or exist only for business, or are either very casual or formal. Some actors leave a permanent mark on our lives because they have been our co-stars in films or plays. What keeps their memory vividly alive is the experiences, problems, and amusing incidents we have shared.

Often the actors of a successful film are cast together again and again in other films. This cements their friendship. This encourages the salacious-minded to see meanings in relationships that do not exist. When a film is being shot, actors are together on the sets for hours together. They spend the time between shots chatting, joking, and ragging each other. The crowds that come to watch shoots are unused to seeing men and women being so free with each other. So they jump to conclusions, linking any old names together. This is not to say that film artists do not misbehave, go overboard, or get caught in awkward situations. But is there any work situation where this does not happen? The only difference is that when this happens in the film world, it hits the headlines.

In June 1980, Prabhat Films celebrated its fiftieth anniversary in its old home, which is now the Film and Television Institute of India. It was a huge get-together of friends and associates. Everybody old and new, from the owners, actors and technicians, down to the smallest errand boy was present.

The film world welcomes people from all social strata, regions, and religions, with their different tempers and temperaments. One's experiences in such a world are bound to be varied. But some friendships turn out to be enduring and genuine. For instance, mine with Prithviraj Kapoor. Prithvi adopted me as a sister and sealed the bond with a rakhi. That was how he felt about me till the very end. He used to call me Dimples (Dimps for short). I met him for the first time in Calcutta when we were shooting for *Rajrani Meera*. We were cast together in six films after that. Of these *Mughal-e-Azam* was the most special.

After this film, Prithvi's health began to gradually deteriorate. I went to see him once when he was very ill. He was in such bad shape that he could not even sit up. He lay there looking at me with tear-filled eyes for a long time and then said, 'Dimps, may God take care of you.' That was Prithvi's farewell message to me. I have carefully preserved a very affectionate letter he once wrote to me, addressing me as 'My darling sister'. The most touching thing is that it is written in Marathi. Prithvi and Mubarak were very old friends from their silent film days. Both knew my husband very well, so we used to meet quite often. I met Mubarak as a co-actor when I returned from Calcutta after finishing my assignments there. P. Jairaj played the lead in the same film. I had acted with him in just one film before I went to Calcutta. I was an inexperienced newcomer then. But he was very supportive. It made a big difference to me. Jairaj is a good-natured, hard-working, and diligent artist. When I returned from Calcutta, I had still not lost my nervousness about working in Bombay studios. Jairaj was very knowledgeable about camera angles and lighting. He would watch carefully when my shot was being set up. If he found there was something amiss he would inform the cameraman and me. We acted in only two films together, but our friendship has endured till today.

Jairaj had named me 'Ba' because he thought I looked like Elizabeth (Ba) from *Barrets of Wimpole Street*. Jairaj (Jai) and Mubarak (Mubi) were both bachelors, and used to spend a lot of time in the homely atmosphere of our Dongersey Road house. Bakul and Harin looked upon them as playmates. They would play cricket and carrom with the boys and perform stunts on their bicycles for them. All four of them used to love their time together. We would also go on picnics quite often to Vesave or Vajreshwari. It was a lovely time for all of us. But once the shooting was over, everybody scattered to shoot for their next films. The boys were very, very disappointed. But even later they continued to talk about Jai and Mubi all the time.

It was nearly two years after this, when we were setting up Natraj films, that Mubarak came with Parshwanath Altekar to discuss setting up the company with me. Unfortunately the company which had been started with so much hope turned into a terrible tragedy. Troubles came hurtling at me one after another, but Mubarak helped me at every step. First and foremost he took the entire burden of Natraj Films on his shoulders and freed me from all responsibility. When the financiers created problems he put in his own money to complete the film on hand. He handled everything, from production hassles and payments to legal matters and paperwork without allowing any problem to touch me. As soon as I became a little stable after the Nataraj Films storm had blown over, he approached producers to get me good roles. It was through him that I was cast in a very good part in Ranjit Movietone's *Adhuri Kahani*. That film put my career on course again.

Mubi is not in very good health these days. Even then he makes a point of coming over to our place once or twice in the year, simply to meet everyone and inquire after them. My family loves him. Mubi Kaka is everybody's favourite and everybody is Mubi Kaka's favourite.

Our Parshwanath Altekar was a simple, straight, no-nonsense man. Whenever and wherever we met, he would raise both hands high and come lumbering towards me shouting, 'How are you Bai? Where have you been hiding?' He had his own working style. Every time I walked on to the set, he would pretend to scold some studio hand nearest at hand, 'What are you gawping at? Bai's here. Where are the tea and *bhajias?*' When the bill for the tea and bhajias arrived it was passed on to me.

Altekar always shut his eyes tight when a shot was being taken. When I asked him how he could see what I was doing with his eyes shut, he answered, 'I don't have to see your performance, because it's bound to be good. I want to hear your voice.'

Altekar stood by me staunchly throughout the Nataraj Films disaster. Though he was himself in financial straits, he completed the film without charging a fee. But he never forgave me for not acting in his play. I asked for his forgiveness on several occasions and tried to explain to him why I had not been able to do it. But he refused to accept my explanation. And the rift between us never closed.

29

Looking Back Now

I was once asked, 'Have you been happy in life?' In response I would say somewhat circuitously, 'I have not been unhappy....' As I look back, many thoughts crowd my mind. But if I were to add up and subtract all my desires, ambitions, and errors, the remainder would be satisfactory. The greater part of my life has been a one-way thing. The hectic pace at which I have lived for the last fifty years has left me with very little time to find stability or to build close relationships. Home, family life, blood relations, friends, schoolmates, everything passed me by. I tailored my life around my work, the frame being set by my shooting dates. Relationships have to be nurtured, feelings cherished. I could never do that. It is hardly fair then that, in the last days of my life, I should expect my people to organize their lives around mine. Everybody has his own life to live. How can I expect people to take time out to think of me, show me love? Why should they? I made many plans but I could not carry them all out the way I had intended. I made mistakes. I was not always reasonable in my actions. There is a saying in Marathi, 'Too much of anything turns to mud.' It applies to many aspects of my life.

Take my shooting and business schedules, for instance. I needed to do both, no doubt. But when the style of filmmaking changed in recent years, it would have made sense to change my own style accordingly. I wasted a lot of time sitting around in studios. I could have put this time to some other use. But I was egoistic about it. I had to be punctual at all costs. People would say, 'Bai's car is at the gate. It's eight-thirty. Set your watches.' But what purpose did that serve? Time is no longer binding in studios and watches have become showpieces. Not only did my punctual arrival on the dot of eight-thirty make no sense, arriving late became a mark of importance!! I used to have a good laugh at myself. Now I make it a condition that the car should be sent to fetch me only when they are ready to shoot. I often wish I had done this earlier, instead of making a big thing of punctuality.

Again, I have tended to act on emotional impulse, without sufficient thought, and then regretted it. Anjali once opened my eyes to the problem. We were sitting out in the courtyard of the Jhirad house one night, discussing past events. 'Anjali, you help people only to have them turn on you later. That's how it is', I said. Anjali's light eyes filled with laughter at the remark and her dimples looked even more attractive in the moonlight. Still laughing she said, 'Granny you are extremely nice but why do you go out of your way to do things for people and then get hurt because they don't care about your feelings the way you want them to? Don't you know that you can kill people with your kindness and greatness my dear, loving Granny!' That woke me up as if from a long sleep. Had I really burdened my people, my family, dear ones, and admirers with my kindness and desire to be generous? It was truly something to think about.

Once in a while I wonder what I would have done if circumstances had not pushed me into films, and if the Khote fortunes had not gone into decline. Then my identity would have been nothing more than daughter-in-law of an illustrious family. Future events proved that that would not have been a very happy situation. What would I have done then?

The girls in my generation, especially those from well-to-do, educated families, were never taught productive skills. We were taught music, sewing, or painting only as hobbies, to be pursued during our spare time after school and college. You went to college after school only to bide your time till you got married. After you got married you became a housewife. This was the path chalked out for girls. Whether it turned out to be happy or sad depended on your luck. Though Papa and Mummy gave us many facilities, our lives were also fitted more or less into this mould. Once you were married you wrapped up all your talents and hobbies and put them away. Girls were rarely encouraged to feel that they should do something with their lives. Even girls who qualified successfully as doctors could practice only between the time they married and started a family. I had not come across a single woman who had made valuable or consistent use of her education.

Ever since I can remember, I had dreamt of acting with Narayanrao (Bal Gandharva), however small the role. Theatre held a great attraction for me. I was fascinated by the entire ambience of the stage, the costumes, the ornaments, and the emotion-charged performances. The dream must have hidden itself deep within me. Could it have surfaced when I entered films?

I was never really glamour-struck by cinema. To begin with, we did not see too many films in those days. There was a general impression that they were bad for the eyes. I had seen only one Hindi film—Maharashtra Film Company's *Karna*. It was a very successful and popular film. Narayanrao had practically forced us to go with him to see it. Even today I vividly recall one shot of a sea of people and another of an enormous elephant that filled the entire screen. It was a mythological film with no place for razzle-dazzle. Glamour is superficial. But the superficial is what seems to attract today's audiences. In fact it is so transient, so ephemeral, that you can never be sure when the gilt will wear off.

The reason I went into films was very specific. Glamour had nothing to do with it. Moreover, I had no fancy notions about my looks. I had always been considered dark-skinned from my earliest girlhood. A fair skin was the prerequisite of beauty. This was the general belief. However, Prabhat made me aware that my face was expressive and photogenic. But my name did not spell glamour and glamour was not the reason why I was in films.

A question that I have been asked over and over again, probingly, is—How do you feel when you co-star with unknown men? Do you feel attracted, do you feel....

The question always amused me. I did not blame people for not knowing how much pressure the camera puts on actors. Make-up, costumes, jewellery, hairstyles, the rise and fall of the voice, memorizing dialogue, getting the nuances right, the emotions right, laughing one moment, crying the next, the eternal anxiety about how one was performing in comparison with the other, whether the actor opposite you was playing your brother, husband, or enemy. Where was there any place in all this for attraction? There is so much stuff around—the camera, blinding lights, sound equipment.

... I once asked a well known actress who was with me in a film, 'Do you ever feel physical attraction?' Making a sour face she replied, 'Attraction, my foot! All this is sheer technical calculation full of ten rehearsals and fifteen takes. All you want is for the shot to be okayed so you are free of it!' The late Ganpatrao Bodas once said to me, 'Bai, you and your role have to be two separate entities.' That is absolutely true. Even a moment's loss of concentration can affect your work and the impact of the character you are playing. People are attracted to the shadows they see on the screen or stage, not to the people who cast them. Their adoration is for the patron goddess of theatre.

I had an amusing experience of this kind once. *Ayodhyecha Raja* was running in Bombay. Mummy and I had stopped the car near Central Bank for some shopping when we overheard an exchange between two boys. 'Hey that's Taramati's voice', said one. The other, 'Come let's see.' The two stood on tiptoe to peep into the car. Then they looked at each other and said, 'Rubbish. This isn't Taramati. This one's dark. Taramati is so fair. Go see the film.' I think those two boys pointed to the truth of a film artist's identity.

These days 'image' has become a much-used word, particularly in the film world. It is considered to be very important for the actor to be constantly aware of his public image. Therefore it is vital for an actor who wishes to maintain his image to look after his body and paint it with cosmetics. The actor's image is his capital investment. This was not how people felt earlier. Attractiveness had a more limited definition. Being clean, well-dressed, and well-groomed was about it. Beauty was considered to be a natural gift. Today's generation has acquired great expertise in cosmetic skills. I sometimes feel sorry for not having looked at myself from that point of view. Viewers do have very special expectations from artists. If they are not fulfilled they are disappointed just as those two young boys were.

People have often suggested that I should share my experiences with today's actors. But as in other spheres of work, the present generation in films has gone so far ahead so rapidly that they do not need our experiences. Since the work situation itself has changed our experiences will not even be relevant to them. Circumstances have changed, viewpoints have changed, the value system has changed.

Of course we ourselves gained much by stubbing our toes, stumbling, falling, then picking ourselves up again to hack our way through. But many of the problems we faced have now been solved by technology. Most importantly, the film business has acquired legitimacy. Many institutions for teaching film have sprung up. Cinema has become an academic discipline. Artists should consider it their first duty to respect the facilities they now have and the honour that has been accorded to them. Rather than going after glamour, it would be beneficial all round if they helped develop film art, film business, and themselves too in the process. The film industry has expanded to include many areas in which women can find an important place for themselves. Their place is no longer only before the camera, but on the technical side of filmmaking too. No age bar operates here so women are free to explore the possibilities for themselves.

Experience is of paramount importance—from whichever direction it comes. It helps you avoid making the mistakes others have made. With the help of experience, you can anticipate and find solutions for problems that are likely to arise. I gained a lot of experience by acting in films made in different parts of the country. My ears became familiar with many languages. I even learned some. I had opportunities to work with some of the best known directors, producers, and technicians in cinema, and to act with the most popular stars of the day. I played important roles in films that were critically acclaimed and popular too. I have been very fortunate indeed. I would be only too happy if my accumulated experience were of any help to the next generation.

Today, at seventy-six when I look back, I feel it was God's grace that helped me overcome the obstacles that came in my way. The children and their welfare had always been my sole anxiety. They are all mature, self-reliant, and happy, set to face life with confidence and pride, ready to fulfil their responsibilities to the best of their abilities. I was thrown headlong into life's problems at the very beginning of my married life. But I have had the good fortune, thanks to the accumulated merit of my ancestors, to see the fruit of my labour before my eyes. That is my true happiness.

What remains are the wounds inflicted on a mother's heart. Their pain will go with me when I have gone.

Glossary

abhang	:	verse
alaap	:	modulation of the voice in singing
ashirwad	:	blessing
ashram	:	abode of a hermit or devotee
attar	:	perfume
barfi	:	sweet made from thickened milk
bel	:	a tree sacred to Lord Shiva
bhajia	:	savoury fritters made from assorted vegetables dipped in chick pea flour and deep fried
bhaubeej	:	the last day of Diwali when a sister prays for her brother's well-being by circling his face with an oil lamp on a salver, and he gives her a gift
champa	:	fragrant yellowish-white flower, *Michelia campaca*
dandpatta	:	martial exercise using a fencing stick and a long, double-edged sword
darbar	:	royal court; hall of audience
dhoti	:	garment worn round the lower body, one end of which passes between the legs
	:	and is tucked in behind
durrie	:	carpet, matting made of cotton
Ekadashi	:	the eleventh day of the bright half of the lunar month
ghat	:	slope, or flight of steps to water, a river bank
ghati	:	person from the Sahyadri mountains on the west coast of Maharashtra
gulab jamun	:	sweet made from soft milk cheese, fried, and then soaked in syrup
halwa	:	sweet made from flour/semolina/grated bottle

		gourd or carrot etc, with milk, ghee, sugar and nuts added.
Hargange	:	calling upon the river Ganga which flows out of Lord Shiva's matted locks
jalebi	:	sweet (shaped like a pretzel) made from chick pea flour, fried, and then glazed
	:	with syrup
kaka	:	father's brother; also used to address senior male family friend
kaki	:	father's brother's wife, also used to address senior female family friend
karvanda	:	small, black, sour-sweet fruit of the Corinda tree.
kavath	:	wood apple
kavathi-chafa	:	ivory coloured, thick petaled, heavily scented flower of the champak family
laddoo	:	ball-shaped sweet made of gram-flour or thickened milk, with sugar, saffron, nuts, etc., added
Manginbaay	:	a goddess
mangalsutra	:	the necklace containing a minimum of five black beads put around the bride's neck by the husband, in one of the last rituals of a Hindu wedding ceremony in Maharashtra. The necklace is an auspicious marriage symbol, not to be kept on by a woman after her husband's death
mazaar	:	tomb, grave
mogra	:	double jasmine (type of flower)
mull	:	muslin
namaskar	:	greeting; respectful salutation
Navratra puja	:	a festival celebrating the day Lord Ram marched upon Ravan, the king of Lanka, to free his wife Sita, abducted by Ravan
paan	:	betel leaf
pagdi	:	a large turban-type headgear
Pahadi	:	belonging to a hill tribe
pallu	:	end of sari (usually decorative) which is draped around upper part of the body
parijat	:	coral tree, one of the five trees of paradise produced by the mythological churning of the

		ocean. The flowers are delicate, translucent white with bright orange stalks.
pedhas	:	sweets made from milk reduced to a malleable consistency
pedhi	:	shop or place of business
Peshwa	:	one of the dynasty of chancellors who administered the Maratha empire from their seat in Pune
prajakta	:	coral tree (parijat, parijatak are alternative names)
prasad	:	food offered to an idol and distributed to devotees as sacred.
puja	:	worship, adoration (of a deity)
qawwali	:	religious songs sung to accompaniment
rakhi	:	protective talisman, tied ceremonially on a protector's or patron's wrist on the full moon of the month of Sravan (August-September); especially by a sister to a brother.
rangoli	:	decorative patterns made with coloured powders on the floor outside the front doors of homes, especially on festivals or auspicious occasions
sais	:	one who hires out pack-horses
Sankranti	:	festival that falls on January 14.
Sant Ramdas	:	a seventeenth century saint poet immensely revered in Maharashtra
Shambho!	:	calling upon Shambhu, one of the names of Lord Shiva
shamiana	:	canopy, awning
Shenvi	:	one of the upper castes in Maharashtra
sloka	:	Sanskrit couplet consisting of lines of sixteen syllables
taan	:	musical note, tone, melody
tanpura	:	stringed instrument used as an accompaniment by singers
tulsi	:	sweet basil
tutari	:	a long upward-curving pipe. The Prabhat Films logo shows a young woman bent backwards holding a tutari to her lips
vaidya	:	Ayurvedic doctor
Vyankatesh	:	one of the avatars of Lord Krishna

wada   :   a mansion, specifically one built in the traditional
                   style of Maharashtra, where rooms give onto a
                   verandah that surrounds a central courtyard

Appendix

TINA AND HER FAMILY

Tina's family, the Skorzewskis, were landed gentry in Poland before World War II. They left Poland at the start of the war, as her father's opposition to the German war preparations was well known, and the family would not have survived German occupation. Father, mother, and two very small children escaped to England. As it was difficult to settle in a country at war, the family decided to try Brazil, and finally settled in Canada. Tina's father died unexpectedly soon after the move to Canada, and Tina and her brother were brought up in difficult circumstances by their mother. After school, Tina worked for the International Civil Organization in Montreal, and with her savings decided to go to Paris to continue her studies and enlarge her life's horizons. After a course of studies at Sorborne University, she secured a job at IATA (because of her knowledge of four languages). I had gone to Paris to attend an international conference. And that is how we met. This, in brief, is the background of Tina's family, and how she came into our lives.

BAKUL KHOTE